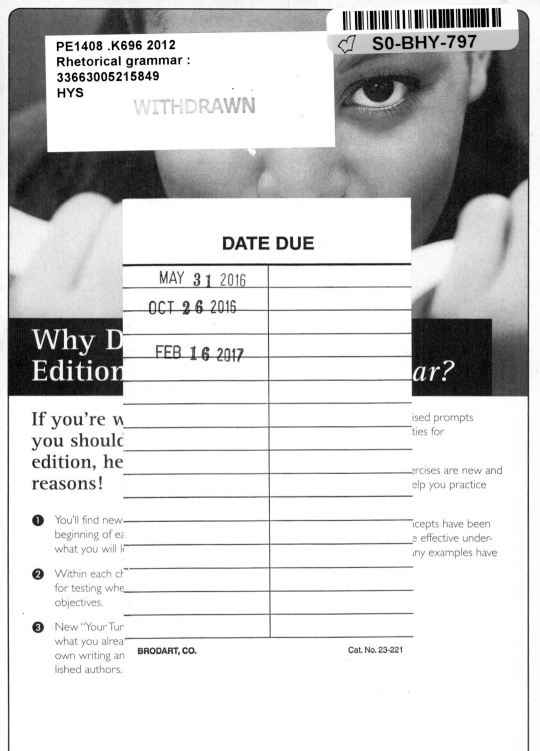

S0-BHY-797

DATE DUE

MAY 31 2016	
OCT 26 2016	
FEB 16 2017	

BRODART, CO.   Cat. No. 23-221

Why D
Edition   ar?

If you're w   ised prompts
you should   ties for
edition, he   ⸺rcises are new and
reasons!   elp you practice

❶ You'll find new⸺   ⸺cepts have been
   beginning of ea   ⸺e effective under-
   what you will l   ⸺ny examples have

❷ Within each ch
   for testing whe
   objectives.

❸ New "Your Tur
   what you alrea
   own writing an
   lished authors.

PEARSON

Rhetorical Grammar

Grammatical Choices, Rhetorical Effects

SEVENTH EDITION

Martha Kolln

The Pennsylvania State University

Loretta Gray

Central Washington University

PEARSON

Boston Columbus Indianapolis New York San Francisco Upper Saddle River
Amsterdam Cape Town Dubai London Madrid Milan Munich Paris Montreal Toronto
Delhi Mexico City São Paulo Sydney Hong Kong Seoul Singapore Taipei Tokyo

Senior Vice President and Publisher:
Joseph Opiela
Senior Sponsoring Editor:
Katharine Glynn
Editorial Project Manager: Denise Phillip
Editorial Assistant: Rebecca Gilpin
Director of Marketing: Megan Galvin-Fak
Senior Marketing Manager:
Sandra McGuire
Senior Managing Editor:
Donna deBenedictis

Production Project Manager: Debbie Ryan
Art Director: Jayne Conte
Cover Designer: Bruce Kenselaar
Cover Art: Donatas1205 / Shutterstock
Full-Service Project Management:
Sudip Sinha
Composition: PreMediaGlobal
Printer/Binder: STP/RRD/Harrisonburg
Cover Printer: STP/RRD/Harrisonburg
Text Font: Adobe Garamond Pro

Credits and acknowledgments borrowed from other sources and reproduced, with permission, in this textbook appear on the appropriate page within text.

Many of the designations by manufacturers and sellers to distinguish their products are claimed as trademarks. Where those designations appear in this book, and the publisher was aware of a trademark claim, the designations have been printed in initial caps or all caps.

Library of Congress Cataloging-in-Publication Data
Kolln, Martha.
   Rhetorical grammar : grammatical choices, rhetorical effects / Martha Kolln, Loretta
     Gray.—7th ed.
     p. cm.
   Includes bibliographical references and index.
   ISBN 978-0-321-84672-3
   ISBN 0-321-84672-9
   1. English language—Rhetoric.   2. English language—Grammar.   I. Gray, Loretta S.
   II. Title.
   PE1408.K696 2012
   808'.042—dc23   2012025459

10 9 8 7 6 5 4 3 2

ISBN 10: 0-321-84672-9
ISBN 13: 978-0-321-84672-3

Contents

PART II
Controlling the Message   *81*

Chapter 5
Cohesion   82

Chapter 6
Sentence Rhythm   101

Chapter 7
The Writer's Voice   117

PART III
Making Choices: Form and Function   139

Chapter 8
Choosing Adverbials   141

PART V
Punctuation   *239*

Chapter 13
Punctuation: Its Purposes, Its Hierarchy, and Its Rhetorical Effects   *240*

Preface

Grammatical choices. Rhetorical effects. These two phrases tell the story of rhetorical grammar, the marriage of grammar and rhetoric for the composition classroom. Writers who recognize the choices available to them will be well-equipped for controlling the effects of their words. As we explain to students in the Introduction,

> To study grammar in this way—that is, to consider the conscious knowledge of sentence structure as your toolkit—is the essence of rhetorical grammar.

But is there really a place for the study of grammar in the composition class? Is there time for grammar in a syllabus already filled with prewriting, drafting, and revising and with reading what others have written? The answer is "yes." In fact you are already spending time on grammar—when you discuss cohesion and transition; when you explain in a conference why a structure is misplaced or awkward; when you help students understand the effects of certain words on the reader; when you point out redundancy; when you suggest sentence revision; when you praise gems of precision. These are principles of grammar and style and revision that are now part of your writing class. *Rhetorical Grammar: Grammatical Choices, Rhetorical Effects* will help you teach these and many more such principles—and it will do so in a systematic way.

And while the book is addressed to student writers in the composition classroom, we are gratified to know that it is also being used successfully in grammar courses for teacher preparation. In addition to the basics of grammar, those future language arts teachers will gain valuable insight into the teaching of writing.

You'll discover that the lessons in this book are not the definitions and categories and rules of traditional grammar that your students encountered back in middle school. Rather, *Rhetorical Grammar* brings together the insights of composition researchers and linguists; it makes the connection between writing and grammar that has been missing from our classrooms. It also avoids the prescriptive rules and error correction of handbooks, offering instead explanations of the rhetorical choices that are available. And, perhaps what is most important, it gives students confidence in their own language ability by helping them recognize the intuitive grammar expertise that all human beings share.

This difference in the purpose of *Rhetorical Grammar* is especially important. Too often the grammar lessons that manage to find their way into the writing classroom are introduced for remedial purposes: to fix comma splices and misplaced modifiers and agreement errors and such. As a consequence, the study of grammar has come to have strictly negative, remedial associations—a Band-Aid for weak and inexperienced writers, rather than a rhetorical tool that all writers should understand and control.

This book, then, substitutes for that negative association of grammar a positive and functional point of view—a rhetorical view: that an understanding of grammar is an important tool for the writer; that it can be taught and learned successfully if it is presented in the right way and in the right place, in connection with composition. The book can also stimulate class discussion on such issues as sentence focus and rhythm, cohesion, reader expectation, paraphrase, diction, revision—discussions of rhetorical and stylistic issues that will be meaningful throughout the writing process. And the students will learn to apply these grammar concepts to their own writing. This is the kind of knowledge—this toolkit of conscious grammar understanding—that will support not only their academic career but their lifelong literacy as well.

Those of you who are acquainted with past editions will see important changes here in the seventh edition:

- New introductory objectives for each chapter and exercises for testing whether those objectives have been achieved.
- New "Your Turn" activities, which ask students to use what they already know to talk about their own writing and about the writing of published authors.
- New and revised prompts for group discussions, many of which are conducive for use in online courses.
- One-third of all exercises are new; others have been revised.
- Clarified discussions of concepts and updated examples.

Retained in this edition are the closing sections—Key Terms, Rhetorical Reminders, and Punctuation Reminders—all designed to help students organize and review material. The updated Glossary of Terms provides easy access to definitions of new vocabulary; the Index directs students to other pages where topics are discussed. A self-instructional Answer Key gives students the opportunity to check their work on odd-numbered items in the exercises.

The primary focus throughout the book remains on revision and style, on the importance to students of understanding the writer's tools. For students interested in further study, we have placed at the end of the book a bibliography of sources relevant to the topics discussed.

Depending on the goals of your course, you may find that *Rhetorical Grammar* is the only text your students need; on the other hand, it can certainly work well in conjunction with a reader or rhetoric. In either case, you'll discover that class time can be used much more efficiently when your students come to class with the shared background that the text provides. The Instructor's Manual includes answers to the even-numbered items in the exercises, further explanations of grammatical principles, and suggestions for class activities.

ACKNOWLEDGMENTS

We would like to thank the reviewers, whose astute feedback and thoughtful suggestions helped us improve this edition of *Rhetorical Grammar*—Cheri Crenshaw, Dixie State College; Cecil ("Jay") Jordan, University of Utah; Rob Schnelle, Central Washington University; Eve Wiederhold, George Mason University; and Leah Zuidema, Dordt College. We'd also like to acknowledge the support of students enrolled in English 320 at Central Washington University. Their frank and insightful remarks have helped us to clarify passages and create new activities. We are especially grateful to those students who allowed us to publish their work in this text. Their writing makes the ideas we've presented come alive.

We owe special thanks to our new editor, Katharine Glynn, and her assistant, Rebecca Gilpin, for encouragement and support. Their valuable suggestions and timely responses kept our collaboration on track.

To our friends and family, we offer heartfelt gratitude. Without their unwavering support, this book would not be possible.

Martha Kolln
Loretta Gray

Introduction

WHAT IS RHETORICAL GRAMMAR?

To understand the subject matter of a book with the title *Rhetorical Grammar*, you'll obviously have to understand not only the meaning of both *rhetoric* and *grammar* but also their relationship to each other. *Grammar* is undoubtedly familiar to you. *Rhetoric*, on the other hand— as well as *rhetorical*—may not be familiar at all. So, to figure out what rhetorical grammar is all about, we'll begin with the familiar *grammar*.

If you're like many students, you may associate the idea of grammar with rules—various dos and don'ts that apply to sentence structure and punctuation. You may remember studying certain rules to help you correct or prevent errors in your writing. You may remember the grammar handbook as the repository of such rules.

But now consider another possibility: that YOU are the repository of the rules. You—not a book. It might help you to understand this sense of grammar if you think of a grammar rule not as a rule or law created by an authority but rather as a description of language structure. Stored within you, then, in your computer-like brain, is a system of rules, a system that enables you to create the sentences of your native language. The fact that you have such an internalized system means that when you study grammar *you are studying what you already "know."*

According to linguistic researchers[1], you began internalizing the rules of your language perhaps before you were born, when you began to differentiate the particular rhythms of the language you were hearing. In the first year of life you began to create the rules that would eventually produce sentences.

---

[1]See the section Language Development in the Bibliography.

You were little more than a year old when you began to demonstrate your grammar ability by naming things around you; a few months later you were putting together two- and three-word strings, and before long your language took on the features of adult sentences. No one taught you. You didn't have language lessons. You learned all by yourself, from hearing the language spoken around you—and you did so unconsciously. When you started to read, your acquisition of language continued. In fact, you are still acquiring language: As you learn new words, you learn (not necessarily through studying) the sentence structures in which those words commonly appear.

This process of language development is universal—that is, it occurs across cultures, and it occurs in every child with normal physical and mental development. No matter what your native language is, you have internalized its basic grammar system. By the time you were five or six years old, you were an expert at narrating events, at asking questions, at describing people and places, probably at arguing. The internalized system of rules that accounts for this language ability of yours is our definition of *grammar.*

When you study grammar in school, then, you are to a great extent studying what you already "know." Note that the verb *know* needs those quotation marks because we're not using it in the usual sense. Your grammar knowledge is largely subconscious: You don't know consciously what you "know." When you study grammar you are learning *about* those grammar rules that you use subconsciously every time you speak or write—as well as every time you make sense of what you hear or read.

But as you know, learning to write involves other rules, the conventions of writing. When you write, you must pay attention to rules about paragraphing and sentence completeness and capital letters and quotation marks and apostrophes and commas and, perhaps the trickiest of all, spelling.

To be effective, however, writing also requires attention to rhetoric—and here is where the term *rhetorical* comes into the picture. *Rhetoric* is the art of using language effectively. Attending to your rhetorical situation means that your audience—the reader—and your purpose make a difference in the way you write on any given topic. To a large degree, that rhetorical situation—the audience, purpose, and topic—determines the grammatical choices you make, choices about sentence structure and vocabulary, even punctuation. Rhetorical grammar is about those choices.

This meaning of *rhetoric* is easy to illustrate: Just imagine the difference between texting a friend and writing a letter to the dean of your college, requesting funds for a new film club. Think of the differences there might be in those two different rhetorical situations. One obvious difference, of course, is vocabulary; you wouldn't use the same words with two such different audiences. The grammatical structures are also going to be different, determined in part by your tone or level of formality.

Understanding rhetorical grammar, then, means understanding both the grammatical choices available to you when you write and the rhetorical effects those choices will have on your reader. The dean of your college will probably recognize—and approve of—your letter as evidence of a serious-minded, articulate student. She will feel assured that any funding she provides will benefit the students on campus. The good friend who gets your text message will recognize your texting style and understand your abbreviated note.

You can think of the grammatical choices you have as tools in your writer's toolkit. You have a variety of tools for the differences in language that different rhetorical situations call for. To study grammar in this way—that is, to consider the conscious knowledge of sentence structure as your toolkit—is the essence of rhetorical grammar.

We begin this study of the tools by focusing, in Part I, on the words and phrases that constitute basic sentences, the patterns these sentences typically follow, the important role of verbs, and techniques for joining sentences (really *clauses*, but we'll discuss that term later). In Part II, you'll learn to put these tools to good use in controlling your message to account for reader expectations, while at the same time developing your writer's voice. Part III looks in more detail at expanding sentences and the rhetorical reasons for doing so.

In Part IV, you'll find yourself consulting—and appreciating—your subconscious language expertise in the chapter covering word classes. The final chapter, in Part V, describes the purpose and hierarchy of punctuation. The Glossary of Punctuation that follows Chapter 13 pulls together all the punctuation rules you have studied in context throughout the book.

The Bibliography that follows the Glossary of Punctuation lists the works mentioned in the text, along with other books and articles on rhetoric and grammar. The future teachers among you will find them useful for research purposes and for your teaching preparation.

Throughout the book you'll find exercises on the topics you've studied. Answers to the odd-numbered exercise items are included in the back of the book. You'll also be able to keep a style inventory, revise your own essays, and participate in group discussions on topics related to your reading.

Be sure to use the Glossary of Terms and the Index if you're having problems understanding a concept. They are there to provide help.

We'd like to conclude this brief introduction with a piece of advice: Don't be deceived by the bad press the word *grammar* has been given over the years. The study of grammar is not dull, and it's not difficult. If you take the time to read the pages in this book carefully and study the language you hear or read every day, you will easily fill your writer's toolkit to the brim and become confident and skillful at creating sentences appropriate for the rhetorical situations you encounter.

PART I

The Structure of Sentences

Using a language may be compared to riding a horse: much of one's success depends upon an understanding of what it can and will do.

—RICHARD WEAVER

You read in the Introduction that it's useful to think of your grammatical choices as tools in your writer's toolkit. Consider the tools filling the drawers in the mechanic's toolbox and the tools in the carpenter's shop. Each has its name and its place and its particular job to do. The same is true for your writer's tools.

In these first four chapters you'll learn about your writing tools: their names, their places, their jobs, what they can and will do:

Chapter 1: A Review of Words and Phrases

Chapter 2: Sentence Patterns

Chapter 3: Our Versatile Verbs

Chapter 4: Coordination and Subordination

You'll discover that understanding the tools available to you—knowing the terminology of grammar and using it to think about and talk about your writing—will give you confidence as you compose and as you revise.

Some of the terminology will already be familiar. After all, you have spent a dozen years learning to read and write, learning the conventions of spelling and punctuation and paragraphing. In other words, you're not encountering an exotic new subject in these pages. So as you read, don't make the mistake of trying to memorize every new term, every grammatical concept. Instead, filter what you are reading through your own experience; ask yourself how and where that concept fits into your understanding.

CHAPTER
1

A Review
of Words and Phrases

CHAPTER PREVIEW

The purpose of this chapter is to review words and phrases. For the most part, we'll be using the terms of traditional grammar; however, instead of discussing the traditional eight parts of speech, we'll introduce you to two broad categories for classifying words: form classes and structure classes. (Pay attention to any words in boldface; they constitute your grammar vocabulary. Definitions for these terms are provided in the Glossary.) This review will lay the groundwork for the study of the sentence patterns and their expansions in the chapters that follow. By the end of this chapter, you'll be able to

- distinguish between the form classes and the structure classes of words;
- identify features of the four form classes: nouns, verbs, adjectives, and adverbs;
- identify the main components of phrases;
- recognize the subject–predicate relationship as the core structure in all sentences;
- recognize how your subconscious grammar knowledge can contribute to your conscious study of sentences and their parts.

FORM CLASSES

Instead of the traditional eight parts of speech, we'll introduce the word categories of the structural linguists, who classified words in two broad groups: **form classes**[1] and **structure classes**. In the middle of

---

[1]Words in bold type are defined in the Glossary of Terms, beginning on page 260

the twentieth century, linguists recognized that the traditional classification of words—eight parts of speech based on Latin—did not accurately describe the way words functioned in English. For example, they emphasized that content words—our **nouns**, **verbs**, **adjectives**, and **adverbs**—have special qualities that the other word classes do not have. Their numbers alone make them special: These four word classes constitute over 99 percent of our vocabulary. They are also different from other word classes in that they can be identified by their forms. Each of them has, or can have, particular endings, or suffixes. And that, of course, is the reason for the label *form classes*.

NOUNS AND VERBS

Here are two simple sentences to consider in terms of form, each consisting of a noun and a verb:

> Cats fight.
> Mary laughed.

You're probably familiar with the traditional definition of *noun* as the name of a person, place, or thing and *verb* as an action word. These definitions based on meaning are certainly useful (*noun* actually means "name" in Latin) although they're not always accurate. For example, a noun like *kindness* is not exactly a thing, nor is *expect* an action. And many, if not most, so-called action words, including *fight* and *laugh*, are also nouns: *The fight lasted only a few minutes; Mary's laugh filled the room.*

So in the case of our form classes, we'll go beyond meaning and consider a word's form in our definitions. Our two sample sentences illustrate one suffix for nouns and one for verbs: the **plural** marker, *-s*, on the noun *cat;* the **past tense** marker, *-ed,* on the verb *laugh.* We'll use these "formal" characteristics as criteria in our definitions of *noun* and *verb.*

The plural *-s* is one of two noun endings that we call **inflections;** the other noun inflection is the **possessive-case** ending, the apostrophe-plus-*s* (*Mary's laugh*)—or, in the case of most plural nouns, just the apostrophe (*the readers' expectations*).

When the dictionary identifies a word as a verb, it begins with the **base form** (*laugh*). This form is also known as the **infinitive**, which is often written with the infinitive marker *to* (*to laugh*). Comprehensive dictionaries will also list inflected forms. The **third-person singular**, which adds an *-s* to the base form, is used with the pronouns *he, she, it,* or with nouns these pronouns can replace. The **present participle** adds *-ing* to the base form. The addition of *-ed* to the base form produces a verb's **past tense** and **past participle**. We'll look at these forms more closely in Chapter 3.

But for now, let's revise the traditional definitions by basing them not on the meaning of the words but rather on their forms:

A noun is a word that can be made plural and/or possessive.
A verb is a word that can show tense, such as present and past.

FOR GROUP DISCUSSION

Many words in English can serve as either nouns or verbs.

> I made a *promise* to my boss. (noun)
> I *promised* to be on time for work. (verb)

Write a pair of short sentences for each of the following words, demonstrating that they can be either nouns or verbs.

> *visit   plant   point   feature   audition   offer*

Compare your sentences with those of a classmate. First, identify the nouns and verbs. Put an N next to each sentence that contains one of these words as a noun. Put a V next to each sentence that uses one of these words as a verb. Next, explain your reasoning. Can the word you identified as a noun be made plural or possessive? Can the word you identified as a verb be inflected?

THE NOUN PHRASE

The term **noun phrase** may be new to you, although you're probably familiar with the word **phrase,** which traditionally refers to any group of words that functions as a unit within the sentence. A phrase will always have a head, or **headword**; and as you might expect, the headword of the noun phrase is a noun. Most noun phrases also include a noun signaler, or marker, called a **determiner**. Here are three noun phrases you have seen in this chapter, with their headwords underlined and their determiners shown in italics:

> *the* <u>headword</u>
> *a* <u>unit</u>
> *the* traditional <u>definition</u>

As the third example illustrates, the headword may be preceded by a **modifier**. The most common modifier in preheadword position is an adjective, such as *traditional*.

As you may have noticed in the three examples, the opening determiners are the **articles** *a* and *the*. While they are our most common determiners, other word groups also function as determiners, signaling noun phrases. For example, the function of nouns and **pronouns** in the possessive case is almost always that of determiner:

> *Mary's* laugh
>
> *her* new car

Other common words functioning as determiners are the **demonstrative pronouns**—*this, that, these, those:*

> *this* old house
>
> *those* expensive sneakers

Because noun phrases can be single words, as we saw in our earlier examples (*Cats fight, Mary laughed*), it follows that not all noun phrases will have determiners. **Proper nouns,** such as the names of people and places (*Mary*), and plural nouns with a general meaning (*cats*) are among the most common that appear without a noun signaler.

In spite of these exceptions, however, it's accurate to say that most noun phrases do begin with determiners. Likewise, it's accurate to say— and important to recognize—that whenever you encounter a determiner *you can be sure you are at the beginning of a noun phrase*. In other words, articles (*a/an, the*) and certain other words, such as possessive nouns and pronouns, demonstrative pronouns, and numbers, tell you that a noun headword is on the way.

We can now identify three defining characteristics of nouns:

A noun is a word that can be made plural and/or possessive; it occupies the headword position in the noun phrase; it is usually signaled by a determiner.

In the study of syntax, which you are now undertaking, you can't help but notice the prevalence of noun phrases and their signalers, the determiners.

EXERCISE 1

Identify the determiners and headwords of the noun phrases in the following sentences. Two noun phrases do not have determiners. How do you know they are still noun phrases?

Note: Answers to the odd-numbered exercises are provided, beginning on page 274.

1. The guitar is a universal instrument.
2. The electric guitar became popular in the 1930s.
3. This innovation rocked the world, so to speak.
4. The electric guitar has played an important role in our culture.
5. Experience Music Project has an exhibit of famous guitars.
6. The exhibit includes Jimi Hendrix's Fender Stratocaster from the Woodstock Festival in 1969.

THE VERB PHRASE

As you'd expect, the headword of a **verb phrase** is the verb; the other components, if any, will depend in part on the subclass of verb, for example, whether it is followed by a noun phrase: A noun phrase follows a **transitive verb** (*The cat chased the mouse*) but not an **intransitive verb** (*Cats fight*). In many, if not most, sentences, the verb phrase will include modifiers (*Mary laughed loudly*). Our two earlier examples—*Cats fight; Mary laughed*—illustrate instances of single-word noun phrases and single-word verb phrases. In the sections that follow, you'll learn how phrases are expanded.

NP + VP = S

This formula, NP + VP = S, is another way of saying "**Subject** plus **Predicate** equals Sentence." Our formula with the labels NP and VP simply emphasizes the form of those two sentence parts, noun phrase and verb phrase. The NP functions as the subject of the sentence; the VP functions as the predicate. The following diagram includes labels of both form and function:

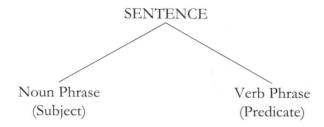

Given what you have learned so far about noun phrases and verb phrases—and with the help of your intuition—you should have no trouble recognizing the two parts of the following sentences. You'll notice right away that the first word of the subject noun phrase in all the sentences is a determiner.

> Our county commissioners passed a new ordinance.
>
> The mayor's husband spoke against the ordinance.
>
> The mayor was upset with her husband.
>
> The merchants in town are unhappy.
>
> This new law prohibits billboards on major highways.

As a quick review of noun phrases, identify the headwords of the subject noun phrases in the five sentences just listed.

You probably had little difficulty identifying the headwords: *commissioners, husband, mayor, merchants, law.*

To find the subject (NP) and predicate (VP) of a sentence, you can use your subconscious knowledge of pronouns. Simply substitute a **personal pronoun** (*I, you, he, she, it, they*) for the subject. What remains is the predicate.

EXERCISE 2

Find the border between the subject and the predicate of the sentences from the previous discussion; then supply a pronoun for the subject.

Examples: The guitar / is a universal instrument. (It)

1. Our county commissioners passed a new ordinance. (   )

2. The mayor's husband spoke against the ordinance. (   )

3. The mayor was upset with her husband. (   )

4. The merchants in town are unhappy. (   )

5. This new law prohibits billboards on major highways. (   )

....

As your answers no doubt show, the personal pronoun stands in for the entire noun phrase, not just the noun headword. Making that substitution, which you do automatically in speech, can help you recognize not only the subject/predicate boundary, but the boundaries of noun phrases throughout the sentence.

Recognition of this subject–predicate relationship is the first step in the study of sentence structure. Equally important for the classification of sentences into sentence patterns is the concept of the verb as the central, pivotal position in the sentence. Before moving on to the sentence patterns, however, we'll look briefly at two other word classes, adjectives and adverbs, which, like nouns and verbs, can often be identified by their forms. We'll then describe the prepositional phrase, perhaps our most common modifier, one that adds information to both the noun phrase and the verb phrase.

ADJECTIVES AND ADVERBS

The other two form classes, **adjectives** and **adverbs,** like nouns and verbs, can usually be recognized by their form and/or by their position in the sentence.

The inflectional endings that identify adjectives and some adverbs are the **comparative** suffix, *-er,* and the **superlative,** *-est:*

Adjective	Adverb
big	near
bigger	nearer
biggest	nearest

When the word has two or more syllables, the comparative and superlative markers are generally *more* and *most,* rather than the *-er* and *-est* suffixes:

beautiful	quickly
more beautiful	more quickly
most beautiful	most quickly

Another test of whether a word is an adjective or adverb, as opposed to a noun or verb, is its ability to pattern with a **qualifier,** such as *very:*

> very beautiful   very quickly

You'll notice that these tests (the inflectional endings and *very*) can help you differentiate adjectives and adverbs from the other two form classes, nouns and verbs, but they do not help you distinguish the two word classes from each other.

There is one special clue about word form that we use to help iden-tify adverbs: the *-ly* ending. However, the *-ly* is not an inflectional suf-fix like *-er* or *-est;* when we add one of these to an adjective—*happier, happiest*—the word remains an adjective (just as a noun with the plural inflection added is still a noun). In contrast, the *-ly* ending that makes adverbs so noticeable is actually added to adjectives to turn them into adverbs:

Adjective				Adverb
quick	+	ly	=	quickly
pleasant	+	ly	=	pleasantly
happy	+	ly	=	happily

Rather than inflectional, the *-ly* is a **derivational suffix:** It enables us to *derive* adverbs from adjectives. Incidentally, the *-ly* means "like": quickly = quick-like; happily = happy-like. And because we have so many adjectives that can morph into adverbs in this way—many thousands, in fact—we are not often mistaken when we assume that an *-ly* word is an adverb. (In Chapter 12 you'll read about derivational suffixes for all four form classes.)

In addition to these "adverbs of manner," as the *-ly* adverbs are called, we have an inventory of other adverbs that present no clue of form; among them are *then, now, soon, here, there, everywhere, afterward, often, sometimes, seldom, always.* Often the best way to identify an adverb is by the kind of information it supplies to the sentence—information of time, place, manner, frequency, and the like; in other words, it answers such questions as where, when, why, how, and how often. Adverbs can also be identified on the basis of their position in the predicate and their movability.

As you read in the discussion of noun phrases, the position between the determiner and the headword is where we find adjectives:

this <u>new</u> recipe   an <u>enormous</u> crowd

Adverbs, on the other hand, modify verbs and, as such, will be part of the predicate:

> Some residents spoke <u>passionately</u> for the ordinance.
> Mario <u>suddenly</u> hit the brakes.

One of the features of adverbs that makes them so versatile for writers and speakers is their movability: They can often be moved to a different place in the predicate—and they can even leave the predicate and open the sentence:

> Mario hit the brakes <u>suddenly</u>.
> <u>Suddenly</u> Mario hit the brakes.

Bear in mind, however, that some adverbs are more movable than others. We probably don't want to move *passionately* to the beginning of its sentence. And in making the decision to move the adverb, we also want to consider the context, the relation of the sentence to others around it.

◀ FOR GROUP DISCUSSION

Identify the adjectives and adverbs in the following sentences. Are the adverbs moveable? If so, rewrite the sentence, moving the adverb to another position in the sentence. Compare your revised sentences with those of your classmates.

1. I have finally finished my annual report.
2. Maria has now made great progress toward her goal.
3. The hunters moved stealthily through the deep woods.
4. The young activists organized rallies everywhere.
5. My best and oldest friend occasionally surprises me with a visit.

PREPOSITIONAL PHRASES

Before discussing sentence patterns, we'll take a quick look at the **prepositional phrase**, a two-part structure consisting of a **preposition** followed by a noun phrase called the **object of the preposition**. Prepositions are among the most common words in our language. In fact, the paragraph you are now reading includes eight different prepositions: *before, at, of* (four times), *by, among, in* (twice), *throughout,* and *as* (twice). Prepositional phrases appear throughout our sentences, sometimes as part of a noun phrase and sometimes as a modifier of the verb.

In a noun phrase, the prepositional phrase adds a detail or makes clear the identity of the noun, which it follows in postheadword position.

>Fans <u>in the ballpark</u> celebrated boisterously.

In this sentence the *in* phrase is part of the subject noun phrase. Notice that *they* can replace *fans in the ballpark*:

>They celebrated boisterously.

Because this *in* phrase functions like an adjective, telling us "which fans," we call it an **adjectival** prepositional phrase. In a different sentence, that same phrase could function adverbially:

>Fans celebrated boisterously <u>in the ballpark</u>.

Here the *in* phrase in the predicate functions like an adverb, telling "where"—so we refer to its function as **adverbial.** Another good clue that the phrase is adverbial is its movability; it could open the sentence:

><u>In the ballpark</u> fans celebrated boisterously.

Remember that the noun's *adjective* and *adverb* name word classes; they name forms. When we add the *-al* or *-ial* suffix—*adjectival* and *adverbial*—they become the names of functions—functions that adjectives and adverbs normally perform. In other words, the terms *adjectival* and *adverbial* can apply to structures other than adjectives and adverbs—such as prepositional phrases, as we have just seen.

Modifiers of nouns are called *adjectivals*, no matter what their form. They usually answer the question "*Which [noun]*"?

Modifiers of verbs are called *adverbials*, no matter what their form. They answer the questions "*When?*" "*Where?*" "*How*"?

EXERCISE 3

Underline the prepositional phrases in the following sentences and identify them as either adjectival or adverbial:

1. You will often find a cake at special parties.
2. Birthday cakes are common in many Western cultures.

3. Birthday cakes in ancient Rome contained nuts and honey.

4. Cupcakes are a popular alternative to birthday cakes.

5. Most people add candles to the top of the birthday cake.

Unlike the form classes, a preposition cannot be distinguished by its form; that is, there are no special endings that identify it. Prepositions are one of the word classes called **structure classes**. Other structure classes include determiners, qualifiers (such as *very*, which you saw in the discussion of adjectives and adverbs), **auxiliaries,** also known as helping verbs, and **conjunctions**. We discuss auxiliaries and conjunctions in Chapters 3 and 4, respectively.

Because prepositional phrases are such common structures in our language, you might find it helpful to review the lists of **simple** and **phrasal prepositions** in Chapter 12. You'll find them on page 225.

FOR GROUP DISCUSSION

Add modifiers (adverbs, adjectives, or prepositional phrases) to the five sentences that follow. Then exchange your sentences with a classmate and identify the modifiers added. As a class, vote on your favorite sentences.

Example: The pipes caused contamination.

The *rusty* pipes *under the sink* caused *serious* contamination *of our water.*

1. The tulips are finally blooming.
2. The children annoyed the neighbors.
3. The carpet matches the furniture.
4. The water glistened in the light.
5. Thunderstorms frightened the hikers.

KEY TERMS

In this chapter you've been introduced to many basic terms that describe sentence grammar. This list may look formidable, but some of the terms were probably familiar already; those that are new will become more familiar as you continue the study of sentences.

Adjectival
Adjective
Adverb
Adverbial
Article
Auxiliaries
Base form of verb
Comparative
Conjunctions
Derivational suffix
Demonstrative
  pronoun
Determiner
Form classes
Headword

Infinitive
Intransitive verb
Inflection
Modifier
Noun
Noun phrase
Object of the
  preposition
Past participle
Past tense
Personal pronoun
Phrase
Plural
Possessive case
Predicate

Preposition
Prepositional phrase
Present participle
Pronoun
Proper noun
Qualifier
Structure classes
Subject
Superlative
Third-person singular
Transitive verb
Verb
Verb phrase

Sentence Patterns

CHAPTER PREVIEW

This chapter extends your study of sentence structure, focusing on seven sentence patterns that account for the underlying skeletal structure of nearly all sentences in the language. These basic patterns will give you a solid framework for understanding the expanded sentences presented in the chapters that follow. This chapter will help you to

- recognize four types of verbs: *be*, linking, intransitive, and transitive;
- identify seven basic sentence patterns;
- distinguish among verb complements;
- discuss the placement and function of optional adverbials;
- recognize imperative and interrogative sentences (commands and questions);
- use short sentences to good effect.

RHETORICAL EFFECTS

We open our study of sentence patterns by looking at the opening paragraph of an essay by Annie Dillard, a well-known essayist and observer of nature:

> A weasel is wild. Who knows what he thinks? He sleeps in his underground den, his tail draped over his nose. Sometimes he lives in his den for two days without leaving. Outside, he stalks rabbits, mice, muskrats, and birds, killing more bodies

than he can eat warm, and often dragging the carcasses home. Obedient to instinct, he bites his prey at the neck, either splitting the jugular vein at the throat or crunching the brain at the base of the skull, and he does not let go. One naturalist refused to kill a weasel who was socketed into his hand deeply as a rattlesnake. The man could in no way pry the tiny weasel off, and he had to walk half a mile to water, the weasel dangling from his palm, and soak him off like a stubborn label.

—Annie Dillard, *Teaching a Stone to Talk*

Dillard's opening sentence couldn't be simpler. She has used what may be our most common sentence pattern: "Something is something." You won't have to read far in most modern essays, or in this textbook, to find the use of *be* as a linking verb. (Notice the first sentence following the weasel quotation!) *Be* is the infinitive; the other forms you may encounter are *am, is, are, was, were,* or *been.*

Dillard could easily have come up with fancier words, certainly more scientific-sounding ones, if she had wanted to:

Scientists recognize the weasel, genus *Mustela,* as a wild creature. As with other wild animals, one can only speculate about the weasel's thinking process, if, indeed, animals do think in the accepted sense of the word.

Are you tempted to read on? (If you have to, maybe—if there's a weasel test coming up!) It's possible that some people might continue reading even if they didn't have to—weasel specialists, perhaps. But for the average reader, the effect—the rhetorical effect—of this stodgy rewrite is certainly different from the breezy,

A weasel is wild. Who knows what he thinks?

Dillard's reader is likely to think, "Here comes an essay that promises a new glimpse of nature—one that I will understand and enjoy. It's written in my kind of language."

The **linking-*be*** sentence pattern provides a good illustration of both our subconscious grammar ability and the concept of rhetorical awareness, of recognizing the effect our sentences can have on readers. As native speakers, we learn to use *be,* including its irregular past forms—*was* and *were*—and its three present tense forms—*am, are,* and *is*—perhaps without even realizing they are related to the infinitive *to be.* If you are not a native speaker of English, you have probably spent a great deal of time learning the various forms of *be* and how they are used, just as native

English speakers studying a foreign language must do when learning its equivalent of *be*.

The linking-*be* pattern is one of seven basic sentence patterns we describe in this chapter. These seven represent the underlying skeletal structure of nearly all sentences in English—perhaps 95 percent of them. As you study the patterns, you'll find it useful to think of them in terms of their required parts. You've already seen the two basic sentence units: the subject and predicate. The next step is to differentiate among the seven patterns on the basis of the structures in the predicate. Here are the two units in the predicate of the weasel sentence:

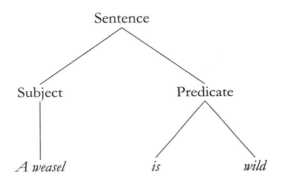

In this pattern the structure following the linking *be* is called a **subject complement** because it says something about the subject: The adjective *wild* is a modifier of *weasel.* The word *complement* comes from the verb meaning "to complete"; it's useful to think of a complement as a completer of the verb.

There are four categories of verbs that produce our seven patterns: ***be*** **patterns,** the **linking verbs,** the **intransitive verbs,** and the **transitive verbs.** These categories are differentiated on the basis of their complements. The patterns add up to seven because *be* is subclassified into two groups and the transitive verbs into three.

THE *BE* PATTERNS

Because *be* plays such an important part in sentence structure, not only as a main verb but also as an auxiliary, we put our *be* sentences into patterns separate from the linking verbs. And while most *be* sentences do have a subject complement, like the one we saw in the weasel sentence, some do not. The first pattern describes those sentences in which the second unit in the predicate contains an **adverbial** of time or place rather than a subject complement. Pattern 1 is not generally considered the linking use of *be*.

PATTERN 1	SUBJECT	*BE*	ADVERBIAL
	The weasel	*is*	*in his den.*
	The final liftoff	*was*	*yesterday.*

In Pattern 2, the subject complement describes or renames the subject. If it's a noun phrase, it has the same **referent** as the subject. *Referent* means the person or thing or event or concept that a noun or pronoun stands for; in other words, *I* and *an optimist* refer to the same person—in this case, the writer or speaker.

PATTERN 2	SUBJECT	*BE*	SUBJECT COMPLEMENT
	I	*am*	*an optimist.* (Noun phrase)
	The winters	*are*	*quite cold.* (Adjective phrase)

When the subject complement contains an adjective, as we have seen in two examples—*A weasel is wild; The winters are quite cold M-dash_* that complement names a quality of the subject. An alternative way of modifying the subject is to shift the adjective to the position before the noun headword: *a wild weasel; the cold winters.* That, of course, is precisely what the subject complement means; the difference between the two structures, the prenoun modifier and the subject complement, has to do with emphasis and purpose rather than meaning. The subject complement position puts greater emphasis on the adjective.

THE LINKING VERB PATTERN

The term *linking verb* applies to all verbs other than *be* completed by a subject complement—the adjective or noun phrase that describes or identifies the subject. Among the common linking verbs are the verbs of the senses—*taste, smell, feel, sound,* and *look*—which often link an adjective to the subject. *Become* and *remain* are the two most common ones that connect a noun or noun phrase. Other common linking verbs are *seem, appear,* and *prove.*

PATTERN 3	SUBJECT	LINKING VERB	SUBJECT COMPLEMENT
	The trail	*looked*	*steep.* (Adjective phrase)
	My sister	*became*	*a nurse.* (Noun phrase)

As with Pattern 2, the subject complement is in line for emphasis.

THE INTRANSITIVE VERB PATTERN

In the intransitive pattern, the predicate has only one requirement: the verb alone.

PATTERN 4	SUBJECT	INTRANSITIVE VERB
	Mary	*laughed.*
	Accidents	*happen.*

As you know, such skeletal sentences are fairly rare in actual writing. The point here is that they are grammatical: No complements are required. In the section "The Optional Adverbial" later in this chapter, we'll look again at adverbial modifiers, structures that add information about time and place and manner and reason, which are commonly added to all the sentence patterns, including this one. However, adding a modifier does not change the basic pattern. The following variations of our samples remain Pattern 4 sentences:

> Mary laughed at my silly hat.
>
> Accidents happen quickly.

Other common intransitive verbs are *change, happen, live, meet, occur, smile, wait*—and literally thousands more. These are among the many verbs known as **action verbs**.

EXERCISE 4

Identify the boundaries of the sentence units in each of the following sentences. Then identify the pattern number. The adverbials are identified with italics. (Remember the trick you learned in Chapter 1 of substituting a pronoun to find the boundaries of a noun phrase.)

Example: The world of computers / remains / a mystery / *to my grandmother.* (Pattern ____3____)

1. Annie Dillard is a keen observer of nature. (Pattern _____)

2. Our committee meeting is *in the library.* (Pattern _____)

3. His excuse sounded plausible. (Pattern _____)

4. The weasel sleeps *in his underground den.* (Pattern _____)

5. The bus from Flagstaff arrived *at two o'clock.* (Pattern _____)

6. The players were *at spring training.* (Pattern _____)

7. The public transportation in our area is unreliable. (Pattern _____)

8. Seemingly invisible bits of nature become visible *with Annie Dillard's words.* (Pattern _____)

THE BASIC TRANSITIVE VERB PATTERN

Transitive verbs are the other action verbs. Unlike intransitive verbs, all transitive sentences have one complement in common: the **direct object.** Pattern 5 is the basic pattern for transitive verbs.

PATTERN 5	SUBJECT	TRANSITIVE VERB	DIRECT OBJECT
	Weasels	*stalk*	*rabbits.*
	My roommate	*borrowed*	*my laptop.*

Transitive verbs are traditionally defined as those verbs in which the action is directed to, or transmitted to, an object—in contrast to the intransitive verbs, which have no object. The direct object tells "what" or "whom."

In Pattern 3 we also saw a noun phrase following the verb, and it too answers the question of "what":

My roommate and I became *good friends.*

The distinction between Patterns 3 and 5 lies in the relationship of the complement noun phrase to the subject: In Pattern 3, the two units have the same referent; they refer to the same people. We could, in fact, say

My roommate and I *are* good friends,

using the linking *be,* turning the sentence into Pattern 2.

In Pattern 5, on the other hand, the two noun phrases, the subject and the direct object, have different referents. We obviously cannot say, with any degree of seriousness,

> Weasels are rabbits.

Incidentally, the pronoun trick you learned for identifying the boundaries of the subject works for all noun phrases in the sentence, including direct objects. For example, in the right context the second sample sentence could be stated,

> My roommate borrowed it,

perhaps in answer to the question "Where's your laptop?" However, the use of the pronoun *it* changes the emphasis: When you say the sentence aloud, you'll notice that the main focus is now on the verb rather than on the direct object, as it is in the original sentence, the one with *my laptop.* You'll read about sentence focus again in Chapter 6.

TRANSITIVE PATTERNS WITH TWO COMPLEMENTS

The last two patterns have two complements following the verb: In Pattern 6 an **indirect object** precedes the direct object; in Pattern 7 an **object complement** follows the direct object.

PATTERN 6	SUBJECT	TRAN-SITIVE VERB	INDIRECT OBJECT	DIRECT OBJECT
	Marie	*sent*	*Ramon*	*a birthday gift.*
	Annie Dillard	*gives*	*her readers*	*insights into nature.*

In this pattern, two noun phrases follow the verb, and here all three—the subject, the indirect object, and the direct object—have different referents. We traditionally define *indirect object* as the recipient of the direct object or the person to whom or for whom the action is performed. In most cases this definition applies accurately. A Pattern 6 verb—and this is a limited group—usually has a meaning like "send" or "give" (for example, *bring, buy, offer*), and the indirect object usually names a person who is the receiver of whatever the subject gives.

An important characteristic of the Pattern 6 sentence is the option we have of shifting the indirect object to a position following the direct object, where it becomes the object of a preposition:

Marie sent a birthday gift to *Ramon.*

You might choose this order if, for example, you want to focus on Ramon, or if you want to add a modifier. A long modifier often fits the end of the sentence more smoothly than it would in the middle. Compare the two:

Marie sent a birthday gift to Ramon, *a friend from her old neighborhood in Northridge.*

Marie sent Ramon, *a friend from her old neighborhood in Northridge,* a birthday gift.

The original order will be more effective if it's the direct object you wish to emphasize or expand:

Marie gave Ramon a birthday gift, *a necktie she had made herself.*

PATTERN 7	SUBJECT	TRANSITIVE VERB	DIRECT OBJECT	OBJECT COMPLE-MENT
	The director	*considered*	*the performance*	*a success.*
	The critic	*called*	*the acting*	*brilliant.*

In this pattern the direct object is followed by a second complement, called an **object complement,** a noun phrase or an adjective that describes the direct object. Note that the relationship between these two complements is the same as the relationship between the subject and the subject complement in Patterns 2 and 3. In fact, we could easily turn these two complements into a Pattern 2 sentence:

The performance was a success.

The acting was brilliant.

It's obvious that this linking-*be* version of the relationship changes the meaning: To call the acting brilliant does not mean that it really *is* brilliant.

Other verbs common to this pattern are *elect, find, make,* and *prefer:*

> Voters elected her governor.
> Some runners found the course challenging.
> Calculators made bookkeeping easier.
> I prefer my coffee black.

SENTENCE PATTERN SUMMARY

1. Subject | ***Be*** | | **Adverbial**
The weasel | *is* | | *in his den.*

2. Subject | ***Be*** | | **Subject Complement**
I | *am* | | *an optimist.* (NP)
The winters | *are* | | *quite cold.* (AP)

3. Subject | **Linking Verb** | **Subject Complement**
The trail | *looked* | *steep.* (AP)
My sister | *became* | *a nurse.* (NP)

4. Subject | **Intransitive Verb**
Mary | *laughed.*

5. Subject | **Transitive Verb** | **Direct Object**
Weasels | *stalk* | *rabbits.*

6. Subject | **Transitive Verb** | **Indirect Object** | **Direct Object**
Marie | *sent* | *Ramon* | *a birthday gift.*

7. Subject | **Transitive Verb** | **Direct Object** | **Object Complement**
The director | *considered* | *the performance* | *a success.* (NP)
The critic | *called* | *the acting* | *brilliant.* (AP)

THE OPTIONAL ADVERBIAL

The units that make up the sentence pattern formulas can be thought of as the basic requirements for grammatical sentences. In other words, a linking verb requires a subject complement in order to be complete; a transitive verb requires a direct object. But there's another important unit that can be added to all the formulas, as mentioned in connection with the intransitive pattern: an optional adverbial, a structure that adds information about time, place, manner, reason, and the like.

Pattern 4, the intransitive pattern, rarely appears without at least one adverbial. Sentences as short as our two examples (*Mary laughed; Accidents happen*) are fairly rare in prose; and when they do appear, they nearly always call attention to themselves. The adverbials in the following sentence are underlined:

An accident happened <u>downtown</u> <u>during rush hour</u>.

As you learned in Chapter 1, the term *adverbial* refers to any grammatical structure that adds what we think of as "adverbial information." It adds the kind of information that adverbs add. In the example, *downtown* tells "where"; *during the rush hour* tells "when."

It's important to recognize that when we use the word *optional* we are referring only to grammaticality, not to the importance of the adverbial information. If you remove those underlined adverbials, you are left with a grammatical, albeit skeletal, sentence However, even though the sentence is grammatical in its skeletal form, many times the adverbial information is the very reason for the sentence—the main focus. For example, if you tell your readers

An accident happened downtown during rush hour,

you're probably doing so to provide information for readers to envision the scene; the adverbials are important information.

The variety of structures available for adding information makes the adverbial a remarkably versatile tool for writers. You can add a detail about frequency, for example, by using a single word, a phrase, a whole clause—or a combination—depending on the writing situation:

My friends and I have pizza <u>regularly</u>.

My friends and I have pizza <u>with persistent regularity</u>.

My friends and I have pizza <u>for breakfast, lunch, and dinner nearly every day of the week</u>.

My friends and I have pizza <u>whenever the mood strikes</u>.

And it's not just their form that makes adverbials so versatile. Perhaps even more important is their movability: They can open the sentence or close it; they can even be inserted between the required units for special effect. Many of the discussions about cohesion and rhythm that you'll read in the next few chapters are concerned with the placement of movable structures, including adverbials.

FOR GROUP DISCUSSION

Although the movability test is useful for identifying adverbials, it isn't infallible. Look at how *for everyone* is used in the following sentences. Would you label it "adverbial" or "adjectival"? Are there instances in which both labels would be possible?

1. The budget was a problem for everyone.
2. A problem for everyone was the budget.
3. For everyone the budget was a problem.

EXERCISE 5

A. Draw vertical lines to separate the sentence units, paying special attention to the various adverbials. Identify the verb category: *be*, linking, intransitive, or transitive.

Example: The Lincoln penny / first /appeared / in 1909.

Verb: intransitive

1. Many people now consider the penny a nuisance coin.

   Verb:

2. Early Lincoln pennies are very valuable today.

   Verb:

3. During World War II the government required large amounts of copper for war production.

   Verb:

4. In 1943 zinc-coated steel replaced the copper in the production of pennies.

   Verb:

5. The Philadelphia Mint unwittingly produced twelve copper pennies that year in addition to the new model.

   Verb:

6. The copper blanks for those twelve pennies were still in the press hopper during the production of the zinc-coated coins.

   Verb:

7. Those twelve 1943 copper pennies soon became valuable collectors' items.

   Verb:

8. Even after 100 years, the production of the Lincoln penny continues today.

   Verb:

B. Now revise the sentences in Part A by shifting the adverbials to other locations. You'll find that some are more movable than others.

....

QUESTIONS AND COMMANDS

This two-part structure—subject and predicate—underlies all of our sentences in English, even those in which the two parts may not be apparent at first glance. For example, in questions—also called **interrogative sentences**—the subject is sometimes located in the predicate half of the sentence; to discover the two parts, you have to recast the question in the form of a **declarative sentence,** or statement:

> *Question:* Which chapters will our test cover?

> *Statement:* Our test / will cover which chapters.

In the **command,** or **imperative sentence,** the subject—the "understood" *you*—generally doesn't show up at all; the form of the verb is always the base form:

> (You)   Hold the onions!
> (You)   Be a good sport.
> (You)   Come with me to the concert.

Questions and commands are certainly not structures to worry about: You've been an expert at using them for many years.

PUNCTUATION AND THE SENTENCE PATTERNS

There's an important punctuation lesson to be learned from the sentence patterns with their two, three, or four required units:

Do not mark boundaries of the required sentence units with punctuation.

That is, never use a single comma to separate

- **the subject from the verb.**
- **the direct object from the object complement.**
- **the indirect object from the direct object.**
- **the verb from the subject complement.**

And, with one exception, never separate

- **the verb from the direct object.**

The one exception to this rule occurs when the direct object is a direct quotation following a verb like *say:*

> He said, "I love you."

Here the punctuation convention calls for a comma before the quoted words.

Even though the separate units in the following sentences may be long and may require a pause for breath, there is simply no place for commas:

> All the sessions during Orientation Week / were / extremely helpful / for incoming freshmen. (Pattern 2)

> Every sportswriter who saw the preseason contest between the Buckeyes and the Aggies / said / that it was a game that will be remembered for a long time to come. (Pattern 5)

In discussions of modifiers in later chapters, you'll encounter sentences in which punctuation is called for *within* a unit:

> My roommate, who grew up in New York City, now lives on a farm in Vermont.

> Weasels, because they are wild, should be approached with great caution.

In both cases, the only reason for the commas is to set off the modifier. Note that the rule, highlighted at the beginning of this section, refers to a *single* comma as a boundary marker.

EXERCISE 6

A. Draw vertical lines between the separate units of the following sentences, and then identify their sentence patterns. You might want to use pronoun substitution to find all the noun phrases in the sentence: subject, direct object, indirect object, subject complement, object complements, as well as the objects in prepositional phrases. Optional adverbials are in italics. You can disregard them when identifying patterns.

1. *In 1747* a physician in the British navy conducted an experiment *to discover a cure for scurvy.*

2. *For sailors* scurvy was a serious problem.

3. Dr. James Lind fed six groups of scurvy victims six different remedies.

4. *When the men consumed oranges and lemons every day,* they recovered miraculously.

5. *Although fifty years passed before the British Admiralty Office recognized Lind's findings,* a daily dose of fresh lemon juice became a requirement.

6. *Interestingly,* Lind's discovery also affected the English language.

7. *In the eighteenth century,* the British called lemons *limes.*

8. *Because of that navy diet,* people call British sailors *limeys.*

9. This word is in the dictionary, *though it is labeled "derogatory."*

EXERCISE 7

Explain why the following sentences are punctuated *in*correctly.

1. The first American winner of a Nobel Prize, was Theodore Roosevelt.

2. After the assassination of President William McKinley, Roosevelt, took office at the age of 42.

3. Voters elected Roosevelt, president of the United States in 1904.

4. Roosevelt told, veterans in Illinois "A man who is good enough to shed his blood for his country is good enough to be given a square deal afterwards."

BASIC PATTERNS IN PROSE

You really don't need instruction for writing or punctuating short sentences—as you have seen, most of them need no punctuation—but you may need instruction in using them. Or maybe *encouragement* is a better word: You may need encouragement to use short sentences. It's not unusual for inexperienced writers to believe that writing calls for long sentences rather than short ones, just as they may believe that writing calls for fancy words rather than plain ones. Both notions are oversimplified. In Chapter 7 we take up the topic of fancy words in the discussion of diction. Here we consider the effectiveness of short sentences, many of which are bare-bones patterns.

The bare sentence pattern as a paragraph opener is a common strategy, especially the Pattern 2, something-is-something sentence like Annie Dillard's "A weasel is wild." Dillard uses many such sentences in her prose—sometimes with other patterns, sometimes with an added adverbial, but still very short. The following examples are from her book *Pilgrim at Tinker Creek*:

> Today is the winter solstice.
> In September the birds were quiet.
> I live in tranquility and trembling.

Richard Ellis opens the first paragraph of his book *The Search for the Giant Squid* with our familiar *be* pattern:

> The giant squid is a real-life enigma.

In his biography of President Harry Truman, David McCullough often introduces a long paragraph with a short *be* sentence:

> He had been a big success as a soldier.
> His real love, however, was politics.
> Politics was personal contact.

But short sentences like these commonly appear in other positions as well. It's not unusual to find a short sentence in the middle of a paragraph of longer sentences—especially when the writer wants to draw the reader's attention, to focus on a particular point. In the following example, from a *Time* article by J. Madeleine Nash dated July 11, 2005, on the movement to demolish dams, the reader can't miss the focus of the short third sentence. Notice, too, how it changes the focus of the paragraph:

> Shaping up as an important milestone is the demolition of two
> large dams in Washington State's Elwha River, which flows

from the mountains of Olympic National Park into the Juan de Fuca Strait. Their removal . . . would occur in states, and if it goes as planned, the Pacific Northwest will lose only a tiny amount of hydropower and regain a legendary salmon fishery. <u>But there could be problems.</u> Behind Elwha dams are some 18 million cubic yards of accumulated sediment, enough to fill four superdomes, and if a lot of that sediment starts to move down-stream at once, the ecological consequences could be severe.

Short, focused sentences like this one are bound to draw the attention of the reader.

The linking-*be* pattern, so often used in short sentences, is one you may have been warned about using. And such a warning is well taken; you'll certainly want to consider an alternative to *be*, especially if you find yourself using it to the exclusion of other verbs. But bear in mind that, given a particular context, *be* sentences can be just as effective as those of any other verb category. As these examples illustrate, they are commonly used by professional writers to introduce paragraph topics.

Are there other types of sentences that can be used to establish a topic or shift focus? Well, yes, consider using a command or a question, as does Michael Pollan in *The Botany of Desire*:

Start with the taste. Imagine a moment when the sensation of honey or sugar on the tongue was an astonishment, a kind of in-toxication. The closest I've ever come to recovering such a sense of sweetness was secondhand, though it left a powerful impres-sion on me even so. I'm thinking of my son's first experience with sugar: the icing on the cake at his first birthday. I have only the testimony of Isaac's face to go by (that, and his fierceness to repeat the experience), but it was plain that his first encounter with sugar had intoxicated him—was in fact an ecstasy, in the literal sense of the word. That is, he was beside himself with the pleasure of it, no longer here with me in space and time in quite the same way he had been just a moment before. Between bites Isaac gazed up at me in amazement (he was on my lap, and I was delivering the ambrosial forkfuls to his gaping mouth) as if to exclaim, "Your world contains *this*? From this day forward I shall dedicate my life to it." (Which he basically has done.) And I remember thinking, this is no minor desire, and then won-dered: Could it be that sweetness is the prototype of *all* desire?

Pollan not only draws the reader into the paragraph with two opening commands but also raises a question at the end of the paragraph to estab-lish the topic of his book.

FOR GROUP DISCUSSION

A. The following paragraph opens a chapter of William W. Warner's *Beautiful Swimmers: Watermen, Crabs and the Chesapeake Bay.*

Winter

It can come anytime from the last week in October to the first in December. There will be a fickle day, unseasonably warm, during which two or three minor rain squalls blow across the Bay. The sun appears fitfully in between; sometimes there is distant thunder. <u>A front is passing</u>. The first warning that it is more than an ordinary autumnal leaf-chaser comes near the end. The ragged trailing edge of a normal front is nowhere to be seen. Ominously absent is the steady procession of fleecy white puffball clouds that usually presages two or three days of fine weather. Rather, the front picks up speed and passes so rapidly that it is stormy at one moment and unbelievably clear and cloud-free the next. <u>Then it comes</u>. The wind rises in a few minutes from a placid five or ten knots to a sustained thirty or forty, veering quickly first to the west and then to the northwest. <u>The dry gale has begun</u>. Short and steep seas, so characteristic of the Chesapeake, rise up from nowhere to trip small boats. Inattentive yachtsmen will lose sails and have the fright of their lives. Workboat captains not already home will make for any port.

1. Note that the title word *winter*—which is also the topic here—does not appear in the paragraph, represented only by the pronoun *it*. What effect does that omission have? In what way would *Winter* as the first word, instead of *It,* affect the drama?

2. You saw a three-word, a four-word, and a five-word sentence in this paragraph. What purpose do they serve? How did they affect your reading?

B. Imagine an unusual place you've visited. Think of three versions of an opening sentence for a paragraph describing this place. Try using a short sentence, a command, and a question. Ask at least two of your classmates which version they consider most engaging.

THE SHORT PARAGRAPH

Another attention-getter is the short paragraph that appears on a page of long, well-developed ones. In *Pilgrim at Tinker Creek* Annie Dillard adds drama with an occasional paragraph of one or two sentences, often used for transition from one topic to another, much like the newspaper example we saw earlier. Each of these examples is a complete paragraph:

> The woods were restless as birds.
> The world has locusts, and the world has grasshoppers. I was up to my knees in the world.

In his book *Undaunted Courage*, the story of Lewis and Clark's journey to the Pacific, historian Stephen E. Ambrose often uses the short paragraph of transition:

> Thus armed with orders, guns, and goods, Lewis set out to meet the Indians of the Great Plains.

Like short sentences in a paragraph of long ones, these short paragraphs call attention to themselves. They, too, say, "Pay attention!" They, too, should be crafted carefully.

KEY TERMS

Action verbs	Indirect object	Question
Adverbial	Interrogative sentence	Referent
Be patterns	Intransitive verb	Sentence pattern
Command	Linking-*be*	Subject
Declarative sentence	Linking verb	Subject complement
Direct object	Object complement	Transitive verb
Imperative sentence	Predicate	

RHETORICAL REMINDERS

Have I made use of short sentences to focus the reader's attention?

Have I made use of short paragraphs where needed for transition or other special effects?

PUNCTUATION REMINDER

Have I made sure that a comma does not separate the required units of my sentences?

Our Versatile Verbs

CHAPTER PREVIEW

This chapter focuses on the expansion of verbs for expressing subtle variations in time and focus. After you study each section closely, completing all the exercises, you'll be able to

- choose verbs that convey your message clearly and engagingly;
- select verb tenses that maintain a consistent time frame;
- explain why some shifts in time frame are logical;
- recognize effective uses of the passive voice;
- understand the positive effects of showing, not just telling.

THE EXPANDED VERB

In Chapter 1 you were introduced to the five forms that all verbs have. Let's take a minute to review those forms:

Base form	film	test-drive
-s form	films	test-drives
Past tense	filmed	test-drove
Past participle	filmed	test-driven
Present participle	filming	test-driving

All verbs have these five forms. Notice that the past tense and past participle forms are identical in the case of *film,* a **regular verb**. In fact, this characteristic—the addition of *-ed* to the base form to produce a verb's past and past participle—is the essential definition of "regular verb." The verb *drive* and its cousin *test-drive* are among our 150 or so **irregular verbs**, those in which the past tense and the past participle are *not* produced with the regular inflections. Among the irregular verbs, there's a great variety in these two forms.

The verb *be*, our only verb with more than these five forms, has eight forms: *am, are, is, was, were, been, being,* and *be*—the infinitive form. *Be* is our only verb that has an infinitive form that is different from the present tense.

In the first two chapters the verbs provided in examples were limited to the one-word variety, the simple **present** and **past tenses**. As you are well aware, many of the predicates we use go beyond these tenses to include **auxiliary verbs**, also called **helping verbs**. You'll find the auxiliary—sometimes more than one—in the position before the main verb:

Microsoft *is* accepting internship applications until May 1.

My little brother *has* read all the Harry Potter books three times.

Jamal *has been* volunteering at the food bank on Saturdays.

Sometimes the auxiliary and the main verb are separated by an adverb:

Microsoft *is* now accepting internship applications.

Although the way auxiliaries are combined with main verbs may seem chaotic, in fact, it's very systematic. To understand this system, you must be able to distinguish between the two ways verb tenses are labeled. The first is perhaps familiar to you: Verbs are labeled according to time as *present, past,* or *future.* The second is probably less familiar: Verbs are also labeled as *simple, progressive, perfect,* or *perfect progressive.* The following chart shows how these two different ways of labeling combine to create the traditional names for our wide array of tenses. In the chart we use the verb *drive* as our example. Note that the three columns designate time.

Verb Tenses			
	PRESENT	PAST	FUTURE
Simple	drive, drives (simple present)	drove (simple past)	*will* drive (simple future)
Progressive	*am* (*is, are*) driving (present progressive)	*was* (*were*) driving (past progressive)	*will be* driving (future progressive)
Perfect	*has* (*have*) driven (present perfect)	*had* driven (past perfect)	*will have* driven (future perfect)
Perfect progressive	*has* (*have*) *been* driving (present perfect progressive)	*had been* driving (past perfect progressive)	*will have been* driving (future perfect progressive)

As you can see, in the first row, a verb in the simple present or simple past does not team up with an auxiliary. A verb in the simple future, though, does take an auxiliary, the **modal auxiliary** *will* (which is discussed further on page 42). In the second row, you will find that the **present participle** (the *-ing* form of the verb) appears in all progressive tenses along with *be,* the form of which is determined by the time: *am, is,* and *are* for the present tense, *was* and *were* for the past tense, and *will be* for the future tense. Similarly, in the third row, the **past participle**, *driven,* appears in all the perfect tenses along with a form of the auxiliary *have: Has* and *have* are in the present tense, *had* is in the past tense, and *will have* is in the future tense. The fourth row is a combination of the previous two: In each of the perfect-progressive tenses, you'll see *been,* the past participle of *be,* as one auxiliary followed by the main verb, the present participle *driving;* the first auxiliary in the string is a form of *have.*

You may be wondering why there is more than one auxiliary listed in each cell. The form of the auxiliary verb depends on the subject of the sentence. For example, when *I* is the subject, the verb in the present progressive will be *am driving;* the verb will be *are driving* when *you, we,* or *they* is the subject; *he, she,* or *it* as subject calls for *is driving.* (These variations will come up again in connection with point of view in Chapter 7; you'll also read about personal pronouns in Chapter 12.)

Using the Expanded Verbs

In this section you'll be encouraged to pay attention to the verb tenses used in prose. Consider the verb forms in the following paragraph from Scott Turow's essay "An Odyssey That Started with Ulysses":

> At the age of eighteen, after my freshman year in college, I worked as a mailman. This was merely a summer job. My life's calling, I had decided, was to be a novelist, and late at night I was already toiling on my first novel.

This passage includes five main verbs: *work, be, decide, be,* and *toil.* They occur, however, in different tenses:

worked—simple past

was—simple past

had decided—past perfect

was—simple past

was toiling—past progressive

When you check the chart on page 37, you'll discover that Turow's verbs are all in the "Past" column. By using the past tense throughout the paragraph, Turow is able to provide a consistent **time frame** for his narrative. This point may seem obvious. But sometimes, amid the fury of producing that first draft, the writer may inadvertently shift tenses.

> Because the library will be open long hours, my uncle spends his free time there.

Something sounds off beat here. You might be asking yourself why the verb *will be* is in the future tense, but *spends* is present. Is the library open long hours now? If it isn't, how can the uncle spend time there? This is the type of confusion that can occur when verb tenses are inconsistent.

You may remember hearing the rule to "avoid shifting tenses" in your writing. What does it mean? Don't writers shift tenses all the time? Yes and no. It's true that Scott Turow has shifted from simple past to past perfect to simple past to past progressive. But as we pointed out, he has stayed in one time frame: All of his verbs fit in the past column. A more accurate statement of the rule is "avoid shifting *time frames* when writing." As long as you use one time frame (present, past, or future), your tenses will be consistent.

There are times, however, when you may want to shift from one time frame to another. You can do this by using a time marker, very likely an adverbial, such as *today, yesterday, soon, in 2010, when I was younger.*

> We <u>take</u> our old magazines to a recycling center. *Soon,* however, we <u>will leave</u> them in curbside recycling bins.

The tense in the first of these two sentences is present; the tense in the second is future. The time marker *soon* signals the shift in time frame.

It is also possible for writers to shift time frames without using a specific time marker—but only when the reason for shifting is easily understood. The second sentence in the following pair of sentences provides historical information to support the assertion in the first sentence, so the shift from a present time frame to a past time frame is appropriate.

> Our recycling center <u>has moved</u>. The owners of the barn housing the center <u>refused</u> to renew our lease.

Another common shift occurs when a writer wants to add a comment that might aid the reader's understanding. In this example, the opening sentence is in the past tense, but the second sentence, the comment, is in the present.

> We recently <u>established</u> a website for reporting local air quality.
>
> Our reports <u>are</u> important to citizens with respiratory diseases.

FOR GROUP DISCUSSION

1. Read the passage below from Robert Grudin's *Time and the Art of Living.*

> In the late November of 1968, I <u>spent</u> a few days in a hotel just off the Piazza San Marco in Venice. At 6 one morning, hearing the loud warning bells, I <u>jumped</u> out of bed, <u>grabbed</u> my camera and <u>rushed</u> out to see the famous Venetian flood. I <u>stood</u> in the empty and as yet dry Piazza and <u>looked</u> out toward the Gulf, for I <u>expected</u> the flood tides to come in from the open water. Many minutes <u>passed</u> before I <u>turned</u> to see that the Piazza <u>was flooding</u>, not directly from the Gulf, but up through its own sewers. The indented gratings in the pavement <u>had</u> all but <u>disappeared</u> under calm, flat silver puddles, which <u>grew</u> slowly and silently until their peripheries <u>touched</u> and the Piazza <u>had become</u> a lake. That morning I <u>experienced</u> vividly, if almost subliminally, the reality of change itself: how it <u>fools</u> our sentinels and <u>undermines</u> our defenses, how careful we <u>are</u> to look for it in the wrong places, how it <u>does</u> not <u>reveal</u> itself until it <u>is</u> beyond redress, how vainly we <u>search</u> for it around us and <u>find</u> too late that it <u>has occurred</u> within us.

   Notice how Grudin begins with one time frame—then shifts to another. Why does he make this shift? Is it effective? Why or why not?

2. Reread Annie Dillard's weasel paragraph at the opening of Chapter 2 with time frames in mind. You'll find that she too has shifted. Did she have a good reason? Does it work? Why or why not?

EXERCISE 8

Correct any unnecessary tense shifts in the following paragraph.

1 The exchange of wedding rings during the wedding ceremony came into fashion in the late nineteenth century.

2 Before the Great Depression, it is more common for just women to wear wedding rings.

3   However, successful advertising campaigns after the Second
World War convinces couples to exchange rings.

4   This custom is now widespread.

Special Uses of the Present Tense

Although you might assume that the present tense is used only to refer
to present time, this is not the case. In some rhetorical situations writers
use the present tense to refer to past events. For example, fiction writers
sometimes use the simple present tense to make action more immediate
or suspenseful. The following passage is from the first chapter of William
Trevor's novel *Felicia's Journey*. In this scene Felicia is riding on a train:

> The train <u>judders</u> on, rattling on the rails, slowing almost to
> a halt, gathering speed again. Felicia <u>opens</u> her eyes. A hazy
> dawn <u>is distributing</u> farmhouses and silos and humped barns
> in shadowy fields. Later, there <u>are</u> long lines of motor cars
> creeping slowly on nearby roads, and blank early-morning
> faces at railway stations.

The present tense is also used in the analysis of literature. In this passage,
John Elder discusses Robert Frost's poem "Directive":

> Frost's opening lines not only <u>point</u> up to the ridge above Bristol,
> they also <u>identify</u> a tension fundamental to America's environ-
> mental movement. We <u>long</u> to save wild beauty from heedless de-
> velopment, to guarantee a modicum of biodiversity in the world
> of internal combustion engines and electronic monoculture.

We also use the simple present form of the verb to refer to habitual actions:

> The news comes on at six o'clock.
>
> I always vote a straight party ticket.

And we use the present in reference to propensities of nature:

> Bears hibernate in winter.
>
> Thunder follows lightning.

Other Auxiliaries

Do-Support. So far we have looked at three auxiliary verbs: *be, have,* and
will. Another common auxiliary is *do.* We call on *do*, or one of its other two
forms, *does* and *did*, when we need an auxiliary for converting a positive

sentence into a negative or turning a statement into a question or for carry-ing the emphasis—but only when the sentence has no other auxiliary:

> The crew *didn't film* at night.
> *Did* the crew *film* at night?
> The crew *did film* at night.

This auxiliary use of *do* is called **do-support**. In other words, *do* comes to the rescue when an auxiliary is needed. Like *be* and *have, do* can also serve as a main verb; in fact, all three are among our most common verbs.

Modal Auxiliaries. You're already familiar with one of the **modal auxil-iaries**: *will,* sometimes called "the sign of the future." Unlike *be, have,* and *do,* the job of the modals is to add nuances to the meaning of the main verb. The other modal auxiliaries are equally familiar: *can, could, may, might, must, shall, should, would, ought to.* These verbs signal a variety of meanings:

> Citizens *can* register to vote. (ability)
> Citizens *should* register to vote. (advisability)
> Citizens *must* register to vote. (obligation)

THE PASSIVE VOICE

You're probably familiar with the definition of a verb as an "action word," a description commonly applied to both intransitive and transitive verbs:

> The students graduated in June. (Pattern 4)
> My roommate wrote the play. (Pattern 5)

In these sentences the subjects are performing the action; they are making something happen. Linguists use the term **agent** for this "doer" of the verbal action. Another term that describes this relationship of the subject to the verb is **active voice**.

What happens when we turn the Pattern 5 sentence around, when we remove the agent from the subject position and give that role to the origi-nal direct object, *the play?*

> The play was written by my roommate.

This reversal has changed the sentence from active to **passive voice**. However, while *my roommate* is no longer the sentence subject, it is still the agent; and while *the play* is no longer the direct object, it is still the so-called receiver of the action. What has changed are their functions, their roles, in the sentence, not their relationship to each other.

The transformation from active to passive involves three steps:

1. An object, usually the direct object, becomes the subject.
2. A form of *be* is added as an auxiliary (in this case the past form *was,* because *wrote* is past); it joins the past participle of the main verb.
3. The original agent, if mentioned, becomes the object of the preposition *by* (or, in some cases, *for*). In the majority of passive sentences, no agent is mentioned.

Forms of the Passive Voice

The core of the passive verb is the auxiliary *be* and the past participle. Here is an abbreviated form of the tense chart you studied earlier; this time, though, it is filled with verbs in the passive voice.

Verb Tenses (Passive Voice)			
	PRESENT	PAST	FUTURE
Simple	*am, is, are* assigned	*was, were* assigned	*will be* assigned
Progressive	*am, is, are being* assigned	*was, were being* assigned	*will be, being* assigned
Perfect	*has, have been* assigned	*had been* assigned	*will have been* assigned

Using the Passive Voice

The passive voice has an important purpose: to shift the focus of the sentence, changing the topic under discussion. This shift is an important tool for sentence cohesion, a feature of writing you will explore in Chapter 5.

The passive voice may also be called for when the agent is unknown or has no bearing on the discussion:

> The Vikings have had a bad press. Their activities <u>are equated</u> with rape and pillage and their reputation for brutality is second only to that of the Huns and the Goths. Curiously, they also <u>have been invested</u> with a strange glamour which contradicts in many ways their fearsome image.
> —James Graham-Campbell and Dafydd Kidd (*The Vikings*)

The authors' purpose in this passage is not to explain who equates the Vikings with rape and pillage or who invests them with glamour. The use of the passive puts these statements in the category of accepted beliefs. Notice the absence of *by* phrases.

In some cases the passive voice is simply more straightforward:

> Joe <u>was wounded</u> in Iraq.

And sometimes, in order to add modifiers to the agent, we put it where we can do so more conveniently, at the end of the sentence:

> Early this morning a campus van <u>was hit</u> by a delivery truck traveling at high speed through the intersection of James Avenue and Water Street.

Note that if we switched the agent to the subject position, the result would be a fairly wide separation of the subject headword and the verb:

> Early this morning a delivery truck traveling at high speed through the intersection of James Avenue and Water Street hit a campus van.

The choice, of course, also depends on where the main focus should be. The passive voice is especially common—and deliberate—in technical and scientific writing, in legal documents, and in lab reports, where the researcher is the agent, but to say so would be inappropriate:

> *Active:* I increased the heat to 450° and allowed it to remain at that temperature for twenty minutes.
>
> *Passive:* The heat was increased to 450° and allowed to remain at that temperature for twenty minutes.

EXERCISE 9

It's important to recognize the passive voice when you see it—so that you'll know how to use it deliberately and effectively. Remember that the passive voice must have a form of the auxiliary *be* and the past participle of the main verb.

A. Transform the following active sentences into the passive voice; remember that the object of the active functions as the subject in the passive.

1. My roommate penned the lead article in today's *Collegian.*

2. Bach composed some of our most intricate fugues.

    3. The county commissioners are proposing a new tax-collection system this year.

    4. The young researcher developed a new drug for migraines.

B. Transform the following passive sentences into the active voice; remember that the subject of the passive is an object in the active. (Note: If the agent is missing, you will have to supply one to act as the subject for the sentences in the active voice.)

    1. This year's cheerleading squad was chosen by a committee last spring.

    2. The election of the class officers will be held on Tuesday.

    3. Your car's oil should be changed on a regular basis.

    4. The suspect is being kept in solitary confinement.

C. First decide if the following sentences are active or passive; then transform them.

    1. You should read the next six chapters before Monday.

    2. After the dot-com bubble burst, many employees of financial institutions were cheated out of their retirement savings.

    3. Our company is trying out a new vacation schedule this year.

    4. The streetlights on campus are finally being repaired.

FOR GROUP DISCUSSION

A. Review the sentences in Exercise 9. When is the use of the active voice more effective? When is the passive voice called for? When could a sentence be written in either the active or the passive voice?

B. Surely the most famous words in the history of the United States are those written by Thomas Jefferson in the Declaration of Independence. Here is the opening of the Declaration's second paragraph:

We hold these truths to be self-evident, that all men are created equal, that they are endowed by their Creator with certain unalienable Rights, that among these are Life, Liberty and the pursuit of Happiness. That to secure these rights, Governments are instituted among Men, deriving their just powers from the consent of the governed. That whenever any Form of Government becomes destructive of these ends, it is the Right of the People to alter or to abolish it, and to institute a new government, laying its foundation on such principles and organizing its powers in such form, as to them shall seem most likely to effect their Safety and Happiness. Prudence, indeed, will dictate that Governments long established should not be changed for light and transient causes; and accordingly all experience hath shown, that mankind are more disposed to suffer, while evils are sufferable, than to right themselves by abolishing the forms to which they are accustomed.

Underline the passive sentences. Rewrite all or some of them in the active voice and compare the two versions.

The Obscure Agent

Certainly the passive voice has a place in every kind of writing; it is a legitimate tool—but like any tool it must be right for the job. Too often the purpose of the passive voice is simply to obscure the agent. For example, one of the most common responses that governmental investigative committees hear from individuals accused of mismanagement is

"Yes, Senator, mistakes <u>were made</u>."

And the passive is common in the "official" style used by bureaucrats:

It <u>was reported</u> today that the federal funds <u>to be allocated</u> for the power plant would not be forthcoming as early as <u>had been anticipated</u>. Some contracts on the preliminary work <u>have been canceled</u> and others <u>renegotiated</u>.

Such "officialese" or "bureaucratese" takes on a nonhuman quality because the agent role has completely disappeared from the sentences. In the foregoing example we do not know who is reporting, allocating, anticipating, canceling, or renegotiating. This kind of faceless passive does an efficient job of obscuring responsibility, but it is neither efficient nor graceful for the writing that most of us do in school and on the job.

Sometimes writers use the passive to avoid the first-person *I,* perhaps because the paper has too many *I*'s already or because the teacher has ruled out the first-person point of view:

The incessant sound of foghorns <u>could be heard</u> along the waterfront.

But remember that English is a versatile language; first person is not the only alternative to the passive. You don't have to write, "I [or we] heard the sound of foghorns. . . ." Here's a version of the sentence using *sound* as the verb:

> The foghorns <u>sounded</u> along the waterfront.

And here's one that describes the movement of the sound:

> The incessant sound of foghorns <u>floated</u> across the water.

Many times, of course, the writer simply doesn't realize that the passive voice may be the culprit producing the vagueness or wordiness of that first draft. For example, a student writer ended his family Christmas story with an impersonal, inappropriate passive:

> That visit from Santa was an occurrence that <u>would never be forgotten</u>.

Clearly, he needed to ask himself, "Who was doing what?"

> The family would never forget that visit from Santa.

And if for purposes of transition or rhythm he had wanted to retain *visit* as the subject, he could easily have done so in an active way:

> That <u>visit</u> from Santa <u>became</u> part of our family legend.

EXERCISE 10

The writer of the following passage has managed to avoid using the first-person point of view but in doing so has obliterated any resemblance to a personal voice. Revise the passage, avoiding both the passive and the first person. Remember to think about the agent as subject.

> The woods in the morning seemed both peaceful and lively. Birds could be heard in the pines and oaks, staking out their territory. Squirrels could be seen scampering across the leaves that covered the forest floor, while in the branches above, the new leaves of the birches and maples were outlined by the sun's rays. The leaves, too, could be heard, rustling to the rhythm of the wind.

WELL-CHOSEN VERBS: SHOWING, NOT TELLING

When writing teachers promote the virtues of "showing" rather than "telling," what do they mean? They mean that you don't have to tell us that the old woman on the park bench is sad; you can show us:

> The old woman on the park bench wept quietly.

You don't even have to tell us that she's old:

> Wearing a shawl around her shoulders, the woman on the park bench wept quietly, wisps of gray hair escaping the woolen cap, frail bony fingers clutching her handkerchief.

Annie Dillard doesn't tell us that building a road through the Everglades between Miami and Tampa was an arduous job; she shows us:

> To build the road, men stood sunk in muck to their armpits. They fought off cottonmouth moccasins and six-foot alligators. They slept in boats, wet. They blasted muck with dynamite, cut jungle with machetes; they laid logs, dragged drilling machines, hauled dredges, heaped limestone. The road took fourteen years to build up by the shovelful.
>
> —*An American Childhood*

And Barbara Ehrenreich doesn't tell us that she was glad her day of hard work as a housecleaner was over; she shows us:

> I rush home to the Blue Haven [Motel] at the end of the day, pull down the blinds for privacy, strip off my uniform in the kitchen—the bathroom being too small for both a person and her discarded clothes—and stand in the shower for a good ten minutes, thinking all this water is *mine*. I have paid for it. In fact, I have earned it.
>
> —*Nickel and Dimed*

A well-chosen verb not only heightens the drama of a sentence and makes its meaning clear but also sends a message to the reader that the writer has crafted the sentence carefully, that the idea matters. We certainly get that message from the examples of prose we have just seen.

The overuse of the linking-*be* is a common signal that a writer is telling rather than showing: "The old woman *is* sad." "The old woman *is* old." "Building a road through the Everglades between Miami and Tampa *was* an arduous job." "She *was* glad her day of hard work as a housecleaner *was* over."

You saw in Chapter 2 that the *be* patterns commonly serve not only as topic sentences but also as supporting sentences throughout the paragraph. You may be surprised, in checking a paragraph or two of your own prose, at how often you've used a form of *be* as the main verb. An abundance of such examples—say, more than two or three in a paragraph—constitutes a clear "revise" message.

Certainly, the potential drama and meaning of your prose are weakened or missing altogether when the verbs don't pull their weight. Sometimes the culprit is one of our other common, garden-variety verbs, such as *have, make, go, do, say, get, take*. Because these verbs have so many nuances of meaning, you can often find a more precise one. For example, where you have selected the verb *make*, you could probably express yourself more exactly with *constitute, render, produce, form, complete, compel,* or *create*, all of which are indexed under *make* in *Roget's Thesaurus*, along with *make believe, make good* (demonstrate), *make out* (discover, know, interpret), and *make up* (complete).

It's important to note, too, that these alternatives to *make* are not uncommon or esoteric words; they're certainly a part of your active vocabulary. Unfortunately, however, the precise verb doesn't always come to mind when you need it—especially when you're composing the first draft. Rather than stop right there in midsentence or midparagraph to find it, just circle the word you've used—or highlight it with boldface type if you're using a word processor. Then, during the revision stage you can take time to think about it again. At that point, in fact, you may want to consult your dictionary or thesaurus just to remind yourself of some of these more specific verbs.

(*A word of warning:* Every word in the thesaurus is not for you. If you're not sure of it or if it doesn't sound natural in your voice, then don't use it. Consulting a dictionary can help you choose words: It often provides synonyms in context, along with the distinctive meanings of each.)

FOR GROUP DISCUSSION

Find time today to watch someone doing something for five or ten minutes. Then write a paragraph-long description of the person in action. Try to use as few *be* patterns as possible. The next time you're in class, compare your paragraphs with those of your classmates, underlining the verbs used in one another's paragraphs.

Alternatively, you and your classmates could compose a fictional story together. One by one, everyone can contribute to a story that begins with this sentence: *They found themselves in an unfamiliar part of the city.*

KEY TERMS

Active voice
Agent
Auxiliary verb
Be patterns
Do-support
Helping verb

Intransitive verb
Linking-*be*
Modal auxiliary
Passive voice
Past participle
Past tense

Present participle
Present tense
Showing
Telling
Time frame
Transitive verb

RHETORICAL REMINDERS

Have I remembered to show, not tell?

Have I kept my use of the linking-*be* to a minimum?

Have I put the agent in subject position whenever possible?

Have I used the passive voice effectively?

Have I used time frames consistently?

Are the shifts I make in time frames signaled by a time marker? If they aren't, will my readers understand why I have made the shifts?

CHAPTER 4

Coordination and Subordination

CHAPTER PREVIEW

In Chapter 2 we introduced basic sentence patterns, emphasizing the separate units of each; here we examine the ways in which we expand units and even sentences themselves, using coordination, subordination, or both, and their effective punctuation. This chapter will help you to

- coordinate and subordinate structures to good advantage;
- ensure that subjects and verbs agree in number;
- use parallel structure and climax to enhance the rhythm of sentences; and
- apply the tools of coordination effectively: commas, semicolons, colons, correlative conjunctions, and conjunctive adverbs.

COORDINATION WITHIN THE SENTENCE

The technique of **coordination**, of putting together like structures in sentences, is old hat; you've been using it all your life. Coordination is a natural part of language, one that develops early in speech. If you pay attention to sentence structure the next time you're within hearing distance of a small child, you'll hear the **coordinating conjunction** *and* used frequently to link parts of sentences:

> We built a new snow fort <u>and</u> threw snowballs.
>
> Robbie is mean, <u>and</u> I'm not going to play with him anymore.

Coordination shows up early and often in writing as well. Certainly in this book you can't read very far without coming to a coordinating conjunction—an *and* or a *but* or an *or.* Your own writing is probably filled with these conjunctions, too.

As you study coordination, you'll find it useful to think again about the sentence parts you studied in Chapters 1 and 2. Most of the coordination that takes place within the sentence results from compounding one or more of those parts. *Compounding* means simply "joining" or "linking." Here we've compounded the subject:

<u>Gino's father</u> *and* <u>my uncle</u> flew helicopters in Vietnam.

In the following sentence the complete predicate is compounded:

The kids <u>played outdoors all morning</u> *but* <u>stayed inside all afternoon.</u>

In the following sentence, only the direct object is compounded:

You can take <u>a taxi</u> *or* <u>a shuttle</u> from the airport.

Now is a good time to review the important punctuation rule you learned in Chapter 2:

> **Do not mark boundaries of the required sentence units with punctuation.**

Here's another, a non-comma rule of sorts, that describes the sample sentences you've just seen:

> **Do not use a comma with a coordinating conjunction when it joins phrases.**

The connectors in the preceding examples—*and, but, or*—are the three primary coordinating conjunctions we use for connecting both full sentences and their parts; you can think of them as "the big three."

You may have had a teacher in elementary or middle school who taught you a list of seven conjunctions—and perhaps helped you remember them with an acronym: *fanboys.* (The *a, b,* and *o* of *fanboys,* of course, stand for *and, but,* and *or.*) That list also includes *for, yet, so,* and *nor.* All of these lesser conjunctions are certainly words you use in writing from time to time, but they do not have the wide range of use that the big three have.

Although the non-comma rule will apply to most of your sentences containing coordinate pairs, you may at times want to give special emphasis to the second part of the pair, in which case, a comma can be used to signal a slight pause:

> I didn't believe her, and said so.
>
> The running back charged ahead, but missed the goal line by an inch.

The emphasis is even stronger with a dash instead of a comma:

> I didn't believe her—and said so.
>
> The running back charged ahead—but missed the goal line by an inch.

The dash also sends the message that the punctuation was deliberate—not a comma error, a judgment some readers might make. Because an emphatic comma can be misjudged, be sure to use it with care.

Use a comma or a dash only sparingly to emphasize an additional comment.

Parallel Structure

One of your most important writer's tools is the concept of **parallel structure**, or **parallelism**. A coordinate structure is parallel only when the parts are of the same form. The parallel structure is an effective one—and this feature is just as important—only when the two ideas are equal, when they belong together. Annie Dillard clearly understood the effectiveness of parallel forms when she wrote this sentence:

> We could live under the wild rose as weasels, <u>mute</u> and <u>uncomprehending</u>.

For contrast, examine this compound structure that is unparallel in form:

> *This new exercise program and going on a strict diet will make me healthier.

Here the conjunction *and* connects the parts of a compound subject. The first part (*This new exercise program*) is a noun phrase in form; the second (*going on a strict diet*) is a special type of verb phrase, a **gerund**. (*Gerund* is the label we give an *-ing* verb when it is used as a noun. Gerunds are discussed further in Chapter 10.) In this case the ideas are equal, so in that sense they belong together. But for the sentence to be grammatical, the two parts of the compound must be the same form:

> <u>This new exercise program</u> **and** <u>a strict diet</u> (NP+NP)
>
> <u>Sticking to this exercise program</u> **and** <u>going on a diet</u> (VP+VP)

You may be thinking that unparallel structures sound perfectly normal—like sentences you hear every day. And you're right. We use sentences like these in our conversation all the time—and no one accuses us of being ungrammatical. But writing is different. We want to be as precise and effective as possible. And as writers we have a second (and third and fourth!) chance to improve our sentences. We don't have to show that first draft to anyone. Sentences with unparallel features can always be improved in subsequent drafts.

Coordination of the Series

In the **series**—a coordinate structure with three or more components—we use commas to separate the parallel coordinate elements:

> Among the lands on the frozen fringes of the Arctic Ocean are <u>Alaska, Canada, and Greenland</u>.

These commas represent the pauses and slight changes of pitch that occur in the production of the series. You can hear the commas in your voice when you compare the series of three with a two-part structure, which of course has no comma:

> Among the lands on the frozen fringes of the Arctic Ocean are <u>Alaska and Canada</u>.

You probably noticed a leveling of your voice in reading the pair, a certain smoothness that the series does not have.

Some writers—and some publications as a matter of policy—leave out the **serial comma**, the one immediately before the coordinating conjunction. One such publication is *The New York Times*. Here is the sentence from which the previous example was taken, as published in the *Times:*

> Unlike Antarctica, a continent surrounded by ocean, the Arctic is mostly ocean ringed by land—the frozen, inhospitable fringes of Alaska, Canada, Greenland, Iceland, Scandinavia and Russia.
>
> —Darcy Frey

The open, or light, punctuation style leaves out the comma where a boundary is otherwise marked. Here, of course, the conjunction *and* marks the final boundary of the series.

This punctuation style, however, does have a drawback: It may imply a closer connection than actually exists between the last two elements of the series, such as the connection in the following sentence:

> Throughout college Herbie survived on pizza, ramen, and <u>macaroni and cheese</u>.

In most academic writing, the serial comma is required, so if you're writing a paper for a class, be sure to include it.

Climax. In addition to parallelism, a second structural principle should be emphasized in connection with the series: **climax**, the arrangement of words or phrases or clauses in the order of increasing scope, length, or importance. Consider the three-part series in this sentence:

> With <u>his bright sunflowers, searing wheat fields and blazing yellow skies</u>, Vincent van Gogh was fanatic about light.

> —Paul Trachtman

This parallel series consists of three noun phrases functioning as the object of the preposition *with*. Notice also the climactic ordering of these phrases, starting with *sunflowers,* moving to *wheat fields,* and ending with *skies.* When you use climactic ordering, you might think of yourself as a photographer, shifting a camera's focus from close-up to wide angle. To get a sense of the effect when a sentence follows neither of these principles, compare Trachtman's sentence with the following version:

> With his searing wheat fields, bright sunflowers, and skies that are blazing yellow, Vincent van Gogh was fanatic about light.

In this example, the first two elements in the series begin with adjectives (*searing* and *bright*), but the third begins with a noun (*skies*). The third element makes the series unparallel; the climactic ordering has also been lost, the series now beginning with wheat fields instead of sunflowers.

Let's return now to coordination that *is* effective. The parallel items in the following sentence are also ordered according to length:

> Those of us who manage the public's dollar will be held to account—to spend wisely, reform bad habits, and do our business in the light of day—because only then can we restore the vital trust between a people and their government.

> —Barack Obama

You can probably hear the special rhythm in these examples with **triplets**, the three-item series. Clearly, there must be something special about triplets, a natural inclination of some kind that encourages writers to write them and satisfies the readers who read them.

FOR GROUP DISCUSSION

A. Below you'll find two sentences from Sarah Bakewell's excellent book on the essays of Montaigne. Which of the triplets in these sentences do you think is more effectively written? Why?

> 1. A typical page of the *Essays* is a sequence of meanders, bends, and divergences.

> 2. A person's ideas vary a lot in two decades, especially if the person spends that time traveling, reading, talking to interesting people, and practicing high-level politics and diplomacy.

B. Write two or three versions of a sentence in which you use triplets to describe something (for example, a book, a film, a sporting event). Exchange these versions with a classmate and discuss their merits.

Coordination with Correlative Conjunctions

In Chapter 6 you'll learn about "power words," words that command special attention; among them are the **correlative conjunctions**:

> *both–and*   *either–or*
>
> *not only–but also*   *neither–nor*

The power of the correlatives lies in their ability to change the rhythm and focus of the sentence and so set up different expectations in the reader. Read these two sentences aloud and listen to the change in your voice when you add *both:*

> Individuals <u>and</u> nations must learn to think about the environment.
>
> <u>Both</u> individuals <u>and</u> nations must learn to think about the environment.

The change may seem like a small one. But notice what the added *both* does: It shifts the emphasis from the predicate to the subject, which normally gets little, if any. Now the reader expects to read on about the response of individuals and nations. Here's another example of the difference that *both–and* can make in contrast to *and* alone. This is a revised version of a sentence you just read:

> The power of the correlatives lies in their ability to change <u>both</u> the rhythm <u>and</u> the focus of the sentence and so set up different expectations in the reader.

If you listen carefully, you'll notice that the addition of *both* adds stress, or loudness, to *and.* The same kind of change in emphasis occurs with *not only–but also* (or *not only–but … as well*):

> As citizens of this global village, we must be concerned <u>not only</u> with our own health and safety <u>but</u> with the needs of others <u>as well</u>.
>
> As citizens of this global village, we must be concerned <u>not only</u> with our own health and safety <u>but also</u> with the needs of others.

In reading these two sentences aloud, you'll notice that in the second there is less emphasis on *others;* the main focus falls on *also.*

Probably the least common correlative is *neither–nor;* and it's probably accurate to say that inexperienced writers avoid it. But because it is rare, it sends a strong message, one that says the writer has constructed the sentence carefully:

> <u>Neither</u> individuals <u>nor</u> nations can afford to ignore what is happening to the environment.

Except for *both–and,* correlatives can be used to join two sentences into one.

> The pitcher bats. + The coach sends in a pinch hitter.
>
> *Either* the pitcher bats, <u>or</u> the coach sends in a pinch hitter.

As with other compound structures, the two parts connected by correlative conjunctions should be parallel in structure: two noun phrases, two prepositional phrases, two verb phrases, and so on. In the case of correlative conjunctions, the problem of unparallel structure is usually easy to spot and easy to fix: It's a matter of paying attention to the conjunctions. *Either* signals that *or* is on the way—and your reader knows it! Just be sure that the same form follows both parts of the correlative, because that's what the reader is expecting. The writer of the following sentence suffered a lapse in attention:

> *I could **either** <u>take the train</u> **or** <u>the bus</u>.

Here we have a verb phrase (*take the train*) connected to a noun phrase (*the bus*). To correct this unparallel structure, simply move *either:*

I could take **either** <u>the train</u> **or** <u>the bus</u>.

Now the same form, a noun phrase, follows both *either* and *or*.

EXERCISE 11

Revise the following sentences by substituting correlatives for the coordinating conjunctions. In your revisions, use all four of the correlatives at least once: *both–and, either–or, neither–nor, not only–but also*. Explain how the focus of each of your revised sentences differs from that of the originals.

1. Tea and coffee contain caffeine.

2. Caffeine quickens metabolism and increases the heart rate.

3. Some people drink coffee or tea, but not both.

4. Caffeine cannot make you intelligent, and it cannot ensure a good night's sleep.

SUBJECT–VERB AGREEMENT

The topic of **subject–verb agreement** is often at issue in sentences that have compound subjects. The concept can perhaps best be illustrated by looking at examples where the subject and verb "disagree":

We was at the movies last night.
He don't work here anymore.

The subject–verb pairings in these sentences, though acceptable in some dialects, differ from what is expected in standard English—*We were; He doesn't*. The following chart shows the verb distinctions determined by what is called the **person** of the subject: first, second, or third:

	SINGULAR	PLURAL	SINGULAR	PLURAL
First	I was	we were	I do	we do
Second	you were	you were	you do	you do
Third	she was	they were	he does	they do

A comparison of these differences highlights the importance of understanding when to use the *-s* form of the verb, the third-person singular.

The first comparison—*we was* versus *we were*—shows that in the non-standard dialect, *was* is the only form of the verb *be* used to indicate past tense. In standard English, however, *be* has two forms for the past tense, *was* and *were*. The second comparison—*don't* versus *doesn't*—reveals a similar pattern. The nonstandard dialect has just one form of negative *do* in the present tense (*don't*), whereas standard English has two (*don't* and *doesn't*). When your writing situation calls for standard English (not all writing situations do), be sure to use the two past-tense forms of *be* and the two present-tense forms of *do*.

In writing, too, the issue of subject–verb agreement is concerned with the *-s* form of the verb and the number (whether singular or plural) of the subject. In standard English, we use the *-s* form only when the subject is singular *and* third person (a subject that can be replaced by *he, she,* or *it*). But when subjects are compound, agreement can get a bit tricky.

When nouns or noun phrases in the subject position are joined by *and* or by the correlative *both–and,* the subject is plural:

> <u>Both Democrats and Republicans</u> **are** in agreement on some issues.

However, the coordinating conjunction *or* and the correlatives *either–or* and *neither–nor* do not have the additive meaning of *and.* In compound subjects with these conjunctions, the verb is determined by the closer member of the pair:

> Neither the speaker nor <u>the listeners</u> **were** intimidated by the protestors.
> Either the class officers or <u>the faculty adviser</u> **makes** the final decision.

If the correct sentence sounds awkward because of the verb form, you can simply reverse the compound pair:

> Either the faculty adviser or <u>the class officers</u> **make** the final decision.

When both members of the pair are alike, of course, there is no question:

> Either <u>the president or the vice president</u> **is** going to introduce the speaker.
> Neither <u>the union members nor the management representatives</u> **were** willing to compromise.

For most verb forms, there is no decision to be made about subject–verb agreement; the issue arises only when the present tense *-s* form of the verb or auxiliary is involved. In the following sentences with the past tense, there is no choice:

> Either the class officers or the faculty adviser <u>made</u> the final decision.
>
> Either the faculty adviser or the class officers <u>made</u> the final decision.

Another situation that sometimes causes confusion about number—that is, whether the subject is singular or plural—occurs with subjects that include a phrase introduced by *in addition to* or *along with:*

> *The sidewalk, in addition to the driveway, need to be repaired.
>
> *Mike, along with his friend Emilio, often help out at the food bank.

These additions to the subject are parenthetical; they are not treated as part of the subject. In both sentences, the subjects are singular; the verb should be the *-s* form—*needs* and *helps.* To make the subject compound—to include the additions—the writer could use a coordinating conjunction, such as *and:*

> The sidewalk <u>and</u> the driveway <u>need</u> to be repaired.
>
> Mike <u>and</u> his friend Emilio often <u>help</u> out at the food bank.

EXERCISE 12

Choose the verb that agrees in number and in person with the subject. If a compound subject is joined by *either–or* or *neither–nor,* the verb should agree with the closer member.

1. The students in Biology 101 (goes/go) on a field trip each spring for a full day.

2. Either the students or the instructor (chooses/choose) a site in the region to explore.

3. Neither the instructor nor the students (goes/go) to any other classes that day.

4. A lunch, along with plenty of water, (is/are) essential for the trip.

5. A field guide, as well as a writer's notebook, (finds/find) a place in most students' backpacks.

COMPOUND SENTENCES

The sentence patterns you learned in Chapter 2 can also be called *clause patterns:* The two words **clause** and **sentence** are close in meaning. First, we'll define *clause* as a structure that contains a subject and a predicate. That definition, of course, conforms precisely to the illustration of *sentence* shown in Chapter 1. When a clause functions independently, we call it an **independent clause**. When it begins with a capital letter and ends with a period (or other terminal mark of punctuation), we call it a **simple sentence**:

> A weasel is wild.

As you well know, however, not all sentences in the English language are simple. Often we want to show that the ideas expressed in two independent clauses are related, so we join them together into a **compound sentence**:

> Acupuncture has been effective in healing muscular disorders, **and** it has no side effects.
>
> Acupuncture is cheaper than conventional medicine, **but** most Americans do not understand how it works.

The punctuation convention for compound sentences calls for a comma at the end of the first clause, signaling that another independent clause is on the way. Here, then, is the second punctuation rule in connection with coordination:

Use a comma before the coordinating conjunction joining the two independent clauses of a compound sentence.

As you can see, it's important to understand exactly what it is you're compounding. If it's only two words or phrases within the sentence, then no comma is called for; if it's two independent clauses, then the conjunction needs a comma to send a signal to the reader that a second independent clause is on the way. It's not unusual to see in published works compound sentences without the comma, especially when both independent clauses are short. However, most professional writers follow the rule consistently.

FOR GROUP DISCUSSION

You may remember hearing a rule for writers that warns, "Never begin a sentence with *and* or *but*." Does this rule accurately describe how writers write? Frankly, no. According to the fifteenth edition of *The Chicago Manual of Style,* "a substantial percentage (often as many as 10 percent) of the sentences in first-rate writing begin with conjunctions" (193).

The reason for this common usage is that starting a sentence with a coordinating conjunction can provide a rhetorical punch, as in this example from the introductory chapter to *Earth: The Sequel* by Fred Krupp and Miriam Horn:

> A revolution is on the horizon: a wholesale transformation of the world economy and the way people live. This revolution will depend on industrial technology—capital-intensive, shovel-in-the-ground industries—and will almost certainly create the great fortunes of the twenty-first century. <u>But</u> this new industrial revolution holds a more important promise: securing the world against the dangers of global warming.

A. Rewrite Krupp and Horn's last sentence, following the so-called rule. Has your revision changed the impact of the sentence?
B. To see if the estimate of sentence-opening conjunctions given in *The Chicago Manual of Style* is accurate, check the textbooks or other readings you've done for your classes. Also check daily newspapers and/or weekly news magazines.

Conjunctive Adverbs and Transitional Phrases

In Chapter 5, on the topic of cohesion, you'll read about *metadiscourse,* a term that refers to certain signals that help the reader understand the writer's message. Among the most useful of such signals are the **conjunctive adverbs**, also known as *adverbial conjunctions.* As their name suggests, conjunctive adverbs join sentences to form coordinate structures as other conjunctions do, but they do so in a different way. The following list includes some of the most common adverbs that function as sentence connectors:

Addition: moreover, furthermore, further, also

Time: meanwhile, then, afterward, previously

Contrast: however, instead, rather

Result: therefore, consequently, thus

Concession: though

Reinforcement: indeed, nevertheless, still

Conjunctive adverbs differ from other conjunctions in that, like ordinary adverbs, most of them are movable; they need not only introduce their clause. It is that movability that makes them such an important tool for writers:

> We worked hard for the Consumer Party candidates; <u>however</u>, we knew they didn't stand a chance.
>
> We worked hard for the Consumer Party candidates; we knew, <u>however</u>, that they didn't stand a chance.
>
> We worked hard for the Consumer Party candidates; we knew they didn't stand a chance, <u>however</u>.

Bear in mind, though, that the farther along in the sentence the conjunctive adverb appears, the less value it has as a connector. If the reader needs the signal that the connector carries—such as the message of *however,* indicating that a contrast is coming—you'll probably want the reader to get it in a timely fashion, not wait until the end, especially when the second clause is fairly long.

A different emphasis occurs when the conjunctive adverb is used with no punctuation. Read these pairs of sentences aloud and note where you put the main stress in the second clause of each:

> Our main speaker canceled at the last minute; the rally was <u>therefore</u> postponed until the following weekend.
>
> Our main speaker canceled at the last minute; the rally, <u>therefore</u>, was postponed until the following weekend.

In the version *without* commas, it is the word *following* the conjunctive adverb that gets main stress; *with* commas, it's the word *preceding.*

This punctuation choice occurs with only a limited number of the conjunctive adverbs; most of them require the commas to send their message. And it's also important to recognize that without punctuation they lose some of their connective power, functioning more like adverbials, less like conjunctions.

You'll also want to consider the tone that conjunctive adverbs tend to convey. Some of them—such as *moreover, nevertheless, therefore,* and even the fairly common *however*—may strike the reader as formal, perhaps even stiff. You can often diminish that formality by using coordinating conjunctions: Instead of *however,* use *but;* instead of *moreover,* use *and;* for *nevertheless,* use *yet.*

Many prepositional phrases are also used as sentence connectors. They are called **transitional phrases**. Note that they serve the same purposes as conjunctive adverbs:

> *Addition:* in addition to
>
> *Time:* in the meantime
>
> *Contrast:* in contrast, on the contrary

Result: as a result, in the end

Concession: of course, at any rate, at least

Reinforcement: in fact, above all, in particular

And like conjunctive adverbs, many of these prepositional phrases can appear at various points in a sentence.

> The campaign contributions we had been counting on didn't materialize; <u>in fact</u>, the campaign was broke.

> The campaign contributions we had been counting on didn't materialize; the campaign, <u>in fact</u>, was broke.

> The campaign contributions we had been counting on didn't materialize; the campaign was broke, <u>in fact</u>.

Unless you want to stress the word following the connector, the rule to remember when using either conjunctive adverbs or transitional phrases is as follows:

Use commas to set off conjunctive adverbs and transitional phrases.

Compound Sentences with Semicolons

You've seen a great many semicolons used in the discussions throughout these chapters. And in the previous section you saw them in sentences illustrating the use of conjunctive adverbs. However, you can't assume from these examples that you'll find them in great numbers everywhere. Some people manage to go through life without ever making their acquaintance. If you belong to that group of nonusers, you can be sure of one thing: Your punctuation is not as effective as it could and should be. But take heart! The semicolon is easy to use.

In her book *Woe Is I,* Patricia T. O'Conner calls the semicolon the flashing red of punctuation traffic signals:

> If a comma is a yellow light and a period is a red light, the semicolon is a flashing red—one of those lights you drive through after a brief pause. (139)

Think of the semicolon as the equivalent of the comma-plus-conjunction that connects compound sentences. You could even put this relationship into a formula:

(, + and/but) = (;)

In the last section you saw semicolons in compound sentences with conjunctive adverbs, but don't get the idea that the conjunctive adverb is required. Semicolons can be used with no conjunction at all:

> There was silence; I stood awkwardly, then moved to the door.
> There was silence; white faces were looking strangely at me.
> —Richard Wright

In compound sentences like these, the semicolon sends a message to the reader: "Notice the connection."

These two uses of the semicolon to connect clauses—by itself and with a conjunctive adverb—are perhaps the most common; but there are times when you'll want to use a coordinating conjunction along with the semicolon, as in this compound sentence you're reading. As you can see, the second clause includes a comma, so we use a semicolon before the conjunction *but* to signal clearly the boundary between the two independent clauses. In Chapter 10 you'll read about the one other place we use the semicolon: to separate the parts of a series when the individual parts include punctuation of their own. Here's an example:

> The study of language includes three main areas: phonology, the study of sounds; morphology, the study of meaningful combinations of sounds; and syntax, the study of sentences.

Because each of the three items in the series includes an explanatory phrase set off by commas, the use of semicolons between them helps keep the reader on track. For a review of all the uses of the semicolon, consult the Glossary of Punctuation.

Compound Sentences with Colons

Inexperienced writers often avoid using semicolons simply because they don't understand them; even less understood is the colon as a sentence connector. In Chapter 10 you'll read about the colon in its more familiar role— as a signal of a list of items:

> Three committees were set up to plan the convention: program, finance, and local arrangements.

In this sentence the message of the colon is "Here it comes, the list of committees I promised."

In connecting two complete sentences, the message of the colon is similar. As with the list in the preceding example, the independent clause following a colon also completes, explains, or illustrates the idea in the first clause:

> Easing away, I feel a twinge of regret: it's late July and soon the thrushes will fall silent.
> —Richard Blood, *Heart and Blood*

The preceding example is from a book of nonfiction. The following sentence is from a novel:

> Jem and I found our father satisfactory: he played with us, read to us, and treated us with courteous detachment.
> —Harper Lee, *To Kill a Mockingbird*

Notice how the first clause sets up an expectation in the reader. The colon says, "Here comes the information you're expecting," or "Here's what I promised." In general, if you can mentally insert *namely, that is, in fact,* or *here's the reason,* as you can in the preceding examples, you should consider using a colon to connect the sentences.

It's important to recognize that this way of connecting two clauses is quite different from the connection with semicolons. The two clauses connected with the semicolon have parallel ideas. And unless you include a signal to the contrary, your reader will expect the relationship to be an additive or contrastive one, an *and* or *but* connection. If you try to replace the colon with a coordinating conjunction, you'll see that it won't work.

Two other common structures that the colon signals are questions and direct quotations:

> The formation of snowflakes touches on some fundamental questions: How do crystals grow? Why do complex patterns arise spontaneously in simple physical systems?
> —Kenneth Libbrecht, *The Snowflake*

> A Northwestern University psychiatrist explained the purpose of brain chemicals rather poetically: "A person's mood is like a symphony, and serotonin is like the conductor's baton.
> —*Time*

Another situation that calls for the colon as a signal, which you're probably familiar with, is the block quotation—the long indented quotation.

There is one detail of punctuation in these compound sentences that varies. Except in the case of the direct quotation, you have the choice of using either a capital or a lowercase letter following the colon.

(The first word of a direct quotation following a colon is generally capitalized.) Some publications capitalize all independent clauses following colons (the style of this book); others capitalize only questions; some use lowercase for all independent clauses except direct quotations. Whichever style of punctuation you choose, be consistent. You can find a review of all the uses of the colon in the Glossary of Punctuation.

Punctuation Pitfalls

If you've ever encountered a teacher's "CS" or "FS" or "RO" notation in the margin of an essay, you're in good company. The **comma splice** and the **fused sentence**, sometimes called a **run-on sentence**, are among the most common—and probably the most perplexing to teachers—of all the punctuation errors that writers make. They are perplexing because they are based on such a straightforward and common situation: a sentence with two independent clauses.

Earlier in this chapter you learned that a compound sentence consists of two independent clauses. Let's examine again a sentence we discussed earlier in this chapter.

> Acupuncture has been effective in healing muscular disorders, **and** it has no side effects.

The punctuation in this sentence follows the highlighted rule you saw in the last section:

Use a comma before the coordinating conjunction joining the two independent clauses of a compound sentence.

What happens if we leave out the conjunction?

> *Acupuncture has been effective in healing muscular disorders, it has no side effects.

We've produced a *comma splice.* In other words, we've spliced, or joined, two independent clauses together with a comma. But a comma alone is not strong enough: It needs the support of a conjunction. *Remember, we want the reader to know that another independent clause is coming.*

If you've ever committed a comma splice—left out the *and* (well, maybe *committed* is too strong a word!)—you may have done so for what you thought was a good reason: to create a tighter connection. The sentence may have sounded or looked better. It's true that sometimes the conjunction adds a certain flabbiness, and maybe the sentence would be

better without it. There is a solution, though, and it's often a good one—
the semicolon. Notice how slim and trim the following sentence is with a
semicolon instead of *and:*

> It's true that sometimes the conjunction adds a certain flabbiness;
> maybe the sentence would be better without it.

In the version with the semicolon, the reader will give more emphasis to
the second clause.

However, if we were feeling miserly and decided to leave out the semicolon as well, we would be creating a fused sentence—two sentences run
together without any punctuation—another error best to avoid.

At this point you may be asking yourself, "How about the conjunction
by itself? Is that ever allowed in a compound sentence?"

> *It's true that sometimes the conjunction adds a certain flabbiness
> and maybe the sentence would be better without it.

Again, the wrong message—another fused sentence of sorts, although not as
serious as the one with neither conjunction nor comma. The use of *and* without the comma tells the reader that a coordinate structure, perhaps another
noun phrase, is coming—not that a new independent clause is coming.

In an earlier section, you saw examples of the semicolon used to join
sentences beginning with a conjunctive adverb or transitional phrase:

> We worked hard for the Consumer Party candidates; <u>however</u>, we
> knew that they didn't stand a chance.

> The campaign contributions we had been counting on didn't
> materialize; <u>in fact</u>, the campaign was broke.

Inexperienced writers sometimes use a comma in these sentences where
the semicolon should be, thus creating a sentence with a comma splice.
When you use a conjunctive adverb to begin a clause, be sure that it follows a semicolon (as shown previously) or a period (as in the following):

> We worked hard for the Consumer Party candidates. However, we
> knew that they didn't stand a chance.

> The campaign contributions we had been counting on didn't
> materialize. In fact, the campaign was broke.

It's certainly possible to find examples in both contemporary and older
prose of two sentences, usually short ones, put together with the conjunction alone or with the comma alone—deliberate deviations from conventional punctuation practices. However, most academic and business
writing assignments call for the compound sentence to follow the rules

stated earlier—*comma-plus-conjunction* or *semicolon-plus-conjunctive adverb/transitional phrase*—so that the punctuation provides the reader with information about the kinds of structures that will come after it. These are the rules followed in this book.

The importance of accurate punctuation cannot be overemphasized. Not only will readers be guided efficiently through your ideas, they will also gain confidence in you as a writer—and as an authority on your topic. It's easy for a reader to conclude—perhaps subconsciously and, yes, perhaps unfairly—that slipshod punctuation equals slipshod thinking. Your image, your credibility as a writer, can be enhanced only when you make helpful, accurate, and effective punctuation choices.

THE COMPOUND SENTENCE: PUNCTUATION REVIEW

We have seen five styles of punctuation for joining the clauses in compound sentences. Every writer should understand all five and be able to use them effectively.

1. COMMA-PLUS-CONJUNCTION

> Every ride at an amusement park has a history, and the history of the roller coaster begins with the Russian Ice Slides of the seventeenth century.

Remember that the comma by itself is not strong enough to make that connection; without the conjunction, the result is a comma splice. Without either the conjunction or the comma, the sentence becomes a fused sentence.

2. SEMICOLON

> Every ride at an amusement park has a history; the history of the roller coaster begins with the Russian Ice Slides of the seventeenth century.

You can think of this connection as a tighter version of the comma with *and*.

3. SEMICOLON-PLUS-CONJUNCTION

> Every ride at an amusement park has a history; and the history of the roller coaster begins with the Russian Ice

Slides of the seventeenth century, located primarily in the area around present-day St. Petersburg.

A semicolon, instead of a comma, is used between two independent clauses, especially when one of the clauses already includes a comma.

4. SEMICOLON-PLUS-CONJUNCTIVE ADVERB/TRANSITIONAL PHRASE

The inclusion of a conjunctive adverb has the advantage of being movable, so you can manipulate the rhythm pattern to focus the emphasis on different words. You can decide how the reader reads the sentence:

Every ride at an amusement park has a history; <u>however</u>, the roller coaster has one of the most unusual stories to tell.
Every ride at an amusement park has a history; the roller coaster, <u>however</u>, has one of the most unusual stories to tell.

Strong stress falls on the word preceding the comma.

5. COLON

Many of the ice slides built in Russia were quite elaborate: Some rose to eighty feet and accommodated several large sleds at once.

Here the colon is saying, "Here it comes, the elaboration you're expecting." Note that the full sentence following the colon does not always begin with a capital letter, as it does here. Some publications prefer lowercase in this position.

These, then, are the five ways we connect the two clauses of a compound sentence. Be sure to take time to understand all of them. Using them correctly also means understanding the structure of clauses, their parameters. These two concepts—the structure of clauses and the conventions for connecting them—are basic tools that every writer needs for every writing task.

EXERCISE 13

Add punctuation to the following passages, if necessary. In some cases there may be more than one possibility.

1. The Smithsonian Institution comprises nineteen museums nine research centers and the National Zoo.

2. Most of the museums are located on the National Mall in Washington, DC but the National Air and Space Museum has two locations.

3. You can find one of the museums on the National Mall and the other near Dulles International Airport.

4. The National Air and Space Museum on the National Mall contains in its collection the Wright Flyer Sputnik 1 and the Apollo 11 lunar module.

5. The museum on the National Mall opened in 1976 however, its collection was so large that an additional museum was built near Dulles International Airport.

6. Visitors to the Steven F. Udvar-Hazy Center can view the Boeing B-29 Superfortress *Enola Gay* the MacCready *Gossamer Albatross* and the space shuttle *Enterprise.*

7. Together, these two museums maintain a vast collection of air- and spacecraft they also sponsor vital research into aviation and related technologies.

8. These museums share the same mission they are dedicated to the commemoration of the nation's aeronautic history.

SUBORDINATION: THE DEPENDENT CLAUSES

So far we've discussed sentences in terms of independent clauses: The simple sentence consists of one independent clause; the compound sentence consists of two, sometimes three or more, independent clauses. But a clause need not be independent. It can also function within a sentence as a **dependent clause**, also called a *subordinate clause.*

When a dependent clause begins with a **subordinating conjunction** such as *because, although,* or *when,* it is an **adverbial clause**. Remember that movability is a good clue that a structure is functioning as an adverbial. And as you can see in the second example, when an adverbial clause opens the sentence, it is followed by a comma:

An adverbial clause is followed by a comma <u>when it opens the sentence</u>.

> When an adverbial clause opens the sentence, it is followed by a comma.

We'll discuss this comma rule in more depth in Chapter 8.

Another type of dependent clause functions adjectivally, as the modifier of a noun. In the following sentence a *who*-clause is a modifier of the subject *the scientist:*

> The scientist <u>who received a Blue Planet Prize</u> works at Columbia University.

Again you can recognize the major units of the clause when you use pronouns for the subject and object:

She	received	it.
(subject)	(verb)	(object)

Because this type of dependent clause functions as an adjective to modify a noun (here, *the scientist*), it is called an **adjectival clause**. Like the prepositional phrases you saw in Chapter 1, the adjectival clause follows the headword of the noun phrase:

the Scientist	who received the Blue Planet Prize
fans	in the ballpark

Dependent clauses can also function as **nominals**, filling noun phrase positions. For example, we could use our original weasel clause as a direct object following a transitive verb like *say,* creating a Pattern 5 sentence:

> Annie Dillard says that a weasel is wild.

This sentence has the same three units as this sample Pattern 5 sentence from Chapter 2:

My roommate	borrowed	my laptop.
Annie Dillard	says	something.

But in the Annie Dillard sentence, the "something" in the direct object position is a clause, not a noun phrase. This type of dependent clause is called a **nominal clause** because it functions as a noun. Note that the term *nominal,* the *-al* form of *noun,* is the name of a function, not a form, just as *adverbial* and *adjectival* are. (In Chapter 1 you learned that the terms *adverbial* and *adjectival* apply to all forms that function the way adverbs and adjectives do.)

These then are the three roles that dependent clauses fill in sentences, their three functions: adverbial, adjectival, and nominal. You'll learn more about the functional categories in Chapters 8, 9, and 10, respectively. Another label you may want to add to your repertoire is **complex sentence**. Whereas a compound sentence contains two or more independent clauses, a complex sentence contains at least one independent clause and one dependent clause.

REVISING COMPOUND STRUCTURES

In compound sentences, as well as sentences with compound predicates, verb forms that are unparallel can sometimes produce a kind of fuzziness. Notice in the following sentence that only one of the two verbs includes an auxiliary:

> Experts in sports medicine <u>emphasize</u> the importance of water intake and <u>are recommending</u> a half-ounce per day for every pound of body weight.

A related source of fuzziness can occur in the compound sentence. Our example could easily be turned into a compound sentence with the simple addition of a second subject:

> Experts in sports medicine emphasize the importance of water intake
>
> , and
>
> <u>they</u> are recommending a half-ounce per day for every pound of body weight.

The sentence is now parallel in *form*. But a question remains: Are the two *ideas* parallel? Do they belong together as equal partners? (And remember, that's what the message of *and* is: "These two structures are equal partners.")

If the two ideas were fuzzy partners as predicates—a judgment suggested by the form of the verbs—then they are just as likely to be fuzzy partners as sentences. The problem is not just that one verb has an auxiliary and the other doesn't (*are recommending* and *emphasize*); it's the underlying reason for that difference. We generally use the simple present tense (*emphasize*) to describe an accepted truth or timeless quality; we use the present progressive tense (*are recommending*) for an ongoing action. It's not that the two ideas don't belong together: They do—but not as equal partners. *And* is simply the wrong connection.

Because the sentence is out of context, we don't know which of the two ideas should be emphasized, but a good guess would be the following recommendation:

> Experts in sports medicine, who emphasize the importance of water intake, are recommending a half-ounce per day for every pound of body weight.

Notice that the use of the embedded adjectival clause makes this a complex sentence rather than a compound sentence. We'll look closely at the adjectival clause in Chapter 9.

You may find it helpful to think in terms of **foregrounding** and **backgrounding** when you have two ideas to combine. Which idea should get the foreground, the prominence of the main clause? Which should be thought of as background and given the supporting role of the dependent clause? This concept is related to the concept of known and new information, which you'll study in the next chapter.

The following sentence illustrates another common coordination problem: a fact and a conclusion based on that fact put together as parallel ideas.

> The African killer bees are less predictable than European bees and tend to attack in vast swarms.

One clue that the two predicates don't belong together is a difference in verb classes: linking and transitive. Again, we need context to know which idea should get the main focus, which idea should be foreground, and which should be treated as the background:

> The African killer bees, which are less predictable than European bees, tend to attack in vast swarms.
>
> The African killer bees, which tend to attack in vast swarms, are less predictable than European bees.

A mismatch in verb forms certainly doesn't guarantee a problem, but it's the kind of sentence you'll want to notice when you're revising.

EXERCISE 14

In his textbook *Classical Rhetoric for the Modern Student,* Professor Edward P. J. Corbett reports on a study of style he conducted in his Honors Freshman English class. His students compared the length of their own sentences and paragraphs with those of a professional writer, F. L. Lucas. They selected eight paragraphs from an essay by Lucas, avoiding short transitional paragraphs and any that contained two or more sentences of quoted material. Then they calculated the average number of words per sentence (20.8) and the average number of sentences per paragraph (7.6).

In addition, they calculated the percentage of sentences that were ten words longer than the average (17 percent) and the percentage that were five words shorter than the average (40 percent). Then they did the same with an expository theme of their own.

We cannot, of course, judge the effectiveness of a paragraph on the basis of statistics. However, data gathered can sometimes show us our strengths (or perhaps bad habits); they can also point out structures we might consider using.

Do a contrastive study of your own writing style and that of a professional, following Professor Corbett's model. For the analysis, choose eight paragraphs from an article published in a magazine (e.g., *Harper's, Atlantic Monthly, The New Yorker, Smithsonian, Nature*) or from an article published in a professional journal in your major field. For purposes of this analysis, a sentence is defined as "a group of words beginning with a capital letter and ending with some mark of end punctuation." In some cases these sentences will be fragments; even so, you should include them in your analysis. However, among the eight do not include short transitional paragraphs or any paragraph that contains two or more sentences of quoted material. Do the same analysis with eight paragraphs from an expository essay of your own.

	PROFESSIONAL	STUDENT
1. Total number of words	_____	_____
2. Total number of sentences	_____	_____
3. Longest sentence (in number of words)	_____	_____
4. Shortest sentence (in number of words)	_____	_____
5. Average sentence length	_____	_____
6. Number of sentences with more than ten words *over* the average length	_____	_____
7. Percentage of sentences with more than ten words *over* the average	_____	_____
8. Number of sentences with more than five words *below* the average	_____	_____
9. Percentage of sentences with more than five words *below* the average	_____	_____
longest paragraph (in number of sentences)	_____	_____
shortest paragraph (in number of sentences)	_____	_____
average paragraph (in number of sentences)	_____	_____

EXERCISE 15

Revise the following sentences, paying particular attention to unparallel ideas or structures.

1. At the new recreation center, students have the privilege of deciding whether to lift weights or swimming in an Olympic-size pool.

2. The Baltimore Orioles' stadium at Camden Yards has all the virtues of the beloved ballparks of another era and is in the great tradition of classic baseball architecture.

3. The academic adviser introduced a number of programs and said that we could make individual appointments to see her.

4. Lance Armstrong won the Tour de France seven times but is also known for his philanthropy.

5. I almost never watch television: There is either nothing on that appeals to me, or the picture disappears at a crucial moment.

6. Blue whales are the largest of all animals, and up to 80 percent of them congregate seasonally in Antarctic waters.

FOR GROUP DISCUSSION

The following excerpt is from Malcolm Gladwell's *Outliers: The Story of Success.* Comment on the uses of coordination, subordination, and parallelism. Be sure to go beyond finding examples to discuss the effects the author's choices have on his message and on you, the reader.

> You can't buy your way into Major Junior A hockey. It doesn't matter who your father or mother is, or who your grandfather was, or what business your family is in. Nor does it matter if you live in the most remote corner of the most northerly province in Canada. If you have ability, the vast network of hockey scouts and talent spotters will find you, and if you are willing to work to develop that ability, the system will reward you. Success in hockey is based on *individual merit*—and both of these words are important. Players are judged on their own performance, not on anyone else's, and on the basis of their ability, not on some other arbitrary fact.
>
>   Or are they?

YOUR TURN

We now invite you to take a turn. Instead of discussing sentences we have found or created, we would like to offer you the opportunity to talk about your own sentences, either those you've written yourself or those you've encountered in your reading. Here are the steps we suggest you follow:

A. Your Writing

1. Choose two or three excerpts from a paper you've written. You may choose either sentences or entire paragraphs.

2. Decide whether you would like to revise the excerpt. If you decide to revise it, list the original sentence(s), your revision, and your reasons for making the revision.

3. If you decide to analyze your original, unrevised excerpt, list the original passage and your reasons for believing it to be effective.

Before you start this assignment, review Chapters 1 through 4 for ideas. The following example was written by a student in one of our grammar classes. Notice that his revision is based on suggestions in Chapter 3.

Original: As the horses churn down the lane to the finish line, it is his voice that can be heard above all the screaming fans.

Revised version: As the horses churn down the lane to the finish line, his voice roars above all the screaming fans.

Reason for the revision: The elimination of *be* verbs can result in more pointed writing. I replaced *it is his voice that can be heard* with *his voice roars.* I used an action verb to replace the *be* verb.

B. Published Writing

Follow the same steps to analyze the writing in a published source, either describing the effectiveness of the writing or making recommendations for improvement. Here's another example from the student whose work we just presented. This time he is drawing on the information from Chapter 2.

Original: The noise of the land birds suddenly intensified; the geese and swans increased their calling. He noticed. I saw him swing his head quickly. There was a look that I had never seen in his eyes, a hint of fear perhaps.

Reason the excerpt is effective: The author uses both short and long sentences. He did not have to vary sentence length. He could have simply written *The noise of the land birds suddenly intensified. The geese and swans increased their calling. He noticed because I saw him swing his head quickly. There was a fear that I had never seen.* Obviously, this version is more monotone and less effective. By including a short sentence in the middle of the paragraph, the author is able to emphasize the quickness of the noticing.

KEY TERMS

Adjectival clause	Coordination	Semicolon
Adverbial clause	Correlative	Sentence
Backgrounding	conjunction	Serial comma
Clause	Dependent clause	Series
Climax	Foregrounding	Simple sentence
Colon	Fused sentence	Subject–verb
Comma	Gerund	agreement
Comma splice	Independent clause	Subordinating
Complex sentence	Nominal	conjunction
Compound sentence	Nominal clause	Subordination
Conjunction	Parallel structure	Transitional phrase
Conjunctive adverb	Parallelism	Triplet
Coordinating	Person	
conjunction	Run-on sentence	

RHETORICAL REMINDERS

Parallelism

Do the coordinate structures within the sentence belong together? (Are the ideas equal? Are the forms the same?)

Climax

When writing a series, have I ordered word, phrases, or clauses in the order of increasing importance, scope, or energy?

Coordinating Conjunctions

Have I used coordinating conjunctions to join sentences where I would like to stress addition or contrast?

Correlatives

Have I taken advantage of the strong focus that the correlatives provide: *either–or, neither–nor, both–and, not only–but also?*

Conjunctive Adverbs

Have I used the versatile conjunctive adverbs to good advantage?

Have I placed them where I want the reader to focus?

Colons

Have I used the colon to connect those sentences that set up an expectation in the reader?

PUNCTUATION REMINDERS

Have I remembered that in the case of a two-part compound within the sentence no comma is required?

Have I used commas between elements in a series?

Have I used a comma with the conjunction joining the two independent clauses of a compound sentence?

Have I used commas to set off conjunctive adverbs and transitional phrases, especially when they begin a clause?

Have I used a comma after a dependent clause at the beginning of a sentence?

Have I made good use of a semicolon to connect clauses when it would effectively signal a close connection?

Have I used a colon effectively to signal the expected information that follows in a second independent clause?

Have I used a dash (or dashes) to lighten the comma load?

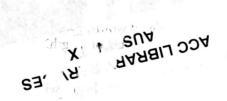

PART II

Controlling the Message

Good prose is a kind of speech, more deliberate and shapely than the words we utter aloud, yet still akin to the living voice.
—SCOTT RUSSELL SANDERS

The writer's toolkit that you brought to this course already had a good many tools in it. As you studied Chapters 1 to 4, you learned the names of many of those tools, along with some new ones. You can think of Chapters 5 to 7 as the training manual for their use:

Chapter 5: Cohesion

Chapter 6: Sentence Rhythm

Chapter 7: The Writer's Voice

These three chapters all focus on helping you gain control of your prose and its effects on your reader: controlling your message. They'll help you feel confident in making choices as you draft and revise. And having that control, that confidence, means more than simply avoiding error: It means creating sentences that flow, that work together to send your readers the message you want them to hear.

In these chapters, you'll learn the *whats* and the *whys*—what options are available to you and why they have the effects they do. By the end of Chapter 7, you'll be able to use your tools to develop your own repertoire of writer's voices, one to suit each of the writing situations you encounter.

Cohesion

CHAPTER PREVIEW

Cohesion refers to the connection of sentences to one another, to the flow of a text, to the ways in which a paragraph of separate sentences becomes a unified whole. Building on what you've studied in previous chapters, you'll now have the opportunity to

- examine connections between sentences in terms of reader expectation;
- discuss the repetition of key terms and related words to improve cohesion;
- use the known–new contract to strengthen cohesion;
- improve clarity by eliminating broad reference; and
- explain how parallel structures across sentences provide cohesion.

READER EXPECTATION

Have you ever come across a teacher's "awk" noted in the margin of a written assignment, or have you yourself ever judged a piece of writing as awkward? Perhaps in reading a composition of your own or one written by a classmate, you've felt that something was amiss—but you couldn't quite put your finger on the something. Such problems can often be traced to thwarted **reader expectations**. Something may have struck you as awkward simply because you weren't expecting it.

Both in reading and in conversation we have a sense of direction about our language. Although we may not know exactly what's coming next, when we hear it—or read it—we recognize if it's appropriate. It's when the ideas take an unexpected turn that the "*awk*" response can set in, when a passage fails to fit that expectation, that sense of appropriateness: "I didn't know exactly what was coming next—but I certainly didn't expect *that!*"

In conversation, we can call a halt to the speaker: "Wait! What was that you just said?" But as readers, we don't have that option. Instead, we find ourselves thinking, "Why am I reading this now?" Even though it's only a fleeting thought, it doesn't take many such interruptions—the pause, the second thought, the backtracking—to obstruct the cohesive flow of a piece of writing.

Where do a reader's expectations come from? Obviously, from what has gone before, from the prior text, or, in the case of an opening paragraph, from the title or, possibly, from the author's reputation. Within a paragraph, reader expectation begins with the opening sentence. The writer, of course, has all manner of possibilities for setting up that expectation. The first sentence of this paragraph, because it is a question, sets up the expectation of an answer—or perhaps a second question.

The effective topic sentence nearly always suggests the direction the paragraph will take, calling up a response in the reader: "Prove it" or "Tell me more." The following sentence opens a paragraph in *Time* about the friendship between Abraham Lincoln and Frederick Douglass, the third paragraph in an article by John Stauffer entitled "Across the Great Divide":

> Despite the immense racial gulf separating them, Lincoln and Douglass had a lot in common.

After reading that statement, we expect to read facts that prove the point. The writer meets our expectations, first with what we might call a subtopic sentence and then the supporting details:

> They were the two preeminent self-made men of their era. Lincoln was born dirt poor, had less than a year of formal schooling and became one of the nation's greatest Presidents. Douglass spent the first 20 years of his life as a slave, had no formal schooling—in fact, his masters forbade him to read or write—and became one of the nation's greatest writers and activists.

The paragraph ends with two additional sentences about Douglass as writer and activist. As you can see, the promise of the topic sentence has been kept. It led us to believe we would be given proof of its proposition—and the sentences that follow do just that.

While you're in the early drafting stage of your essay, you have lots of details to think about: deciding which ideas should be emphasized, which main ideas require support, and which words convey meaning most effectively. At this early stage the response of your reader may not even occur to you. But certainly at the various revision stages along the way, you'll want to think about the reader's expectations.

Remember that, as with many other facets of language, a reader's expectations are not necessarily conscious thoughts. A thwarted expectation may constitute only a fleeting break in concentration, a momentary blip in the flow. But remember, too, it's that blip that produces the *"awk."*

Active readers do more than simply process the words and meanings of a particular sentence as they are reading it. They also fit the ideas of the current sentence into what they already know from having read previous sentences and from their own experience. At the same time, they are developing further expectations.

To become aware of the reader's expectations means to put yourself in the reader's shoes—or head. It requires the ability to read your own ideas objectively, to see and hear your own words as someone else might read them. All the sections that follow in this chapter, covering various features of cohesion, emphasize this relationship between writer and reader.

FOR GROUP DISCUSSION

1. Look again at the weasel paragraph at the opening of Chapter 2. Delete the second sentence, the question. Discuss how that deletion alters reader expectation. In what way does the presence of the question change the expectation set up by the opening sentence? Compose an alternative second sentence in the form of a statement, rather than a question. Compare your version to Dillard's in terms of its effect on a reader's expectation.

2. The following excerpt comes from a paragraph in *The Life and Wars of General Phil Sheridan* by Roy Morris, Jr. For this exercise, the excerpt is divided into four separate sentences. Take a slip of paper and cover all the sentences but the first. Then, read the first and discuss what you expect to follow. Do the same with the second and third sentences. Are the sentences in this excerpt cohesive? Is there anything that could be done to make them more cohesive?

    Before 1870, large buffalo herds still roamed the Southern plains, and many thousands of Native people still lived as they preferred, with the buffalo at the base of their economies.

The slaughter of the vast buffalo herd that roamed the plains and prairies until the 1840s reached a million animals a year during the 1870s.

Along the newly opened tracks, the railroads ran special excursions from which self-styled sportsmen shot buffalo from the comfort of their seats.

General Phil Sheridan remarked that the buffalo hunters had done more in two years to defeat the Indians than the entire regular Army had been able to do in the previous thirty years.

REPETITION

Instead of **repetition**, this discussion could be headed **lexical cohesion**, a term that refers to the contribution of particular words to the cohesion, or continuity, of text. (*Lexicon,* the noun form of *lexical,* means the words of the language; you can think of your lexicon as the dictionary in your head.) The repetition of words from one sentence to another is an obvious cohesive link, one that logically occurs in a paragraph on a particular topic.

In *Constructing Texts,* George Dillon characterizes the conflicting advice about repetition that student writers often encounter as a "no-man's land":

> [A] no-man's-land where they are caught in the crossfire of Never Use the Same Word Twice on a Page and Repeat Key Terms, Use Your Thesaurus to Find Synonyms and Avoid Needless ("Elegant") Variation. (p. 96)

Dillon notes that the journalism class is more often the source of "Never Use the Same Word Twice" and the English class the source of "Repeat Key Terms." He points out that sportswriters are especially good at avoiding repetition, at finding synonyms.

In this paragraph about a Cubs/Cardinals game from the *New York Times,* notice the variety of nouns and verbs:

> [Derrek Lee's] two-run shot off Matt Morris (11–3) with two outs in the fifth sailed over the visitors' bullpen in left before clanging off a guardrail, a drive estimated at 421 feet that put the Cubs ahead, 5–3. Morris gave up all three homers and has allowed 10 this season after surrendering 35 last year.

In the first sentence, the batter's successful hit is referred to as both a *shot* and a *drive*, and the three verbs in the last sentence—*gave up, has allowed, surrendering*—are all synonyms for delivering a home-run pitch. In fact, among the major word classes in the paragraph—nouns, verbs, adjectives, and adverbs—there's not a single repeated word!

On the other hand, you'll find that the paragraphs you've been reading in this textbook reflect the English-class advice that Dillon identifies: "Repeat Key Terms." For example, look at the fourth paragraph under the heading "Reader Expectation" on page 82. You'll see the word *expectation* four times and the word *paragraph* three times, with no synonyms for either word—simply because there are no synonyms that would do the job as well. And, of course, it makes sense to repeat key concepts in a book designed to teach those concepts. But you'll also find from time to time alternative phrasing for the sake of variety or for the purpose of adding a new dimension to the discussion. In the writing you do for your English class, the best advice is probably the middle ground. It would certainly be a mistake to conclude that repetition should be avoided. In fact, the opposite is true: Repetition strengthens cohesion.

But what happens when your teacher writes "rep" in the margin of your essay, a comment usually aimed at unnecessary repetition? How can you tell the difference between the good kind, the repetition that enhances cohesion, and the kind that calls negative attention to itself? Unnecessary repetition goes by the name of **redundancy**. It's possible that the redundant word the teacher noticed is part of a redundant sentence, one that adds nothing new to the discussion. As you'll read in the next section, most sentences contain both known (old) and new information. The lack of new information may be the source of that "rep" comment.

Lexical cohesion also refers to synonyms and other related words, not just actual repetition: *birds/robins, rodents/mice, meal/supper, friend/companion, vacation/trip/holiday*. And of course our grammar itself calls for the use of pronouns in lieu of repeating a noun or noun phrase. Such substitutes constitute strong cohesive ties.

THE KNOWN–NEW CONTRACT

Seeing the sentence as a series of units, as you did in Chapter 2, will help you understand the feature of cohesion called the **known–new contract**. It relates to both what the reader knows and what the reader expects.

The first sentence in a paragraph, like the first paragraph of a chapter or an essay, sets up expectations in the reader about what is coming. Certainly one of those expectations is that the following sentences will stick to the topic. Another is that the sentence will have new information, not just a repeat of what the reader already knows.

The term *known–new* also describes the most common order for that information, with the known information coming first, generally in the subject position, and the new information—the reason for the sentence—in the predicate, where the main emphasis of the sentence naturally occurs. This pattern is obvious in the Lincoln/Douglass paragraph you read earlier in this chapter, with *Lincoln and Douglass* as the subject of the topic sentence, *they* as the subject of the second, and their separate names as subjects in the sentences that follow.

The repeated known information is not always repeated in the exact words, as it is in the Lincoln/Douglass example—as the sports reports in the preceding section clearly demonstrate. We saw another example in the paragraph about dams in Chapter 2, where the known information in the second sentence is a paraphrase of the topic in the first:

> Shaping up as an important milestone is <u>the demolition of two large dams</u> in Washington State's Elwha River, which flows from the mountains of Olympic National Park into the Juan de Fuca Strait. <u>Their removal</u> ... would occur in stages, and if it goes as planned, the Pacific Northwest will lose only a tiny amount of hydropower and regain a legendary salmon fishery.

In other words, *removal* is another way of saying *demolition*.

The Lincoln/Douglass example illustrates a common pattern wherein the repeated topic, information that the reader knows, remains fairly constant throughout the paragraph, in subject position. In some paragraphs, however, the new information that appears in the predicate of one sentence becomes the known information in the next, functioning as the subject. Here, for example, is a newspaper paragraph written by a meteorologist in response to a reader's question about thunderstorms; it begins with a one-sentence paragraph:

> Thunderstorms can be categorized as single cell or multicell.

> Basically, *a single-cell thunderstorm* is the lone thunderstorm that forms <u>on a hot humid day.</u> The *heat and humidity of the day* is the only trigger for the storm. This type of storm forms in an environment with little difference in the wind speed and direction—or wind shear—between the surface and cloud level.
> —Joe Murgo, *Centre Daily Times*

Here's another paragraph in which you can find known–new links:

> This desire to deepen my alternate language [Ojibwe] puts me in an odd relationship to my first love, <u>English.</u> *It* is, after all, the language stuffed into my mother's ancestors' mouths. English is the reason she didn't speak her native language and the reason I can barely limp along in mine. English is <u>an all-devouring language that has moved across North America like the fabulous plagues of locusts that darkened the sky and devoured even the</u> <u>handles of rakes and hoes.</u> Yet *the omnivorous nature of a colonial language* is a writer's gift. Raised in the English language, I partake of a mongrel feast.
> —Louise Erdrich, "Two Languages in Mind,
> but Just One in the Heart"

The ⟶ in these examples highlight this pattern: The new information in the predicate of one sentence (underlined) becomes the known information (italicized) in the next one.

In another paragraph pattern, or information pattern, the topic sentence is followed by supporting details suggested by the topic and expected by the reader. This pattern of development is fairly standard for writing various kinds of description, where the topic sentence sets up the expectation of the details that will prove its point, specific examples to support the generalization in the topic sentence:

> *Our trip to Florida for spring break* turned out to be a disaster. <u>The hotel room</u> we rented was miserable—shabby and stuffy and downright depressing. <u>The food</u> we could afford made our dining hall remembrances from campus seem positively gourmet. <u>The daily transportation</u> to the beach we had been promised showed up only once and even then was an hour late....

Here the subjects of the supporting sentences are what we can think of as subtopics of the main subject, "our trip to Florida for spring break." Paragraphs like this one generally cry out for more details, and the place to add them is under those subtopic sentences, with specifics of the room and the food and other events that make the trip come alive for the reader—in other words, another layer of detail. If, after finishing the disaster details, you decide to add some happy events of the trip, either in the same paragraph or in the next one (assuming there were indeed some happy events), you'll have to signal that change to your reader with *on the other hand, however, but,* or some other indication that you're shifting gears.

If you're writing a descriptive essay about your apartment, perhaps to let a future roommate know what to expect, chances are you'd use this same pattern. You might begin with an overall assessment of the apartment's adequacy or inadequacy, its efficiency or lack thereof, in your topic sentence. The subjects of the sentences that follow would support that assessment with details about cost, location, furnishings, neighbors, and so on.

It might appear that the sentences of such a paragraph, like those in the description of spring break, contain no known information, when each brings up a new topic, or subtopic. But in both cases the subtopics really are known information; they are all part of the domain, the sphere, of apartment living—or of spring breaks in Florida. We can think of them as essentially given information, information that a reader can be expected to recognize as relevant.

FOR GROUP DISCUSSION

The following paragraphs are from Chapter 15 of *Undaunted Courage* by Stephen E. Ambrose, the story of the Lewis and Clark expedition. The passage here describes an event in October 1804, a year into the trip. As you read the sentences, note the information patterns and cohesive ties that Ambrose has used. You might begin by marking the known information in each sentence and noting its connection to the preceding text:

> Beginning in October, as the expedition made its way through present northern South Dakota, it passed numerous abandoned villages, composed of earth-lodge dwellings and cultivated fields. Some of the fields, although unattended, still had squash and corn growing in them. These had once been home to the mighty Arikara tribe. About thirty thousand persons strong in the year the United States won its independence, the tribe had been reduced by smallpox epidemics in the 1780s to not much more than one-fifth that size. Another epidemic swept through in 1803–4, devastating the tribe. What had been eighteen villages the previous year had been reduced to three by the time Lewis arrived.

EXERCISE 16

Revise the following passages to improve their cohesion. Think especially about reader expectation and the placement of known and new information.

1. The Gateway Arch at the edge of the Mississippi River in St. Louis is the world's tallest monument. Eero Saarinen designed the stainless steel structure that commemorates the Westward Movement.

2. Psychologists believe that color conveys emotional messages. Advertisers routinely manipulate consumers using color psychology. The pure white backgrounds and bold primary colors of detergent boxes are thought to influence buyers. Cleanliness and strength are associated with those colors.

3. The relentless heat of California's great Central Valley makes the summer almost unbearable at times. Over 110° is not an unusual temperature reading from June through September. Bakersfield often records the hottest temperature in the valley.

4. Getting chilled or getting your feet wet won't cause a cold. Weather is not the culprit that causes the common cold. Viruses are to blame.

5. The federal witness-protection service began in 1968. The U.S. Marshal Service directs the program. Over four thousand people have been relocated under the program. New identities are created for people in the program. The people are in extreme danger because they have testified against criminals.

The Role of Pronouns

Personal Pronouns. Perhaps our most common known element, equally as strong as the repeated noun phrase, is the pronoun. In Chapter 1, you'll recall, we used personal pronouns—*he, she, it, they, we*—to identify the boundaries of noun phrase units. When we use those pronouns in writing (and we often do use a pronoun instead of repeating a noun phrase), we call that noun phrase the pronoun's **antecedent**. You can think of the antecedent as the pronoun's backup system. And because it has that backup noun phrase, the pronoun is, by definition, known information. But the pronoun will work only when its antecedent is clear to the reader, in the foreground of the reader's consciousness.

Let's look at a portion of the weasel paragraph we saw in Chapter 2:

[1] A weasel is wild. [2] Who knows what **he** thinks? [3] **He** sleeps in **his** underground den, **his** tail draped over **his** nose. [4] Sometimes **he** lives in **his** den for two days without

leaving. [5] Outside, **he** stalks rabbits, mice, muskrats, and birds, killing more bodies than **he** can eat warm, and often dragging the carcasses home.

The pronoun *he* connects the second sentence to the first—only that one word, but clearly a strong grammatical tie. The third sentence repeats *he.* The fourth and fifth sentences both begin with *he.*

As you learned in Chapter 1, personal pronouns in the **possessive case,** such as *his* in the third and fourth sentences of the weasel passage, function as **determiners**, or noun signalers. These **possessive pronouns** also signal a link between new and known information. In the following passage, the possessive pronoun *its* provides strong cohesive ties:

> Portland, sixty miles from the Pacific Ocean, is by no means immune to the suburbanization that has sapped the vitality from many cities. **Its** suburbs now contain about two thirds of the area's 1.4 million residents and about half of the area's jobs. Yet as the suburbs have grown, the downtown has become more attractive and popular than ever.
>
> Downtown Portland has distinct edges. **Its** eastern border is the deep, navigable Willamette River, lined for more than a mile by Tom McCall Waterfront Park, a grassy, mostly level expanse suited to events that draw thousands such as the Rose Festival (Portland calls itself the "City of Roses"), a blues festival, and a summer symphony series. **Its** western border is the steep West Hills, which contain Washington Park, home of the International Rose Test Gardens, where more than 400 varieties of roses are cultivated, and Forest Park, whose 4,800 acres of Douglas fir, alder, and maple constitute one of the largest nature preserves and hiking areas in any American city.
>
> —Philip Langdon, *The Atlantic Monthly*

In the weasel paragraph, *he* constitutes the entire subject; in the Portland paragraph, in all three cases, *its* stands for the possessive noun *Portland's* and acts as a signal for the headwords: *suburbs, eastern border, western border.* But no matter how it functions—whether it occurs by itself or acts as a determiner—the pronoun represents known information. It is this known information that helps provide the cohesive tie between sentences. The three *its* sentences here are typical, with the known information in the subject and the new information in the predicate.

Demonstrative Pronouns. Like the personal pronouns, the **demonstrative pronouns**—*this, that, these,* and *those*—take the place of a noun phrase; in doing so, they provide a strong cohesive tie. And, like the possessive pronouns, they also serve as determiners:

> That sounds like a good plan. (noun phrase replacement)
>
> That plan sounds good to me. (determiner for *plan*)

When you read the second sentence aloud, you can hear the special focusing quality that the demonstrative adds to the noun *plan,* a focus that the determiner *the* would not have:

> The plan sounds good to me.

The demonstratives include the feature of proximity, in reference to both space and time, with *this* and *these* indicating closeness, *that* and *those* more distance. You'll find many sentences in these chapters (note the use of *these*) that demonstrate the close proximity indicated by *these* and *this* in their roles as determiners.

In the following example from Chapter 2, the demonstrative pronoun *these* occurs without a noun headword:

> These seven [sentence patterns] represent the underlying skeletal structure of nearly all our sentences.

When a writer uses a pronoun, the reader has the right to assume that the antecedent is not just known information but that, in fact, the information is located in the foreground of his or her consciousness. The demonstratives, especially *this* and *these,* represent extra emphasis for foregrounding. We saw an example of this emphasis in the Ambrose passage about Lewis and Clark:

> Some of the fields, although unattended, still had squash and corn growing in them. These had once been home to the mighty Arikara tribe.

And in the sentence introducing the quote you just read, there's another example: *this emphasis.*

Writers can easily introduce weak spots when a pronoun has no clear antecedent. For example, in the following sentence there is no specific noun phrase to back up either the demonstrative pronoun *this* or the personal pronoun *it:*

> My roommate told me she has decided to drop out of school and look for a job. This has taken me completely by surprise, and I know it will shock her parents.

The problem here is not one of communication; we can easily figure out what the sentence means. But notice the absence of a specific noun in the first sentence to which the demonstrative *this* refers; rather, the pronoun refers to the idea in the sentence as a whole. This use of the pronoun is called **broad reference**. And while this example may not cause the reader to stumble, sometimes the understood antecedent is a bit troublesome to figure out. The point is that we, as readers, shouldn't have to do the figuring: That job belongs to the writer. Often the best way to fix a vague *this* or *that* is to turn the pronoun into a determiner and supply the missing headword:

> This decision of hers took me completely by surprise.

By turning *this* into a complete noun phrase, we also provide the vague *it* with a backup antecedent.

When you're revising the first draft of your essay—or perhaps rereading a sentence you just wrote—always pay attention to those sentences with a lone pronoun as subject, especially the demonstratives. Make sure that the antecedent of *this* or *that* or *these* or *those* is clear to the reader. If the noun phrase the pronoun stands for is not obvious, consider using the pronoun as a determiner and adding a headword. Pay special attention to *it* and *they* as well. It's important to recognize that pronouns without clear antecedents are in violation of the known–new contract.

FOR GROUP DISCUSSION

You could make the argument that a bare *this, that, these,* or *those* is perfectly capable of communicating without a noun headword, as the example in the Lewis and Clark passage by Steven Ambrose demonstrates. In fact, the original draft of the sentence that introduces the quotation also had a bare determiner: "We saw an example of *this* in the Lewis and Clark passage."

Do you think the revised version with the word *emphasis* added is an improvement? Would the addition of *fields* improve the Ambrose passage? And how about the roommate example? Did it really need the headword added? Check some of your reading material from this or another class to find out how common it is for demonstratives to appear without headwords. Are the missing headwords obvious, easy to retrieve?

EXERCISE 17

Revise the following passages to eliminate the vague pronouns. In some cases the most effective revision will be to turn *this* or *that* into a determiner. Another possibility is to combine the sentences.

1. Many women in the nineteenth century joined the fight for equal legal and political status. This eventually led to the establishment in 1890 of the National American Woman Suffrage Association.

2. Women in the labor force protested against long hours and poor working conditions. The National Consumers' League, founded in 1899, tried to improve that.

3. Some married women in the 1830s were able to have their own property, but it didn't mean they could vote.

4. Elizabeth Cady Stanton and Susan B. Anthony insisted that the fourteenth amendment gave women the rights of citizenship; because of this, they also argued that the fifteenth amendment should be expanded to guarantee a woman's right to vote.

5. In 1920 the Constitution was finally amended to give women the right to vote. That did not, however, provide *all* women with the right to vote: In some states, many African American women (and men) had to pass tests in order to vote.

6. Today equal rights are still denied to women in many countries either because of their sex, their ethnic identity, or their economic status. This will not change without pressure from international organizations dedicated to promoting and protecting human rights.

The Role of the Passive Voice

In Chapter 3 you practiced changing sentences in the active voice to passive by making the direct object of the active sentence the subject of the passive. That shift of focus is one of the main strengths of the **passive voice**, one of its purposes: It allows known information to be in the subject position. Here, for example, is the beginning of a paragraph from a *Time* article by Michael D. Lemonick about the destruction of the Brazilian rain forests. Note how the subject of the passive second sentence provides a cohesive tie:

> If Americans are truly interested in saving the rain forests, they should move beyond rhetoric and suggest *policies* that are practical—and acceptable—to the understandably wary Brazilians. <u>Such policies cannot be presented as take-them-or-leave-them propositions</u>. If the U.S. expects better

performance from Brazil, Brazil has a right to make demands
in return. In fact, the U.S. and Brazil need to engage in face-
to-face negotiations as part of a formal dialogue on the environment between the industrial nations and the developing
countries. [emphasis added]

In the first sentence, *policies* is new information; in the second it is known.
You'll note that the agent is missing from the passive sentence; however,
"by the Americans" is clearly understood. Note also how the information
patterns work in the two sentences following the passive, with the known
information, *U.S.* and *Brazil*—the agents—in subject position and the
new information in the predicates.

The following example of the passive voice appears in a sentence you
read earlier in this chapter in the discussion of the known–new contract.
It opens a paragraph:

> In another paragraph pattern, or information pattern, the
> topic sentence is followed by supporting details suggested by
> the topic and expected by the reader.

Here the term *supporting details* is the new information, so it belongs in
the predicate, where it gets the main emphasis. You'll be reading more
about the connection of information and sentence rhythm in the next
chapter.

Other Sentence Inversions

As you've seen, the *passive transformation,* as the passive voice is sometimes called, inverts the active word order, with the original object shifted
to subject position. Another, much more common, method of rearrang-
ing information is to open the sentence with an adverbial modifier, as
you saw in Chapter 2 under the heading "The Optional Adverbials"
(page 26). Adverbials are called optional because, with few exceptions,
sentences are grammatical without them. However, when we do add
them—and adverbials are very common indeed—they are considered
modifiers of the verb; that is, they are part of the predicate. But they
don't have to stay in the predicate position. Here is an opening adverbial
from the discussion in Chapter 2:

> <u>Because a weasel is wild</u>, it should be approached with great
> caution.

In that discussion, this example was presented without context. But let's assume that it is the opening of a paragraph following our old standby weasel passage. You probably remember its opening sentence: *A weasel is wild.* Clearly, if our *because* clause opened a second paragraph on weasels, the clause itself would be adding no new information, so we don't want it at the end of the sentence. We want to save the sentence end for the new idea—in this case, the idea of great caution. The *because* clause, with its known information, provides the transition from the previous sentence; it is the glue that connects them. One of the main points of the adverbial discussion in Chapter 2 is the movability—and thus the versatility—of the optional adverbial. When you put that feature together with the concept of the known–new contract, you can appreciate how important a tool movable adverbials can be for you as a writer.

Still another inversion of information involves switching the position of the subject and the predicate. Here's the topic sentence of a paragraph you've seen before:

> Shaping up as an important milestone is the demolition of two large dams in Washington State's Elwha River, which flows from the mountains of Olympic National Park into the Juan de Fuca Strait.

Here's the underlying subject–predicate structure:

> The demolition of two large dams ... is shaping up as an important milestone.

The writer's purpose for making that subject–predicate switch is connected to the previous paragraphs in the article, which relate the history and consequences of dam removal. The word *milestone* refers to that history, so it becomes the transition to the new information about these two particular dams. It's an unusual grammatical situation, for the old information to occur in the verb phrase, the predicate. Using her inversion tool, the writer has set aside the subject–predicate order so that the new information is in line for emphasis. The position at the end of the sentence also makes it easier to add those two long modifiers, a prepositional phrase and a *which*-clause. We look more closely at word-order variations in Chapter 11.

FOR GROUP DISCUSSION

The following paragraph is the beginning of a short description of Thomas Jefferson by Lee A. Jacobus:

> Thomas Jefferson, an exceptionally accomplished and well-educated man, is probably best known for writing the Declaration of Independence, a work composed under the

eyes of Benjamin Franklin, John Adams, and the Continental Congress, which spent two and a half days going over every word. The substance of the document was developed in committee, but Jefferson, because of the grace of his style, was chosen to do the actual writing. The result is one of the most memorable statements in American history.

Explain why the author used the passive voice where he did. Try writing a version of the paragraph using only the active voice. Is it equally effective?

PARALLELISM

Early in this chapter you read that it's okay to repeat words, that repetition can have a positive effect on the reader. In this section we look again at a specific kind of repetition called **parallelism**, the repetition of whole structures, such as phrases and clauses. Parallelism is usually thought of as a device for enhancing a writer's style—and indeed it is that—as you learned in Chapter 4. It can certainly add polish and flavor to prose that otherwise might be the plain vanilla variety. But it can also provide cohesion, especially when the repeated elements extend through a paragraph or from one paragraph to the next.

The quality of being parallel means that the repeated elements have the same structure, such as noun phrases with noun phrases, prepositional phrases with prepositional phrases, as we emphasized in the discussion of coordination (page 53). One of the most famous sentences in President Kennedy's inaugural address includes parallel verb phrases: "pay any price, bear any burden, meet any hardship, support any friend, oppose any foe." And we're all familiar with Lincoln's "of the people, by the people, and for the people."

Parallelism becomes an especially strong cohesive device when a structure echoes a structure from a previous sentence or paragraph. In the second paragraph of the Portland passage on page 91, the subject "Its eastern border" names one of the "distinct edges" referred to in the opening sentence. The next sentence not only fulfills the reader's expectation with the word *western,* it does so using parallel structure:

> Its eastern border is the deep, navigable Willamette River ...
>
> Its western border is the steep West Hills ...

In the following passage the author's use of repetition adds intensity and drama to his argument:

> That knowledge has become the key resource means that there is a world economy, and that the world economy, rather than

the national economy, is in control. <u>Every country, every in-dustry, and every business</u> will be in an increasingly competi-tive environment. <u>Every country, every industry, and every business</u> will, in its decisions, have to consider its competitive standing in the world economy and the competitiveness of its knowledge competencies.

— Peter F. Drucker, *The Atlantic Monthly*

The two repeated series as subjects are the most obvious repetitions, but note also in the first sentence two instances of *world economy* contrasted with *national economy* and a third repetition of *world economy* in the last sentence. And in the second and third sentences we read *competitive standing, competitive environment,* and *competitiveness.*

The repeated series in this paragraph by Stephen Jay Gould from *Ever Since Darwin* illustrates another fairly common feature of paral-lelism, that of **antithesis**, the introduction of contrasting, or dissimi-lar, ideas:

Why imagine that specific genes for <u>aggression, dominance, or spite</u> have any importance when we know that the brain's enormous flexibility permits us to be <u>aggressive or peaceful, dominant or submissive, spiteful or generous?</u> <u>Violence, sex-ism, and general nastiness</u> are biological since they represent one subset of a possible range of behaviors. But <u>peacefulness, equality, and kindness</u> are just as biological—and we may see their influence increase if we can create social structures that permit them to flourish.

— Stephen Jay Gould, *Ever Since Darwin*

These examples should make it clear that parallelism is more than mere stylistic décor: The parallel structures are, in fact, among the strongest cohesive ties that the writer has available. They highlight those ideas that should be in the foreground of the reader's consciousness, sending the message that the parallel structures are not only connected but also significant.

Repetition Versus Redundancy

Rather than commending these authors for effective parallelism, you may be tempted to accuse them of redundancy. How do we distinguish between them? How do we tell the difference between good repetition and bad?

Parallelism of the kind we see here—parallelism as a stylistic device— invariably calls attention to itself. Did these authors intend to do that, to call attention to these structures? Clearly, the answer is "Yes—and for good reason." In both passages, the use of repetition has added a dramatic dimension to the prose.

The repetition in these passages might also tempt you to accuse the authors of wordiness; their sentences certainly don't pass the test of brevity or conciseness, features of writing so often touted in composition textbooks. Clarity, of course, is always a goal. And, yes, sometimes clarity calls for brevity, for a lean version of a sentence. But there are many occasions that call for a celebration of words. We certainly don't expect the president to be brief in an inaugural address; neither should we expect a writer to be brief in explaining the concept of a world economy or in arguing for the biological basis of kindness.

In Chapter 8 redundancy is addressed in a section called "The Proliferating Prepositional Phrase." And the use of repetition as a stylistic device is discussed further in Chapter 11, "Making Stylistic Choices."

FOR GROUP DISCUSSION

A. Find the parallel structures in the following paragraph from Jay Wink's *The Great Upheaval* and explain how they provide cohesion:

> Soldiers marched that day in Manhattan. For almost as long as anyone could remember, the sight of soldiers had invariably meant the same thing, whether they were French or Russian, Austrian or English, whether they belonged to kings or were battle-hardened mercenaries, whether they moved in great formations or galloped along on horseback. Too often their presence was ominous, signaling that the campaign was beginning and the war was deepening, that the dead would increase and the bloodshed would continue, and the suffering would go on. But today their footsteps were unique, booming out the rites of nationhood. They called out a celebration of victory and the raising of the flag—the American flag. It was November 25, 1783. Evacuation Day in New York City.

B. Not only is repetition the topic in this paragraph from Nicholas Carr's *The Shallows,* it also repeats forms. Discuss the ways Carr links form and content without sounding monotonous.

> During the course of a day, most of us with access to the Web spend at least a couple of hours online—sometimes much more—and during that time, we tend to repeat the

same or similar actions over and over again, usually at a high rate of speed and often in response to cues delivered through a screen or a speaker. Some of the actions are physical ones. We tap the keys on our PC keyboard. We drag a mouse and click its left and right buttons and spin its scroll wheel. We draw the tips of our fingers across a trackpad. We use our thumbs to punch out text on the real or simulated keypads of our BlackBerrys or mobile phones. We rotate our iPhones, iPods, and iPads to shift between "landscape" and "portrait" modes while manipulating the icons on their touch-sensitive screens.

C. Think of a repetitive action or experience and write a paragraph similar to Carr's. Then exchange your paragraph with a classmate and discuss what makes your paragraphs cohesive. Use the rhetorical reminders at the end of this chapter to help you.

KEY TERMS

Antecedent	Determiner	Possessive case
Antithesis	Known–new contract	Possessive pronoun
Broad reference	Lexical cohesion	Pronoun
Cohesion	Parallelism	Reader expectation
Demonstrative	Passive voice	Redundancy
pronoun	Personal pronoun	Repetition

RHETORICAL REMINDERS

Have I anticipated my reader's expectations?

Do my paragraphs profit from lexical cohesion, the repetition of words?

Is the known information in the beginning of the sentence, where it can provide a cohesive tie to the previous sentence, with the new information in end-focus position?

Have I taken advantage of parallelism as a cohesive device?

Sentence Rhythm

CHAPTER PREVIEW

In this chapter we look at a feature of language you might not have thought about before: its **rhythm**, its regular beat. To help you gain control of the rhythm of your prose, this chapter will help you to

- recognize the importance of end focus;
- use cleft sentences and *there*-transformations to direct the reader's attention;
- shift sentence stress by strategically placing conjunctive adverbs, transitional phrases, and commas; and
- select power words for emphasis.

YOUR SENSE OF RHYTHM

One of the most important aspects of your expertise with sentences is your sense of rhythm. For example, if you read the opening sentence in this paragraph out loud, you'll hear yourself saying "one of the most" in almost a monotone; you probably don't hear a **stress** on a syllable, a strong beat, until you get to *important:*

one of the most imPORTant

And you probably rush through those first four words so fast that you pronounce "of" without articulating the *f*, making "one of" sound like the first two words in "won a prize."

Notice, also, that the following two sentences have the same basic rhythm even though the number of words in each sentence differs:

| She | told her | best friend. |
| She | sent it to her | best friend. |

We would simply pronounce *sent it to her* more quickly than *told her*.

As listeners we pay attention to the stressed words (or syllables within words); that's where we'll hear the information that the speaker is focusing on. And as speakers we manipulate emphasis to coincide with our message, reserving the prominent stress for our main point of focus.

Such sentence manipulation is not something we ordinarily think about, nor is it a skill we were taught; for native speakers it's automatic, part of our native language ability. On the other hand, if you're not a native speaker of English, mastering the rhythm of sentences may be difficult, especially if the sentence rhythm of your native language does not have a regular beat. Recognizing the relationship between the rhythm of a sentence and its message will help you as a writer. You'll also understand more spoken English if you attend to sentence rhythm, especially noting strong beats.

You've probably been told about the importance of reading your written work aloud. The advantage of doing so is that you'll hear which words you've emphasized in your writing. If you note that something doesn't sound right, your hesitance might be due to a disrupted or unhelpful rhythm. Also valuable is listening to someone else read your work out loud. When that person stumbles on a sentence, you'll know to consider that sentence a candidate for revision.

END FOCUS

The rhythm of sentences is closely tied to their two-part structure (subject and predicate) and to the known–new contract. In Chapter 5 you learned that known information often occurs in the subject position. When it does, you'll note the prominent stress occurs in the predicate, on the new information, generally on the last or next-to-the-last unit in the sentence. Linguists describe this common rhythm pattern as **end focus**.

As you read the following, listen for the syllable that gets main stress:

> The common cold is caused by a virus.
>
> Barbara wrecked her motorcycle.
>
> Sentence rhythm is characterized by end focus.

Did you stress *virus, motorcycle,* and *end?* We normally don't read sentences in lists, of course; we read them in context. And as readers we count on the context, on the meaning, to guide the reading, to help us put the emphasis where it belongs. Our job as writers, then, is clear: If we want readers to understand our intentions and to focus on the important information, we must help them by taking sentence rhythm into account.

The following passages provide a simple lesson on the way in which end focus and sentence rhythm work together:

> According to the *Chicago Tribune,* Thomas E. Dewey won the 1948 presidential election. But correspondent Arthur Sears Henning made a huge error. The voters had elected Harry S. Truman.

> According to the *Chicago Tribune,* Thomas E. Dewey won the 1948 presidential election. But correspondent Arthur Sears Henning made a huge error. Harry S. Truman had been elected by the voters.

As you probably noticed, the one difference in the wording of the two passages is the word order in the last sentence. And, when you read the two, that difference probably produced a difference in the rhythm pattern. In the second sentence of both passages the words *but* and *huge* led you to expect information refuting the claim in the first sentence. Recognizing that *Truman* fulfilled your expectation, that's the sentence unit you stressed. However, by putting *Truman* in the opening position, the writer disregarded the reader's expectation that the new, important information would be in end-focus position.

Clearly, using the passive voice in the last sentence of the second passage wasn't a good choice. Not only does it disrupt the reader's expectations, but it also fails to enhance cohesion. Sometimes, though, a sentence in the passive voice both facilitates cohesion and ensures that new information is in the predicate. Compare the following passages. Does the end of the second sentence in each pair focus on known or new information?

> Each year since 1901, scientists, artists, and peacemakers from around the world have received the Nobel Prize for helping humanity. The creator of dynamite and other explosives, Alfred Nobel, founded this award.

> Each year since 1901, scientists, artists, and peacemakers from around the world have received the Nobel Prize for helping humanity. This award was founded by Alfred Nobel, the creator of dynamite and other explosives.

Here, the second passage takes advantage of end focus. And this grammatical choice does have a rhetorical effect. In fact, choosing a passive sentence here has the dual effect of placing new information where it will be stressed and making the second passage more cohesive. The message is thus clear, and the reader satisfied.

The movability of optional adverbials, which you read about in both Chapters 2 and 5, also comes into play in this discussion of end focus. The term *optional* refers only to the fact that most sentences do not need adverbials to be grammatical; however, when we do add them, we usually do so for good reason: to add information about time and place and manner and reason and so on. Often that information provides transition from the prior text, so the opening position is the right place for it. And time adverbials, like *yesterday, in 2010,* or *when I was little,* often belong there at the opening. But not always. If the adverbial is the new information, save it for the end of the sentence, the point of main stress.

EXERCISE 18

How would you rewrite the second sentence in the following pairs of sentences to take advantage of end focus?

1. The word *janitor* found its way into the English language as a synonym for doorkeeper. This word was also the name of a minor school official in Scots usage.

2. The word *janitor* has its roots in ancient mythology: Ianus (later Janus) was the god of gateways, thresholds, and all sorts of beginnings. *January,* the month marking the beginning of the new year (a time for hopeful resolutions), is also rooted in the name *Ianus.*

CONTROLLING RHYTHM

Because end focus is such a common rhythm pattern, we can think of it as part of the contract between writer and reader. The reader expects the main sentence focus to be in the predicate, unless given a signal to the contrary. But of course not all sentences are alike; not every sentence has end focus. In speech, especially, the focus is often shifted elsewhere. The speaker can easily stress the new information, no matter where in the sentence it appears. Consider, for example, these alternative ways of stressing information in speech:

BARBARA wrecked her motorcycle yesterday morning. [Not someone else.]

Barbara wrecked HER motorcycle yesterday morning. [Her own, not someone else's.]

Barbara wrecked her motorcycle yesterday MORNING. [Not in the afternoon.]

And we can add extra stress to *motorcycle*:

> Barbara wrecked her MOTORCYCLE yesterday morning. [Not her car.]

Or we can give the whole sentence added emphasis:

> Barbara DID wreck her motorcycle yesterday morning. [Believe me, I'm not making this up.]

The speaker is in control of the message that the listener is meant to hear. The spoken language is powerful, much more powerful than writing, far more capable of expressing feelings and nuances of meaning.

The It-*Cleft*

It's true that the speaker has a much easier job than does the writer in getting the message across and preventing misinterpretation. But the writer is certainly not powerless—far from it. As we saw earlier, the careful writer can take control simply by understanding the reader's expectations about the sentence and by making sure that the important information coincides with the prominent stress. One way to shift the stress is to use a **cleft sentence** (the term *cleft* comes from the verb *cleave,* which means to divide or split), which divides and rearranges a typical sentence, according to this pattern:

It + form of *be* +	[stressed element] +	*who* or *that* ...
It was	the BUTler	who solved the mystery.

Notice how this version differs from a typical sentence:

> The butler solved the mystery.

The cleft sentence makes use of *it,* called an **expletive**. Without an antecedent, *it* doesn't function in a cleft sentence as a personal pronoun. The ***it*-cleft** enables the writer to shift the emphasis to another unit in the sentence, forcing the reader to focus on the structure following *it was* (or *it is, it has been,* etc.). In the next example, the adverbial receives the focus:

> It was <u>singlehandedly</u> that the butler solved the mystery.

Instead of focusing on the information at the end of the sentence, the reader will stress the word or phrase after the unstressed *it was.* The following *it*-cleft from a *Time* article by Michael D. Lemonick empha-sizes the way a virus causes harm:

> It is by killing individual cells in the body's all-important im-mune system that the AIDS virus wreaks its terrible havoc. The virus itself isn't deadly, but it leaves the body defenseless against all sorts of diseases that are.

The *it*-cleft enables the writer to control the reader's attention, to de-termine precisely what the rhythm of the sentence will be.

FOR GROUP DISCUSSION

The following short article by Dale Conour accompanies a dramatic two-page photograph in *Sunset* (October 2004) of an enormous black cloud of starlings nearly covering the sky. Notice especially the au-thor's methods of controlling rhythm. Part of that control comes with the use of *it*—seven times, in fact: as an expletive *it* and as the personal pronoun. Can you justify all those *it*s? Consider cohesion as well as the rhythm and focus that they produce. Could the essay get by with fewer *it*s?

> It's an eerie sight to anyone—a massive swarm of Euro-pean starlings, some million strong, sweeping over a fal-low field off State 46 north of Bakersfield, California. But to birders, it's even more disturbing: They know it's an invasion.
>
> It began in 1890 when New Yorker Eugene Schiffelin made it his quest to introduce to the New World every Old World bird mentioned in Shakespeare's works. Compelled by a single mention of the starling in *Henry IV,* Schiffelin loosed 60 birds in Central Park.
>
> The result today: Millions of starlings—voracious, aggressive, and smart (they're members of the myna family)—have blanketed the U.S., while the number of cavity-nesting songbirds has plummeted.
>
> It may have been *Henry IV* in which the Bard men-tions the starling directly, but it's *Henry VI* in which he's prophetic: "Hung be the heavens with black, yield day to night!"

The What-*Cleft*

Another kind of cleft sentence uses a *what* clause, usually in subject position; here a form of *be* separates the original sentence into two parts:

> The butler solved the mystery singlehandedly.
>
> <u>What the butler did was solve the mystery singlehandedly.</u>

The **what-cleft** splits the original sentence into known and new information, providing at least two strong beats:

What the butler DID was solve the mystery singleHANDedly.

Here is an example of a sentence with three different *what*-cleft variations:

> Thick fog reduced visibility.
>
> <u>What the thick fog DID was reduce visiBILity.</u>
>
> <u>Thick FOG was what reduced visiBILity.</u>
>
> <u>What reDUCED visibility was the thick FOG.</u>

This example could also be revised as an *it*-cleft:

> It was thick FOG that reduced visibility.

FOR GROUP DISCUSSION

In her essay "Saving the Life That Is Your Own," Alice Walker included the following sentence with a *what*-cleft.

What is always needed in the appreciation of art, or life, is the larger perspective.

Write a similar sentence without the *what*-cleft. How does the rhythm change? Is there anything other than the use of the cleft that affects the rhythm? Compare the rhetorical effect of the original version with that of your own version.

The There-*Transformation*

Another method of changing word order to shift the stress is known as the **there-transformation:**

> A stranger is standing on the porch.
>
> <u>There's a stranger standing on the porch.</u>

No concert tickets were available that morning.

<u>There were no concert tickets available that morning</u>.

Again, this reordering puts the main stress on the subject by shifting its position. Remember that the normal subject position, the opening position, is usually unstressed. This addition of *there,* like *it* in the *it*-cleft, is known as an expletive; it delays the subject, thereby putting it in line for stress.

In addition to its focusing ability, the *there*-transformation gives the writer a way of introducing a new topic, both within the paragraph and at the opening, as the topic sentence. You'll find many such introductory sentences in the books you read. These two come from two different chapters of Tom Vanderbilt's book *Traffic:*

> There is an iron law in traffic engineering: The longer pedestrians have to wait for a signal to cross, the more likely they are to cross against the signal.
>
> There are times when we do not want to signal our intentions.

In *there*-transformations you can hear the main stress on the structure following *there is* or *there are.*

Have you been told to avoid using *it* and *there* constructions? Such advice is generally given in discussions of wordiness and brevity, with suggestions for deleting extra words. While it's true that *it is* and *there are* do add words, when they are used in the right place and for the right reason, they are not redundant, unnecessary words; they are, in fact, doing an important job.

It's certainly possible to overuse these structures (and the passive voice as well)—and it's that overuse you need to worry about. So as you reread that first (or second or third) draft, do pay special attention to sentence focus, to the way the reader will read your sentences: Think about end focus, about known and new information, about sentence rhythm. Make sure you've used these focusing tools for the right reason.

EXERCISE 19

Rewrite the following sentences, shifting the focus by using sentence transformations: the *it*-cleft, the *what*-cleft, and the *there*-transformation. For example, you could use a cleft structure in the first sentence to focus either on the date or the place or the ship.

1. The *Titanic* hit an iceberg and sank in the North Atlantic in 1912.

2. Our defense won the Stanford game in the final three minutes with a crucial interception.

3. Hundreds of angry parents were protesting the senator's position on daycare at yesterday's political rally in the student union.

4. Lightning causes many of the forest fires in the Western states.

5. Countless travelers have lost their lives in the Bermuda Triangle.

6. Herbert Spencer used the phrase *survival of the fittest* to label the competition among human beings.

◄ **FOR GROUP DISCUSSION**

Overuse of *there* constructions can indeed make a paragraph muddy. Clean up the following paragraph by deleting unnecessary *there* constructions and revising the sentences for clarity. Discuss your revisions with your classmates.

There are three good reasons to use a check instead of cash. First, with a check, there is not the necessity to carry large sums of money, which could easily be stolen. There is also the ease with which bills can be paid by mail. Even if the check is lost, there is no loss of money. Finally, there is the receipt that checks provide. This receipt can be used as a legal document.

RHYTHM AND THE COMMA

The sentence transformations with *it* and *what* and *there* are not the only ways we have to control the focus and rhythm of sentences. Other ways, in fact, are more common and, in most cases, more subtle. The phrase *in fact* in the preceding sentence illustrates one such method—a transitional phrase that interrupts the rhythm pattern. The inserted phrase adds emphasis to the subject. We can illustrate the difference with this example showing stress and length:

Other ways are more COMmon.
Other W—A—Y—S, in F—A—C—T, are more COMmon.

The visual signal of the comma causes the reader to give added length and stress to the preceding word. The main focus is still on the new information at the end, but the sentence rhythm has changed, with part of the reader's attention shifted to the subject.

This role for the comma, to shift the peak of stress, is probably one you hadn't thought about before. You've probably considered the comma in the more traditional way, as a signaler of the pause in speech. But, as you learned in Chapter 2 regarding the sentence units, not every pause translates to a comma in writing. And when we do include a comma, the pause goes beyond simple hesitation. It emphasizes and lengthens the pre-ceding word. Even the common *but* gets that extra attention in the third sentence of this paragraph. The inserted *as* clause lengthens the opening *but,* as well as *sentence*:

> B—U—T, as you learned in Chapter 2 regarding S-E-Ntence units, ...

Among the most versatile tools for manipulating sentence rhythm are the **conjunctive adverbs** and **transitional phrases**, which we examined in Chapter 4. The conjunctive adverbs create cohesion with an adverbial emphasis. Their versatility lies in their movability. That earlier sentence could have been written like this:

> Other ways are much more common, in fact.

In this version, the word *common* gets all the attention.

Here are some other examples of sentences with movable phrases—examples from previous passages:

1. One obvious difference, <u>of course</u>, is vocabulary.
2. Consider, <u>for example</u>, these alternative ways of saying the motorcycle sentence ....
3. When you study grammar at school, <u>then</u>, you are studying what you already "know."

Notice especially how many different places in these sentences a conjunc-tive adverb or a transitional phrase occurs: in (1) between the subject and the predicate; in (2) between the verb and the direct object; in (3) be-tween the introductory adverbial and the main clause.

An important point to understand is that there are other places in all three of these sentences where that word or phrase could have been placed. Writers position these words and phrases to help their readers: How do I want the reader to read this sentence? What is important here for the reader to stress? Will the reader understand how this sentence fits in with what follows? Other familiar words and phrases are listed on pages 62 and 63–64.

FOR GROUP DISCUSSION

1. Several of the sentences in the following passage, from *The Birds* by Roger Tory Peterson, illustrate another method of putting the subject in line for main stress. Read the passage aloud and mark the peaks of stress. Using your understanding of the sentence

units, identify the subject and predicate of each clause. What technique has the author used to control the rhythm? In thinking about the subject–predicate order of the sentences, you might want to review the discussion of inversion on pages 95–96. (The sentences are numbered so that the discussion of them will be easier.)

> [1] A bird's feathers have to do many things. [2] Not only must they provide lift surfaces for wings and tail, but they must protect the bird against the weather and insulate it against loss of heat. [3] Feathers come in almost infinite variety, but they fall into four main categories. [4] Most numerous are the contour feathers which coat the body, giving it a streamlined shape. [5] A house sparrow wears about 3,500 of these in winter, and they are so efficient at sealing in heat that it can maintain a normal temperature of 106.7°F without difficulty in below-freezing cold. [6] Lying beneath them are the soft down feathers, also used for insulation. [7] Scattered among both types are the hairlike filoplumes, which sometimes protrude from the coat and may serve as a kind of decoration, or possibly as sensory organs.

2. Read a draft of your own essay (or a classmate's) with sentence rhythm in mind. Think especially about end focus and the difference in rhythm that commas make. Would you make any changes? Share your ideas with your classmates.

POWER WORDS

We've just seen how conjunctive adverbs set off by commas can override the principle of end focus, the expected rhythm pattern. We've also seen how the use of *it* and *there* can change the emphasis. But some words are powerful enough to interrupt the usual rhythm pattern on their own— even without commas or sentence shifts.

Read the following pairs of sentences aloud and listen for the words that get main stress:

> In the first gallery we admired a display of Tiffany glass.
>
> In the first gallery we admired a magnificent display of Tiffany glass.
>
> The senator spoke about the problems of the homeless.
>
> The senator spoke eloquently about the problems of the homeless.

Both its meaning and its length may contribute to a word's inherent attention-getting power, as in the case of the adjective *magnificent* and the adverb *eloquently*. Words that convey strong emotions and words that have a superlative or absolute quality are hard to compete with for attention in most sentences.

Adjectives and adverbs are especially powerful when they are preceded by another modifier (*secretly jealous, cautiously hopeful, quite gracefully, especially powerful*) and when they are in the superlative degree, ending in -est (*loudest, fastest*) or marked by *most* (*most aggressively, most incredible*). Noun phrases too have the power to take control of the sentence, especially when they include one of those powerful modifiers (*complete chaos, dangerous undertaking, overwhelming courage, bewildering array*).

A word of warning is called for here. To label these words as power words is not necessarily to recommend that you use them. The point to remember is that when you do use them they'll command attention. Like movie stars who inevitably create a stir wherever they go, these words change the atmosphere of the sentences they inhabit. Here is what happened to the sentence about the senator's speech:

> The senator spoke about the problems of the HOMEless.
>
> The senator spoke ELoquently about the problems of the homeless.

The word *eloquently* shifts the limelight from the topic of the speech to the senator's style of speaking; and, in doing so, it sets up a different expectation in the reader. We would not be surprised if the subject of the next sentence turned out to be *he* or *she* (the senator) rather than *they* (the homeless).

It's important to recognize that in each example the added word—*magnificent, eloquently*—changes a statement of fact into an arguable proposition. The reader has every right to expect supporting evidence for these opinions. What was there about the speech that was eloquent? In what way is the display magnificent? In other words, those power words that change the rhythm also change the reader's expectations.

Correlative Conjunctions

The correlative conjunctions that you read about in Chapter 4—*either–or, neither–nor, both–and, not only–but also*—are among the power words that change the focus and rhythm pattern of the sentence and change the expectation of readers. When you read the following sentence, you probably give the loudest stress to *environment*:

> Individuals and nations must learn to think about the
> environment.

Now add one word. Instead of the simple conjunction *and,* use the correlative *both–and* and listen to your rhythm pattern.

> *Both* individuals *and* nations must learn to think about the environment.

It's important to recognize that these two different kinds of conjunctions cannot be used interchangeably. In the example with *both–and,* the main stress shifts from *environment* to the subject, so the reader expects to learn more about the responsibilities of individuals and nations.

Now examine another version with *not only–but also* (or ... *as well*):

> *Not only* individuals *but also* nations must learn to think about the environment.
>
> *Not only* individuals *but* nations *as well* must learn to think about the environment.

In these examples, the subject, especially *nations,* has acquired even more emphasis.

Adverbials of Emphasis

As you read in Chapter 2, adverbials provide their information of time, place, manner, and the like, in a variety of shapes; they also give the writer special flexibility because they are movable. And in the previous section on "Rhythm and the Comma," you saw how the conjunctive adverbs can change the focus by shifting position. But there's another group of adverbials, mainly single-word adverbs, whose purpose is to emphasize a particular structure and thus control the pace and rhythm of the sentence.

Read the following sentences and note where you apply the main stress:

> I could hardly sleep last night.
>
> My roommate also had trouble studying.
>
> Some people are always looking for trouble.
>
> The country has never before faced the kind of crisis it faces now with terrorism.

You probably put the emphasis on *hardly, also, always,* and *never before.*

Given these examples, you can think of other words that you use for emphasis: other negatives, such as *seldom, barely, scarcely;* other frequency words, such as *often, sometimes, rarely;* and other adverbs expressing duration, such as *already, no longer, still.*

Negative adverbials produce an even stronger emphasis when they open the sentence, the result of switching the position of the subject and the auxiliary:

> Never before <u>has the country encountered</u> the kind of crisis it now faces with terrorism.

This shift, in fact, requires an auxiliary unless the main verb is a form of *be:*

> I seldom <u>get</u> a good night's sleep on weekends.
>
> Seldom <u>do I get</u> a good night's sleep on weekends.

This is another instance where we call on *do*-support when we need an auxiliary. (This use of *do*-support is discussed briefly on pages 41–42.) And, as you can hear, the auxiliary–subject combination shares the main stress with the adverbial. It's possible, of course, to write sentences in which these words would not have main stress, where the principle of end focus, for example, would still be in effect. But certainly these are words that you, as a writer, need to recognize; they often wield the power in a sentence, controlling its rhythm and making a difference in the message.

The Common *Only*. One of our most versatile—but also most frequently misused—adverbials of emphasis is the common *only*. Like other emphasizers, *only* can change the focus of the sentence by directing the reader's attention to a particular word or phrase:

> My grandfather writes only poetry.
>
> Paul cleans the apartment only on Saturdays.

When you read these sentences you'll find yourself putting nearly equal emphasis on both *only* and the headword that follows it. Such placement of *only* does affect the reader's expectations. Read the following two sentences and guess what the second part of each sentence might be:

> The car only looked old.
>
> Only the car looked old.

Did you think of follow-ups like these?

> The car only looked old; it's really quite new.
>
> Only the car looked old; the pick-up was in good shape.

However, there's also a common problem with *only:* It's frequently misplaced—and most of the time we don't even notice! If we read closely, though, we might be puzzled.

> My grandfather only writes poetry. (He doesn't read poetry?)
>
> Paul only cleans the apartment on Saturdays. (He doesn't do anything else?)

Even songwriters get it wrong:

> I only have eyes for you.

Perhaps the judgments of *wrong* and *misplaced* are not always accurate—too picky perhaps—when we consider how often this placement of *only* occurs both in speech and in the formal prose of respected writers. Nevertheless, in some cases, the reader will get a clear message when the *only* puts emphasis on a specific detail, to strengthen the sentence focus. That message says, "Pay attention! I've crafted this sentence carefully."

FOR GROUP DISCUSSION

Add a conjunctive adverb, a transitional phrase, or a power word to the following sentences and discuss the change in rhythm and rhetorical effect.

1. The sunset astonished everyone.
2. Sunbeams spread across the sky.
3. Clouds lit up.

FOR GROUP DISCUSSION

How does Richard Ellis control the rhythm in this paragraph from *The Search for the Giant Squid?* (Look closely at the words at the beginning of each sentence.)

> There is probably no apparition more terrifying than a gigantic, saucer-eyed creature of the depths with writhing, snakelike, grasping tentacles, a huge gelatinous body, and the powerful beak of a humongous seagoing parrot. Even the man-eating shark pales by comparison to such a horror. In only a few species do octopuses and squids reach the monstrous size required to attack swimmers, but this has not deterred writers and filmmakers from recruiting them when an underwater man-killer is needed.

KEY TERMS

Adverbial of emphasis
Cleft sentence
Conjunctive adverb
Correlative
   conjunction

End focus
Expletive
It-cleft
Power words
Rhythm

Stress
There-transformation
Transitional phrase
What-cleft

RHETORICAL REMINDERS

Sentence Rhythm

Have I considered my reader's expectations by putting the new information in line for end focus, unless otherwise marked?

Controlling Rhythm

Have I used the *there*-transformation and cleft sentences effectively—but not too frequently?

Have I placed interrupting words and phrases and clauses where they'll be the most effective?

Power Words

Have I considered the impact of power words on the rhythm pattern?

Have I considered the contribution that correlative conjunctions could or do make to the rhythm and the reader's expectations?

Have I placed *only* in its most effective position?

PUNCTUATION REMINDER

In punctuating my sentences, have I taken into consideration that a comma changes the rhythm of the sentence, adding length and stress to the preceding word?

CHAPTER
7

The Writer's Voice

CHAPTER PREVIEW

We've already looked at options you have for controlling the reader's attention. Now we turn to features of language that will affect your writer's voice and, of course, the reader's interpretation of that voice. By the time you finish working through the activities in this chapter, you'll be able to

- adjust the tone of your writer's voice for different audiences and purposes;
- choose words appropriate for your rhetorical situation (diction);
- recognize metadiscourse used to guide the reader through the text and to establish credibility; and
- select a point of view from which to best convey opinions or information.

TONE

In conversation there's nothing very mysterious about tone of voice and its contribution to meaning:

> "He was his usual cheerful self."
> "She's got attitude."
> "I think he was kidding."

In a face-to-face encounter, of course it's not only the voice that communicates the tone: There's the red face, the raised eyebrows, the rolling eyes, the smile, the smirk, the pleased expression.

But even on the phone, without visual cues, we usually have no trouble drawing conclusions about tone. A person's voice may exude confidence or trepidation, hostility or pleasure, anger, bitterness, indifference. "How did she sound?" is a question someone might ask you about a phone conversation—not only, "What did she say?"

But how does your *writer's* **voice** sound? What determines its **tone?** Indeed, what does *tone* mean when there is no sound, only words on paper?

To answer these questions, consider what you read in the Introduction about rhetoric—about the choices you make based not only on your topic but also about your audience and purpose. In that discussion we compared your writer's voice in a text message to your best friend with that in a letter to the dean of your college. Or consider the words you would use in a letter to a prospective employer. You would choose words to convey an earnest and confident and businesslike tone—and of course you'd be careful to dot every *i* and cross every *t,* so to speak.

Clearly, it's the rhetorical situation—the topic, the purpose, and the audience—that determines the tone. For example, newspapers and newsmagazines generally call for a neutral, objective voice. But apparently not always—not in this Associated Press article about rodent fossils discovered in South America:

> Eeek! Imagine a rodent that weighed a ton and was as big as a bull.
>
> Uruguayan scientists say they have uncovered fossil evidence of the biggest species of rodent ever found, one that scurried across wooded areas of South America about 4 million years ago, when the continent was not connected to North America.
>
> A herbivore, the beast may have been a contemporary, and possibly prey, of saber-toothed cats—a prehistoric version of Tom and Jerry.
>
> For those afraid of rodents, forget hopping on a chair. Its huge skull, more than 20 inches long, suggested a beast more than eight feet long and weighing between 1,700 and 3,000 pounds.
>
> Although British newspapers variously described it as a mouse or a rat, researchers say the animal, named Josephoartigasia monesi, actually was more closely related to a guinea pig or porcupine.
>
> —Raphael G. Satter

The author's tongue-in-cheek tone here is anything but neutral. His opening with the interjection *eek* is a sure way to signal a playful tone. His use of the imperative—*imagine a rodent, forget hopping on a chair*—invites our participation, our agreement; his choice of details—*big as a bull, a prehistoric version of Tom and Jerry*—keeps us interested.

And in the following short piece, one of several in "Parade's Special Intelligence Report," a regular feature of *Parade* magazine, the use of the word *snafu* in the headline sets the reader up to expect that same kind of flippant tone:

Social Security Snafu

The federal government had to cough up cash last month and mail a "letter of explanation" to 51 million Americans who were short-changed on their Social Security checks. It seems the Bureau of Labor Statistics was supposed to give them 2.5% cost-of-living increases but only added 2.4%, due to faulty math. Recipients won't get rich: It's about $12 to $19 more. (We wonder what it cost to calculate the difference, then print and mail all those letters.) But the blunders didn't stop there: Some folks were sent financial data about their neighbors.

As you can see, the writer fulfills the headline's expectations. It's the choice of words that does it: *cough up, short-changed, faulty math, blunders*. You can be quite sure that a news release on the topic sent by the Bureau of Labor Statistics would have used different words.

In each of these examples, the writer's attitude toward the topic, the writer's take on the topic, clearly sets the tone: tongue-in-cheek, flippant, facetious, derisive.

EXERCISE 20

1. Rewrite the "Snafu" paragraph in a neutral tone, as the Bureau of Labor Statistics might have done in a news release. In addition to the informal words mentioned, you'll also want to consider the appropriateness of *It seems* in the second sentence, the reference to getting rich in the third, and the sentence in parentheses.

2. These five short paragraphs open an article by Jeff Gammage entitled "One Significant Swede" about Carl Linnaeus in the magazine section of the *Philadelphia Inquirer* (June 28, 2005):

   At the Swedish museum in South Philadelphia, the staff is getting ready for a gala, year-long celebration of the 300th birthday of Carl Linnaeus.

   They face just one pesky problem: Most people don't know who the heck he is.

And that's a shame, sponsors say. Because Linnaeus is not just another guy in a powdered wig.

The Scandinavian scientist came up with a big, world-changing idea, a way to tidy up the clutter of the natural universe: He invented a system to name and categorize everything that lives, has lived or will live. And then he got people to follow his rules.

Remember your high school biology teacher pounding *kingdom-phylum-class* into your head? You can thank—or blame—Carl Linnaeus.

As you can see, the first paragraph covers the standard *who–what–when–where–why* of journalistic reporting in a straightforward way. What has the writer done to change the tone of the last four paragraphs?

   A. Revise the last four paragraphs so that they conform to the straight reporting of the first paragraph.

   B. Then, revise the opening paragraph so that it conforms in tone to the final four paragraphs.

For the revisions, you might want to combine paragraphs into perhaps just one or two.

DICTION

All of the published examples in the preceding section, besides illustrating tone, show clearly the connection between tone and **diction**, the choice of words: They are two sides of the same coin. Both are connected to the writing situation as well as to the essential sense of the words. And it may take only a few words to change the tone from neutral to ironic or bitter or skeptical or enthusiastic—depending, of course, on their meanings.

Where do those meanings come from? While the dictionary can give the core meaning of a word—its **denotation**—its essential sense resides in the language user and in the written or spoken context in which it is used. This special sense, association, or overtone carried by the word is called its **connotation**. For example, *economical* and *cheap* are synonyms: They both mean "thrifty." However, their connotations differ. While *an economical car* has a positive connotation, suggesting good gas mileage, *a cheap car* has a negative connotation, bringing to mind the hassles of needing multiple car repairs. Communication takes place when the essential sense of a word is shared between speaker and listener, writer and reader.

Groups of synonyms can often be organized according to levels of formality. You would no doubt be able to sense that of the three verbs *choose, select,* and *pick out* (a phrasal verb), *pick out* is least formal and *select* is most formal. The words you choose are effective only when they are appropriate to the rhetorical situation, appropriate for the audience and purpose, when they convey your message accurately and comfortably. The idea of comfort may seem out of place in connection with diction, but, in fact, words, especially those with negative connotations, can sometimes cause the reader to feel uncomfortable. You've probably experienced such feelings yourself as a listener—hearing a speaker whose words for one reason or another strike you as inappropriate and make you feel uncomfortable. Writing can provoke those same feelings in a reader.

As a reader yourself, you undoubtedly spot an inappropriate word simply because it commands attention—negative, uncomfortable attention. And when words are inappropriate, they set up communication barriers. As a writer you must learn to spot your own inappropriate words. One of the most common such attention-getters is the word that is too formal for the situation. Sometimes, of course, the opposite problem occurs: a word too informal for its purpose. But student writers are more likely to have the mistaken notion that writing calls for a sophisticated vocabulary. And so they look for words that demonstrate that sophistication.

One consequence of that inappropriate word choice is the loss of a **personal voice**. If what you've written doesn't sound like something you'd actually say, then you should reconsider your choice of words or style of phrasing. This is not to suggest that writing is exactly like speech; it's not, of course. In our everyday conversation with family and friends, we use informal words and phrases that we rarely see in writing, and we commonly use sentence fragments. Further, in writing we use certain modifiers and connectors, such as the *further* at the beginning of this sentence, that we rarely use in speaking. But even when we include such structures, we should be able to recognize our words as our own.

The following passage is the opening of a law school applicant's short essay in response to the question, "Why do you want to study law?"

> It has long been a tenet of my value system that as a capable individual I have a social and moral duty to contribute to the improvement of the society in which I live. It seems that the way to make a valuable contribution is by choosing the means that will best allow me to utilize my abilities and facilitate my interests.

In spite of the **first person point of view**—the use of *I*—there's nothing personal in those lines. Here the writer's voice simply doesn't fit the rhetorical situation. If she had been asked in a face-to-face interview why she wanted to go to law school, she certainly would not have begun her answer with "It has long been a tenet of my value system." Never in her life has she begun a sentence that way. Instead, she would have said "I believe" or "I've always thought." But like many inexperienced writers, she associated formal writing with lofty phrases and uncommon words.

A personal voice does not, however, preclude the use of big words or uncommon words. Nor does the expression *big words* refer to the number of syllables. It means pretentious or fancy words, words that call attention to themselves. Pretentious words send the message that the writer is trying too hard. The word *tenet,* as used in the law school statement, is one such pretentious word; it's out of place. Even the Declaration of Independence, with its formal, ceremonial language, uses the simple word *truths:*

> We hold these truths to be self-evident.

There are times, of course, when an uncommon word is called for, a word with the precise meaning you want. All of us have in our passive vocabulary words that we rarely, if ever, use in speaking; and using them when they're called for does not mean giving up our personal voice. The mere fact that a word is infrequent does not make it pretentious. In the opening sentence of the previous paragraph, for example, the verb is *preclude.* It's not a common word, but there's certainly nothing fancy or pretentious about it: It's simply the most precise word for the job.

Another problem with pretentious language is the flabbiness that it produces, such as "utilize my abilities and facilitate my interests." Verbs like *utilize* and *facilitate* may sound impressive, but what do they really mean? *Utilize* simply means *use:* "to use my abilities." And it would probably surprise the law school applicant to learn that *facilitate* does not mean "to carry out," as she apparently assumed; it means "to make easier." So "facilitate my interests" is not only pretentious; it is meaningless.

FOR GROUP DISCUSSION

1. Words are powerful. As a writer you choose words that call up images in the mind of the reader. But to use words effectively, you have to understand the meanings, the associations, they are likely to have for the reader. Consider the following sets of related words: What features do the members have in common? What features separate them? In what context would one be more effective than another?

companion/friend/buddy	careful/stingy/thrifty/tight
picky/careful/prudent	slumber/sleep/snooze
slender/skinny/scrawny	foolhardy/daring/rash/bold

2. Bertrand Russell is credited with the following "conjugation of an irregular verb":

> I am firm. You are obstinate. He is pigheaded.

Using some of the groups of words in item 1, and adding to them as necessary, try your own conjugations.

Example: I am slender; you are skinny; he is scrawny.

3. One characteristic of ineffective diction is the overuse of **clichés**, many of which are **similes**, comparisons that transfer the qualities of one thing (or person or animal) to another. Such comparisons become clichés when the reader knows exactly what's coming—that is, when there is no new information involved. Unlike the message of pretentious words, trying too hard, clichés send the message that the writer isn't trying hard enough. The comparison is much more effective when it evokes a fresh image, when it helps the reader see something or someone in a new way.

Chances are you and most of your classmates can complete the following phrases with identical words:

quiet as a _____   mean as _____

hot as _____   light as _____

cold as _____   pretty as _____

scared as a _____   weak as _____

strong as _____   ugly as _____

fast as _____   tough as _____

avoid like the _____   sell like _____

Now, instead of using the expected word, find one that creates a fresh image. For example, you might say, "Quiet as a cloudy sky."

Note: You'll find it interesting and instructive to compare the answers given by the nonnative speakers of English in the class with those of native speakers.

Metaphor

As you've seen, the choice of words affects the reader's response to the message and no doubt to the writer as well. Selecting just the right word can close the distance between writer and reader. Another technique for closing that distance is the use of **metaphor**, the application of words from one sphere to another.

You were introduced to the grammar of metaphor in Chapter 2 when you read about the linking-*be* followed by a noun phrase as subject complement. A "something is something" sentence becomes metaphor when that equation is figurative rather than literal—in other words, when the two "somethings" belong to different spheres or domains. Shakespeare's

All the world's a stage

and Charlie Brown's (Charles Schulz's)

Happiness is a warm puppy

illustrate the wide range of possibilities—from the profound to the commonplace.

But *be* sentences, like these examples, are by no means the only form of metaphor, or even the most common. In our everyday language we apply words from one domain to another, creating metaphor with just a simple modifier. Language itself is often described metaphorically: flowery prose, gutter journalism, bathroom words, hard-boiled detective novels. Newsmagazines abound with metaphors, many of them overworked. *Time* reported on "an industrial dinosaur like General Motors" the same week that *Newsweek* described the company as "a sinking ship." In *Time*'s story the head of the company "doesn't like sitting in the back seat"; in *Newsweek*'s he's helping to steer "a treasure galleon."

Metaphor can often illuminate and lighten a serious or technical discussion. The following passage opens the third paragraph of a long article by Lauren Resnick and Chris Zurawsky in *American Education,* a publication of the American Federation of Teachers, describing the standards movement in American schools. The two preceding paragraphs introduce the topic in straightforward academic prose.

> At about fifteen years of age, the standards movement is in its adolescence, and many are already preparing to kick it out of the house. Before we give up on our unruly teen, however, let's take a clear look at what we have to be proud of, what flaws we need to address, and what might be the benefits of pressing ahead.

After just two sentences of the teenager metaphor, however, the reader is back to serious business, with the questions that the article goes on to address. Undoubtedly, though, in both of these examples, the metaphor has made the reader stop and think about the topic in a new way.

◀ **FOR GROUP DISCUSSION**

How does Gretel Ehrlich create a personal voice in this passage from *The Future of Ice: A Journey into Cold?* How would you characterize Ehrlich's tone? How does her word choice help her create that tone? What effect does her use of metaphor have?

> A glacier is an archivist and historian. It registers every fluctuation of weather. It saves everything no matter how small or big, including pollen, dust, heavy metals, bugs, and minerals. As snow becomes firm and then ice, oxygen bubbles are trapped in the glacier, providing samples of ancient atmosphere: carbon dioxide and methane. Records of temperatures and levels of atmospheric gases from before industrialization can be compared with those after—a mere 150 years. We can now see that the steady gains in greenhouse gases and air and water temperatures have occurred only since the rise of our smokestack and tailpipe society.

Verbs and Formality

As you might expect, the level of formality in our prose is determined in large part by our choice of verbs—the pivotal unit in the sentence. Among the verbs that send an informal signal to the reader are many **phrasal verbs**, common verbs combined with one or more **particles** (preposition-like words). Some of the verb-plus-particle combinations form **idioms**. The term *idiom* refers to a set phrase whose meaning cannot be predicted from the separate meanings of the words. The meaning of the idiom *give up,* for example, is different from the combined meanings of *give* and *up:* It means "surrender" or "abandon."

Our language is filled with such idiomatic phrasal verbs: *turn down, bring about, bring on, put up with, stand for, think up, take off, take up, look down on, brush aside, get on with, walk out on, come down with, swear off, write off*—the list goes on and on. As you can see, these are common verbs, part of our everyday speech. They lend an air of familiarity, a conversational tone to the writer's voice.

Idioms are certainly appropriate in informal contexts—for example, in a personal essay or narrative, or for a general audience, such as you might address in a letter to the editor of a newspaper. But for research papers or technical reports—and certainly for résumés and letters to prospective employers—a more formal verb may be called for. One way of adding formality, then, is to look carefully at (*scrutinize*) your sentences and do away with (*eliminate*) or at least cut down on (*reduce*) the number of idioms.

EXERCISE 21

A. Substitute a single word for each of the phrasal verbs listed in the second paragraph of the preceding discussion. In some cases there will be more than one possibility.

B. The idioms we've used in writing this book certainly influence its level of formality. Here are some of the sentences you've seen so far. Come up with a more formal version of each.

   1. <u>Come up with</u> a more formal version of each.

   2. The punctuation convention <u>calls for</u> a comma ....

   3. We can <u>think of</u> it as part of the contract between writer and reader.

   4. You can be sure that in reading their own prose, whether silently or aloud, they are <u>paying attention to</u> sentence rhythm.

   5. The pronoun <u>stands in for</u> the entire noun phrase.

   6. We <u>call on</u> *do* when we need an auxiliary ....

Nominalized Verbs and Abstract Subjects

One common feature of formal writing, especially academic writing, is the use of **nominalized verbs**—verbs have been turned into nouns: *occur* → *occurrence, succeed* → *success, combine* → *combination, remove* → *removal.* Writers take advantage of this feature to link sentences together; they use the verb (actually the entire predicate) to present new information and the nominalized verb, often preceded by a demonstrative *this, that, these,* or *those,* to establish known information:

> The grammar of the written language <u>differs</u> greatly from that of the spoken language. <u>This difference</u> is attributable to the constant innovations of spoken language.

In this example *differ* and *difference* affirm the known–new contract.

Though nominalized verbs contribute to cohesion, they should be used with care. Because they are so common and so easy to produce, they can become a trap for the unwary writer, introducing abstraction where concrete ideas belong. It's during the revision stage of writing that you'll want to be on the lookout. Ask yourself, is the **agent**—the initiator of the action—there and, if so, is it functioning as the subject? In other words, does the sentence explain *who is doing what?* If the answer is no, your sentence may be a prime candidate for revision. Can you find the agent in the following sentence?

> High student achievement led to the creation of the Gifted Students Program.

Although *high student achievement* is the subject, it is an abstraction. The agent could be *students,* or it could be the unnamed creators of the program. Here is one possible revision:

> The School Board created the Gifted Students Program for high achievers.

Another possible source of confusion is the sentence with a verb phrase or a clause as subject, rather than the usual noun phrase. When you study these structures in Chapter 10, you'll see that they are common substitutes for noun phrases. But because they are abstractions, they too may be pitfalls for the unwary writer. Again, the source of the problem may be that of the misplaced or missing agent:

> The <u>buying</u> of so many Christmas presents made little sense to us.
> <u>Analyzing</u> the situation in China shows that opportunities for investment are growing.

Although we need context to tell us the best way to revise these sentences, we can see and hear a problem. The sentences seem to be about actions—but they can't show the action in a strong and concrete way because the agents of those actions are not there in subject position. This kind of agentless sentence should send up a red flag—a signal that here's a candidate for revision.

EXERCISE 22

Revise the following passages, paying special attention to unnecessary nominalizations and problems of agency. The first two items are the examples from the preceding discussion. Remember to ask yourself, "Who is doing what?"

1. The <u>buying</u> of so many Christmas presents made little sense to us.

2. Analyzing the situation in China showed that opportunities for investment were growing.

3. In the biography of Lyndon Johnson by Robert Caro, the account of the Senate election of 1948 is described in great detail.

4. One of the requirements for the completion of the application for a scholarship was the submission of a financial statement by the student's parents.

5. The overuse of salt in the typical American diet has had the result of obscuring the natural taste of many foods. Nutritionists maintain that a reduction in people's dependence on salt would lead to an enhancement of taste and heightened enjoyment of food.

Contractions

Contractions affect the rhythm of sentences and, in doing so, affect the reader's perception of the writer's voice. That voice will probably strike the reader as more conversational, less formal, when contractions are part of the message. Contractions help to close the distance between writer and reader.

Although contractions are often seen as too conversational, most writers, even in formal contexts, will contract the negative *not* in such words as *don't* and *can't:*

> If you use ready-made phrases, you not only <u>don't</u> have to hunt about for words; you also <u>don't</u> have to bother with the rhythms of your sentences, since these phrases are generally so arranged as to be more or less euphonious.
> —George Orwell, "Politics and the English Language"

Other frequent contractions are those with the auxiliary verbs *have, had, will, would, is, am,* and *are.* Here are some common examples:

> Negatives: can't, don't, won't, couldn't, doesn't, isn't
> Auxiliaries: I'd, she'll, they're, we've, he's, it's

The contracted forms of *be* can also occur when they function as the main verb:

> <u>You're</u> happy.
> <u>I'm</u> sad.

The contracted *is* is especially common with *it* and *there:*

> <u>It's</u> a nice day today.
> <u>There's</u> a storm due tomorrow.

You may have noticed that none of the examples, either in the lists or in the quoted passages, involve nouns—only pronouns. Contractions with nouns—"My <u>dog'll</u> eat anything"; "The <u>Senate's</u> accomplished a lot lately"—are fairly common in conversation and in written quotations and dialogue, but they are rare in most writing situations. However, contractions with pronouns are anything but rare.

The advice against using contractions that you may have heard or read simply does not reflect actual usage. Even fairly formal written prose commonly includes the contracted *not,* as the Orwell passage illustrates. And in negative questions, the contracted form is essentially required:

> <u>Hasn't</u> the winter weather been wonderful?
>
> <u>Shouldn't</u> the tax laws be revised?

In the uncontracted form, the *not* predominates, changing the intended emphasis, if not the meaning:

> Has the winter weather not been wonderful?
>
> Should the tax laws not be revised?

An interesting feature in negative statements is that often the writer has more than one contraction to choose from.

> She is not here. → She's not here *or* She isn't here.

Both contracted forms are less formal than the original, but there's also a difference between the two: In the version with the diminished *not (isn't),* the reader will probably put more emphasis on *here*—and may then expect a different follow-up sentence:

> She isn't here. She's in class.
>
> She's not here. I don't know where she is.

If you want to ensure that the reader puts strong stress on the negative, you can use the uncontracted *not*—with or without the contracted *is.* Another difference between these two contracted versions is the number of syllables. The sentence with *isn't* has four syllables; the one with *not* has only three—a rhythm difference that in a given situation may be important.

It's important to recognize the connection between the level of formality and the use of contractions: In general, the more formal the writing, the fewer contractions you'll find, or want to use, especially contracted auxiliaries. However, in most of the writing you do for school or on the job, the occasional contraction will certainly be appropriate. It's important to recognize the contribution that contractions can make to your personal voice.

FOR GROUP DISCUSSION

Choose two advertisements that differ in tone and diction. Describe the tone and diction of each. Then rewrite each of the ads using the voice and tone of the other one. Share your ads and rewrites with your classmates. Compare their characterizations of tone and diction with yours.

METADISCOURSE

Metadiscourse refers to certain signals that help the reader understand the writer's message. The word *metadiscourse* actually means discourse about discourse—signals that clarify the purpose or direction of a particular passage, acting as guideposts for the reader. For example, a word like *however* tells the reader to expect a contrasting statement. And when a sentence opens with *for example,* as the previous one does, you know the sentence will discuss an example of the concept just mentioned. The phrase may not be necessary—many examples go unmarked—but sometimes that help is very important.

Some of our most common and useful metadiscourse signals are the conjunctive adverbs you read about in Chapter 4: *however, thus, nevertheless,* and transitional phrases such as *in other words, in addition,* and *in fact* (see the list on pages 62 and 63–64). Other connecting words and phrases you're familiar with, such as *first, in the first place, second, next, finally,* and *in conclusion,* clearly add to the ease of reading. Those that signal contrasting pairs of ideas—*on the one hand/on the other hand*—are especially helpful. Signals like these contribute to the sense of cohesion, the flow of the paragraph—and sometimes to its accurate interpretation—by keeping the reader informed of the writer's intentions.

We can think of these text connectors as primarily informational, to help the reader understand the message. Other structures that we label as metadiscourse have a different purpose and a different effect: They offer guidance for reading the text, informing the reader of the writer's own attitude about the content of the message.

As you read the following passages, think about the role played by the underlined words. If the sentences look familiar, it's because they have all appeared in earlier sections of this book.

1. <u>The point is</u> that we, as readers, shouldn't have to do the figuring.

2. Parallelism is usually thought of as a device for enhancing a writer's style—<u>and indeed it is that</u>—as you learned in Chapter 4.

3. You've <u>probably</u> been told at one time or another to avoid *I or you* or the passive voice—and, <u>very possibly</u>, the *it*-cleft as well.

All of these underlined structures qualify as metadiscourse.

The opener, *the point is,* in (1) emphasizes our take on the importance and validity of the claim we're making. The inserted clause in (2) calls attention to the truth of the statement about parallelism that could be taken wrong, given the wording "is usually thought of." The paragraph goes on to emphasize the importance of parallelism to cohesion.

The use of *probably* and *very possibly* in (3) is called hedging: There's no way we could know for sure that you've been told those things, so we don't want to sound too positive. We don't want you, the reader, to be stopped by a bold statement when it may not be valid in your case. And we certainly don't want you to lose confidence in our authority to write on this topic. Other hedging terms are words like *perhaps,* verbs like *seem* or *indicate* or *suggest* and phrases like *to a certain extent,* as well as the modal auxiliaries *might* and *may* and *could.*

Although you might think that using words like *perhaps* and *probably* would communicate doubt about the author's authority and the reliability of the information, such **hedges** actually have the opposite effect on the reader. In *Constructing Texts,* George Dillon maintains that they "certify the writer as a modest, careful scholar whose tentative conclusions are probably of wider application and greater likelihood than he feels he can claim" (91).[1]

There are many other kinds of metadiscourse markers that allow the writer to guide the reader's understanding: Some of them comment on the context; some of them allow the writer to address the reader directly; some comment on what is coming next—or what the reader has already learned. Some have more than one purpose. Here are some further examples, also taken from earlier sections of the book:

> As you probably noticed, the only difference between the two passages is in the word order in the last sentence.
>
> In this chapter we look at a feature of language you might not have thought about before: its rhythm, its regular beat.
>
> In Chapter 5 you learned that known information often occurs in the subject position.

In the following paragraph, from *Saga of Chief Joseph,* by Helen Addison Howard, the author translates "Nez Perce" in a parenthetical comment, a type of metadiscourse called a **code gloss**, a term applied when the writer clarifies the meaning of a word or phrase. You'll see other obvious metadiscourse signals as well:

> After Lewis and Clark passed through their country (about which more later), French-Canadian trappers came to trade the white

---

[1]Dillon's book is listed in the Bibliography under "Text Analysis."

man's guns, cloth, metal articles, and trinkets for their pelts of beaver. The French traders, it is claimed, applied the name "Nez Perce" (<u>Pierced Nose</u>) to these Indians because a few members of the tribe used to pierce their noses to insert a shell for ornament. This habit was not a tribal custom, but the name clung to them.

Still another example of metadiscourse appears in the first sentence of the paragraph introducing the previous quotation: The sentence beginning "In the following paragraph, from *Saga of Chief Joseph,* by Helen Addison Howard, the author translates" is called an **attributor**, the source of the quoted information. Attributors add authority to the text. In the previous discussion of Dillon's comment about hedges, the attributor phrase begins "In *Constructing Texts*"; the opening "According to" is another common lead-in for an attributor.

All of these metadiscourse markers send messages to the reader from and about the writer. They say, in effect, "I'm helping you out here, trying to make your job of reading and understanding easier."

FOR GROUP DISCUSSION

Consider the use of metadiscourse in the following paragraph, the first paragraph in Chapter 9 of Thomas S. Kuhn's *The Structure of Scientific Revolutions.* This chapter is entitled "The Nature and Necessity of Scientific Revolutions."

> These remarks permit us at last to consider the problems that provide this essay with its title. What are scientific revolutions, and what is their function in scientific development? Much of the answer to these questions has been anticipated in earlier sections. In particular, the preceding discussion has indicated that scientific revolutions are here taken to be those non-cumulative developmental episodes in which an older paradigm is replaced in whole or in part by an incompatible new one. There is more to be said, however, and an essential part of it can be introduced by asking one further question. Why should a change of paradigm be called a revolution? In the face of the vast and essential differences between political and scientific development, what parallelism can justify the metaphor that finds revolutions in both?

Identify all the uses of metadiscourse in the paragraph; characterize their purpose and their effect on the reader.

POINT OF VIEW

In discussing point of view—the perspective from which the writer views the topic—we again take up the discussion of **personal pronouns**. In Chapter 1 we saw personal pronouns as stand-ins for noun phrases and used them to determine those phrase boundaries; in Chapter 5 we recognized their role as cohesive devices. Here we look at their relationship to point of view. The writer's decision about point of view is essentially a choice about **person**, a feature of personal pronouns: Shall I write in **first person**? **Second person**? A combination? Or shall I stick strictly to **third person**?

In the following chart, the first forms shown are **subjective case**, the form used when the pronoun functions as the subject or subject complement in its sentence. The forms shown in parentheses are variations of case (**possessive, objective**): The possessive case is used when the pronoun functions as a determiner; the objective case is used in three of the complement positions (direct object, indirect object, object complement) and as the object of a preposition.

PERSON	NUMBER	
	<u>Singular</u>	<u>Plural</u>
First	I (my, me)	we (our, us)
Second	you (your, you)	you (your, you)
Third	he (his, him)	
	she (her, her)	they (their, them)
	it (its, it)	

(The case of personal pronouns is discussed further on pages 230–231.)

Many kinds of essays are written in first person—more than you might think. Personal narratives, of course, are nearly always first person, but so are many other essays. In fact, it would probably be accurate to say that most essay writers use first person somewhere in their text—an occasional *we* or *our* or *us*. The exceptions are business and scientific reports and historical essays, which are often strictly third person. Newspapers and newsmagazines also stick to third person when they report the news. But writers of editorials and syndicated columns and feature stories regularly use both first and second person. And in textbooks it's certainly common to see both first and second person. In this one you'll find sentences with *we* or *our* or *you* or *your* on every page.

If it's true that first person is a common point of view, then why do teachers so often rule it unacceptable in the essays they assign? You may have had an English teacher in high school or college who required you to stick to third person. One reason for that proscription against first person is undoubtedly the bad writing that so often results, with *I* turning up as the subject of almost every sentence—as if the writer, the "I," were the topic being discussed.

The most common use of first person in professional writing is the plural—*we* and *us* and *our* rather than *I* and *me* and *my*. The result is a kind of collective first person (sometimes referred to as the "royal *we*" or the "editorial *we*"). You'll find that collective first person in the preamble to the Constitution: "We the people ... for ourselves and our posterity ...." The *we* in this book is also often that collective *we*, though at times it refers just to the two authors of this book. Following is another example of the collective *we*, a first-person passage from *A Brief History of Time* by Stephen W. Hawking:

> Now at first sight, all this evidence that the universe looks the same whichever direction <u>we</u> look in might seem to suggest there is something special about <u>our</u> place in the universe. In particular, it might seem that if <u>we</u> observe all other galaxies to be moving away from <u>us</u>, then <u>we</u> must be at the center of the universe.

Here the first-person plural is especially effective, where the writer wants the reader to be included in his description of the universe.

Another point of view that is sometimes ruled out is the second person, the use of *you*. But it too is common for many writing occasions. You'll notice that many of the sentences in the foregoing paragraphs, as well as the sentence you're reading now, include *you* as the subject. This use of *you* not only gets the attention of the reader; it actually involves the reader in the subject matter.

But *you* does not always address the reader; it is often used in a more general sense, with a meaning more like that of the third person. Notice the use of *you* in this passage from *Broca's Brain* by Carl Sagan, describing an excursion into the back rooms of the Museum of Man in Paris:

> Most of the rooms were evidently used for storage of anthropological items, collected from decades to more than a century ago. <u>You</u> had the sense of a museum of the second order, in which were stored not so much materials that might be of interest as materials that had once been of interest. <u>You</u> could feel the presence of nineteenth-century museum directors engaged, in their frock coats, in goniometrie and craniologie, busily collecting and measuring everything, in the pious hope that mere quantification would lead to understanding.

Here *you* takes the place of "one" or "a person"; it is not "you the reader."

Some teachers, however, prefer *one* to this general *you:*

> When <u>one</u> sees the Golden Gate Bridge for the first time, the sight is simply breathtaking.

The use of *one* adds a formality, a distance that *you* does not have. In most informal situations we're more likely to use *you* rather than *one* to convey that third-person indefinite sense:

> When <u>you</u> see the Golden Gate Bridge for the first time, the sight is simply breathtaking.

This use of *you* is technically second person, but the meaning here is closer to the indefinite third-person *one.*

It is not at all unusual to mix the point of view. A first- or second-person passage always includes pronouns in the third person. And many essays that are essentially third person have an occasional *we* or *our* or *you.* There is no rule that says good writing should not have that versatility of view.

FOR GROUP DISCUSSION

1. Revise the point of view in the paragraph by Carl Sagan. What version—first-person, second-person, or third-person—do you prefer? Why?

2. Next, revise the point of view in the paragraph by Stephen W. Hawking. Which version sounds better to you? Why?

3. Now, change the point of view of one of your own paragraphs and discuss the differences you find.

EXERCISE 23

A. Continue the survey of your writing style.

	PROFESSIONAL	STUDENT
1. Number of sentences with first-person pronouns	_____	_____
2. Number with second person: *you* or *your*	_____	_____

3. Number of transitional phrases   _____   _____
4. Number of hedging words   _____   _____
5. Number of code glosses   _____   _____
6. Number of attributors   _____   _____

   B. What do your statistics tell you? Do they tell you anything about
   the kinds of metadiscourse expected in a specific writing situation? Do they suggest any types of metadiscourse that you might
   consider using in the future? If they do, what is it about your
   writing situation that makes you think these metadiscourse signals would be appropriate?

YOUR TURN

Once again it's your turn. At the end of Chapter 4, you had the opportunity to talk about your own writing and about the writing of published
authors. We'd like to offer you that opportunity again, but this time instead of discussing the material in Chapters 1 through 4, try commenting
on cohesion, sentence rhythm, and voice. To refresh your memory of the
steps for this activity, return to page 77. Here's a new student example to
help you get started:

Original: He laid a rough path of flat rock from the heavy door of the
   cabin, around the jutting log ends of the left cabin corner, and
   on down the hill to the lake.

Revision: From the heavy door of the cabin, all the way down the hill to
   the lake, he laid a rough path of flat rock for us to follow.

Reason for the revision: I inverted this sentence to create a little tension
   leading up to the independent clause. The inversion also provides
   a better transition to the next sentence, which features something
   else that my grandfather did (he is mentioned first in my original
   sentence but later in the revised version).

KEY TERMS

Abstract subject	Contraction	Metadiscourse
Agent	Denotation	Metaphor
Attributor	Diction	Nominalized verb
Cliché	First person	Objective case
Code gloss	Hedge	Particle
Connotation	Idiom	Person

Personal pronoun	Possessive case	Third person
Personal voice	Second person	Tone
Phrasal verb	Simile	Voice
Point of view	Subjective case	

RHETORICAL REMINDERS

What is there in my sentence structure and word choice that has established my tone? Have I avoided words that contradict my tone?

Can I hear my personal voice in the words I've written? Have I avoided unusual words that don't really sound like me—words I probably wouldn't use in speech?

Have I been accurate and complete in attributing the ideas and words of outside sources and in using quotation marks for passages that are not my own?

Are my contractions appropriate, given the level of formality I want to achieve? Are my contractions attached only to pronouns (*she's*) and auxiliaries (*can't*)—not to nouns (*John'll go with us; The teacher's talking*)?

Have I used hedging words appropriately, where I need to hedge? Emphatic words where I want to show emphasis? Have I guided the reader where such guidance would help?

PUNCTUATION REMINDERS

Have I set off metadiscourse markers with commas where an emphasis on the marker would be useful?

Have I included apostrophes in contractions to indicate where a letter or letters have been left out?

Have I used quotation marks correctly (e.g., outside the period at the end of a sentence)?

(*Note:* See pages 251–259 in the Glossary of Punctuation.)

PART III

Making Choices: Form and Function

Proper words in proper places make the true definition of style.
—JONATHAN SWIFT

We hope that the first seven chapters have helped you recognize your knowledge of language structure as your writer's toolbox, with tools that can help you make good decisions as you write and revise—or, as Jonathan Swift put it, decisions that help you find the proper words for proper places. By *proper*, Swift is referring to appropriateness, words that are suitable to the occasion: the grammatical choices that produce the desired rhetorical effects.

The four chapters in this section pull together and expand on some of the details of sentence structure you've studied in earlier chapters:

Chapter 8: Choosing Adverbials
Chapter 9: Choosing Adjectivals
Chapter 10: Choosing Nominals
Chapter 11: Other Stylistic Variations

In Chapter 1 you were introduced to the *-al* forms of *adverb* and *adjective*. There, and in subsequent chapters, you learned that forms other than adverbs and adjectives, such as prepositional phrases and dependent clauses, can modify verbs and nouns. In Chapter 4 you again saw *adverbial* and *adjectival*. You were also introduced to the term *nominal*, the *-al* form of *noun*.

In the first three chapters of this section, you'll learn to think about the basic sentence units and their modifiers in terms of both form and function. The following chart will help you organize this two-sided analysis.

You'll discover that all of the general functions listed on the right—adverbial, adjectival, and nominal—can be carried out by all of the general forms listed on the left—words, phrases, and clauses.

FORM	FUNCTION
Word	**Adverbial**
noun	modifier of verb
verb	**Adjectival**
adjective	subject complement
adverb	object complement
Phrase	modifier of noun
noun phrase	**Nominal**
verb phrase	subject
gerund	subject complement
infinitive	direct object
participle	indirect object
prepositional phrase	object complement
Clause	object of preposition
independent clause (sentence)	appositive
dependent clause	

The last chapter in this section, Chapter 11, focuses on ways you can endow your sentences with special effects through punctuation, placement, and other stylistic choices.

CHAPTER 8

Choosing Adverbials

CHAPTER PREVIEW

Many of the structures you've already been introduced to can function as adverbials: adverbs, prepositional phrases, noun phrases, verb phrases, and dependent clauses. In this chapter you will learn to

- identify and discuss the use of adverbials by other writers;
- add variety to your writing by including adverbials;
- place adverbials purposefully, punctuating them appropriately; and
- use adverbials to link short clauses.

THE MOVABLE ADVERBIALS

The Glossary of Terms, beginning on page 260, defines *adverbial* as

Any structure, no matter what its form, that functions as a modifier of a verb—that is, that functions as an adverb normally functions.

You'll recall that the word **adverb** is the name of a word class, one of the four form classes—not the name of a function. But as our definition of **adverbial** makes clear, we generally think of adverbs as modifiers of the verb—in other words, part of the predicate. Likewise, all the other forms that function as adverbs—in other words, all the adverbials—are considered part of the predicate as well. However, one of the adverbial's most versatile features is its ability to be placed elsewhere in the sentence. For example, consider how often in a story or essay the opening adverbial sets the scene:

> When in the course of human events …
>
> Four score and seven years ago …
>
> Once upon a time …

Many of the Chapter Previews in this book begin with that scene-setting adverbial:

> In this chapter …

Another important function of the opening adverbial is to provide cohesion, the tie that connects a sentence to what has gone before. Opening adverbials can also provide road signs that connect the sentences in special ways—for example, to orient the reader in terms of time or place. Notice in the following paragraph from *The Sea Around Us* how Rachel Carson opens her sentences with adverbials:

> <u>Sometimes</u> the disintegration [of islands] takes abrupt and violent form. The greatest explosion of historic time was the literal evisceration of the island of Krakatoa. <u>In 1680</u> there had been a premonitory eruption on this small island in Sunda Strait, between Java and Sumatra in the Netherlands Indies. <u>Two hundred years later</u> there had been a series of earthquakes. <u>In the spring of 1883</u>, smoke and steam began to ascend from fissures in the volcanic cone. The ground became noticeably warm, and warning rumblings and hissings came from the volcano. <u>Then</u>, <u>on 27 August</u>, Krakatoa literally exploded. <u>In an appalling series of eruptions, that lasted two days</u>, the whole northern half of the cone was carried away. The sudden inrush of ocean water added to the fury of superheated steam to the cauldron. <u>When the inferno of white-hot lava, molten rock, steam, and smoke had finally subsided</u>, the island that had stood 1,400 feet above the sea had become a cavity a thousand feet below sea level. <u>Only along one edge of the former crater</u> did a remnant of the island remain.

Opening adverbials like these are especially common in narrative writing, the story or explanation of events through time. You'll notice that most of Carson's adverbial openers provide information of time. And she has used a variety of forms:

Adverbs:	*Sometimes, Then*
Prepositional phrases:	*In 1680, In an appalling series of eruptions ...*
Dependent clause:	*When the inferno ... subsided*

FOR GROUP DISCUSSION

Carson's opening adverbials are clearly there for the purpose of cohesion, for guiding the reader through the events in time, introducing the details in sequence. It is at the end of each sentence where we find the new information, the reason for the sentence, as in this dramatic main clause:

Then, on 27 August, Krakatoa literally exploded.

The paragraph's last sentence opens with an adverbial prepositional phrase telling *where:*

Only along one edge of the former crater did a remnant of the island remain.

The time adverbials in the other sentences are clearly there to create cohesion. Why has Carson used this information of place to open the sentence? In spite of its length, this opener is not set off by a comma. What else do you notice about this final sentence?

EXERCISE 24

Revise the following paragraph about the eruption of Mount St. Helens in 1980, using the passage by Rachel Carson as a model.

[1] Natural events quite frequently exceed all expectations. [2] The explosion of Mount St. Helens certainly did. [3] Small earthquakes showed signs, beginning in March of 1980, of a volcano coming to life after being dormant for 123 years. [4] Ash sent by steam explosions fell not only locally but also in Spokane, Washington, 285 miles east of the volcano by the end of March. [5] Dixy Lee Ray, governor of Washington, declared a state

of emergency in April, after stronger tremors had been detected. [6] Teams of scientists monitored the volcano closely because the threat of an eruption was so great. [7] However, measurements radioed in at 7:00 in the morning on May 18 showed no unusual changes. [8] Mount St. Helens erupted an hour and a half later.

ADVERBS

As we've seen, many of our adverbs provide information about time and place and frequency: *today, here, sometimes*. You read about their meaning and **movability** in Chapter 1. Some of the adverbs are the adverbs of manner, which are produced by adding -*ly* to adjectives: *quickly, slowly, carefully, gracefully*, and literally thousands more—given the thousands of adjectives available. They are also among our most movable adverbs, appearing not only at the beginning and end of the sentence, but also between the subject and the predicate, even within the main verb:

> My roommate *is <u>seriously</u> thinking* about changing her major.

The movability of adverbs allows the writer to take charge of the way the reader emphasizes certain words in the sentence. Read the roommate sentence aloud; then compare your reading with this version:

> My roommate *is thinking <u>seriously</u>* about changing her major.

You will probably hear more stress given to the adverb when it follows the verb.

We should note that if you open the sentence with an adverb set off by a comma, it will often become a **sentence modifier**, saying something about the sentence as a whole, rather than as simply modifying the verb. Bear in mind as well what you learned in Chapter 5 about the effect a comma can have: The word preceding it will get strong stress:

> <u>Seriously</u>, my roommate is thinking about changing her major.

In this case, it's not the thinking that is serious. This shift in meaning does not generally occur with the time and place adverbs, like those we saw earlier: *sometimes, then, now, here, there, everywhere*. Single-word sentence modifiers are more commonly the -*ly* adverbs:

> <u>Clearly,</u> something has to be done about the health system.
> <u>Luckily,</u> we survived the accident with only minor injuries.

PREPOSITIONAL PHRASES

No doubt our most common adverbial—perhaps even more common than the adverb—is the **prepositional phrase**, introduced in Chapter 1, where you saw both adverbial and adjectival prepositional phrases. Following are examples of adverbial information that prepositional phrases provide:

Direction:	*toward the pond, beyond the ridge, across the field*
Place:	*near the marina, on the expressway, along the path*
Time:	*on Tuesday afternoon, at noon, in modern times, in the spring of 1883*
Duration:	*until three o'clock, for several days, during spring break, throughout the summer months*
Manner:	*in an appalling series of eruptions, without complaint, with dignity, by myself, in a frenzy*
Cause:	*because of the storm, for a good reason*

The Proliferating Prepositional Phrase

Our two most common prepositions, *of* and *to,* are especially vulnerable to proliferation. Both occur in countless idioms and set phrases. For example, we regularly use *of* phrases with numbers and with such pronouns as *all, each, some,* and *most:*

> all of the people, each of the parts, some of the students, most of the problems

Of is also used to indicate possessive case, as an alternative to *'s:*

> the capacity of the trunk, the base of the lamp, the opening night of the new show, the noise of the crowd

And we use it to show direction and position and time:

> the front of the house, the top of the bookcase, the back of the page, the end of the play

Because there are so many such situations that call for prepositions, it's not at all unusual to find yourself writing sentences with prepositional phrases strung together in chains. You can undoubtedly find many such sentences in the pages of this book. In fact, the sentence you just read ended with two: "*in* the pages *of* this book." It would be easy to add even more: "*in* the pages *of* this book *about* the grammar *of* English *for* writers." As you edit what you've written, it's important to tune in to the rhythm of the sentence: A long string of short phrases is a clue that suggests revision. Ask yourself if those prepositional phrases are proliferating awkwardly.

Awkwardness is not the only problem—nor is it the most serious. The sentence that ends with a long string of prepositional phrases often loses its focus. Our usual rhythm pattern follows the principle of end focus; it calls for the new information to be the last or next-to-the-last structural unit. Notice, for example, what happened to that altered sentence in the previous paragraph. Here's the original; read it aloud and listen to the stress:

> You can undoubtedly find many such sentences in the pages of this book.

Chances are you put stress on *many* and on *this book*. Now read the altered version:

> You can undoubtedly find many such sentences in the pages of this book about the grammar of English for writers.

Because you expected the sentence to have end focus, you probably found yourself putting off the main stress until you got to *writers*. But that last unit (starting with *about*), consisting of three prepositional phrases, is known information. Not only should it get no stress, *it shouldn't be there at all.* That kind of unwanted repetition of known information is another example of **redundancy**.

Here's an additional illustration of this common source of redundancy—an edited version of the opening sentences from the previous paragraph:

> Awkwardness is not the only problem <u>with those extra prepositional phrases in our sentences</u>—nor is it the most serious <u>of the writer's problems</u>. The sentence that ends with a long string of prepositional phrases often loses its focus <u>on the main point of the sentence that the writer intended it to have</u>.

Those redundant modifiers add to the total number of words—and that's about all they add. Clearly, they have added no new information. And they have obliterated the original focus.

NOUN PHRASES

The **noun phrases** that function adverbially constitute a fairly small category, compared with the other adverbials. Many of them resemble

objects of prepositions—that is, prepositional phrases with their prepositions missing:

> They worked [for] <u>ten solid hours</u>.
> The film festival began [on] <u>July 1.</u>

In some cases, the noun or noun phrase following an intransitive verb
may look surprisingly like a direct object rather than an adverbial:

> The hikers walked <u>single file</u> up the steep trail.
> I studied <u>every night</u> until 1:00 a.m.

While these noun phrases may look like objects following transitive verbs,
the questions they answer are the adverbial *where* or *when* or *how,* not the
what or *whom* of the direct object. In addition, whereas sentences with
direct objects can undergo the passive transformation, sentences with intransitive verbs followed by adverbial noun phrases cannot:

> *Single file was walked by the hikers.

VERB PHRASES

Another kind of phrase that functions as an adverbial is the verb phrase—
in this case, the **infinitive phrase**:

> Jack got up early that morning <u>to go fishing</u>.

The infinitive is usually easy to recognize: the base form of the verb preceded by *to,* sometimes called the *infinitive marker.* There's an understood "in order to" meaning underlying most adverbial infinitives:

> Jack got up early that morning in order to go fishing.

The problem known as "dangling" sometimes occurs with the adverbial
infinitive phrase. As with other verbs, the infinitive needs a subject; the
reader assumes that its subject will be the subject of the main clause, as it
is in the example with *study.*
   When the subject of the infinitive is not included, the infinitive dangles:

> *<u>To keep your grades up</u>, a regular study schedule is important.
> *For decades the Superstition Mountains in Arizona have been
>   explored in order <u>to find the fabled Lost Dutchman Mine</u>.

Certainly the problem with these sentences is not a problem of communication; the reader is not likely to misinterpret their meaning. But in

both cases a kind of fuzziness exists that can be cleared up with the addition of a subject for the infinitive:

> To keep your grades up, <u>you</u> ought to follow a regular study schedule.
>
> For decades <u>people</u> [or <u>adventurers</u> or <u>prospectors</u>] have explored the Superstition Mountains in Arizona to find the fabled Lost Dutchman Mine.

The dangling infinitive, which is fairly obvious at the beginning of the sentence, is not quite so obvious at the end, but the sentence is equally fuzzy:

> *A regular study schedule is important to keep your grades up.

Two rules will help you use infinitives effectively:

> **The subject of the adverbial infinitive is also the subject of the sentence or clause in which the infinitive appears.**
>
> **An infinitive phrase that opens the sentence is always set off by a comma.**

DEPENDENT CLAUSES

One of the most important adverbial forms is the **dependent clause**, which you saw briefly in Chapter 4:

> <u>Because the weasel is wild</u>, it should be approached with great caution.
>
> Roads were closed and air travel was interrupted <u>while volcanic ash caused poor visibility</u>.

Its importance lies in the information-bearing potential of its subject–predicate structure; it has the information-bearing quality of a complete sentence. As you can see in our two examples, without their opening conjunctions, the dependent clauses are, in fact, complete sentences:

> The weasel is wild.
>
> Volcanic ash caused poor visibility.

The **subordinating conjunction** indicates the relationship of the dependent **adverbial clause** to the independent sentence, the main clause. The clause introduced by *because* adds a reason; *while* adds time information.

We have many such subordinating conjunctions, words and phrases that connect the clause for a specific purpose:

Time:	*when, whenever, after, as, before, once, since, till, until, now that, while, as long as, as soon as*
Concession:	*though, although, even though, if, while*
Contingency:	*if, once*
Condition:	*if, in case, as long as, unless, provided that*
Reason:	*because, since, as long as*
Result:	*so, so that*
Comparison:	*as, just as, as if*
Contrast:	*while, whereas*

Adverbial clauses are certainly common structures in our language. We use them automatically and often in conversation. But in writing they are not automatic, nor are they always used as effectively as they could be. Two problems that show up fairly often are related to the meaning of the sentence:

1. The wrong idea is subordinated.
2. The meaning of the subordinating conjunction is imprecise.

Here, for example, are two related ideas that a writer might want to combine into a single sentence:

We worked hard for our candidates.
We suspected that our candidates didn't stand a chance.

Here are two possibilities for connecting them:

<u>Although</u> we worked hard for our candidates, we suspected they didn't stand a chance.

We worked hard for our candidates, <u>even though</u> we suspected they didn't stand a chance.

We need context, of course, to know precisely how the relationship between hard work and the chances of winning should be expressed; but given no other information, the second version expresses what would appear to be the logical relationship.

Perhaps an even more common problem than the imprecise subordinating conjunction is the compound sentence with no subordination—the sentence with two independent clauses, two equal focuses, that might be more accurate and effective with a single focus. The most common culprit is the compound sentence with *but* as the connector. Here, for example, is a paragraph opener in a *New York Times Magazine* article about sleep. The paragraph preceding this one gives examples of accidents on the job connected with work schedules:

> The biological clock is flexible enough to adjust to slight changes in a person's work schedule, *but* in many industries rotations in shift work are so drastic that they play havoc with body rhythms, leaving employees unable to sleep at home and impairing their productivity at work. [Italics added]
>
> —Erik Eckholm

Here the two clauses are clearly not equal: The main idea is the second clause. The idea in the first one, although it has not previously appeared in the article, is presented as understood, the known information. The new information is in the second clause. Revising the sentence to make the first clause dependent, or subordinate—a way of identifying it as background information—will help the reader focus on the new idea:

<u>Although</u> the biological clock is flexible enough ...

Subordination of the first clause signals the reader that the main idea— the foreground—is coming later. Quite frequently *while*-clauses and *since*-clauses communicate this same kind of message, telling the reader that the information in the dependent clause is already known, knowledge that the reader and writer share.

EXERCISE 25

Turn the following complete sentences into dependent clauses by (1) adding a subordinating conjunction in the opening position and (2) adding the resulting clause to another sentence as a modifier, either at the beginning or at the end. You will have to supply the main clause. See page 149 for a list of subordinating conjunctions; use at least six different ones in your sentences; try for ten.

Example: The party ended at midnight.

We got home earlier than expected because the party ended at midnight.

or

If the party ended at midnight, why did they get home at 3:00 a.m.?

1. Cleo couldn't pay her phone bill last month.

2. There is simply no way to avoid the problem.

3. The building across the street burned to the ground last weekend.

4. The service sector is a large part of the economy.

5. Traffic came to a halt.

6. We could hear someone singing.

....

Punctuation of Adverbial Clauses

There is one standard punctuation rule that applies to the adverbial clause:

An adverbial clause that opens the sentence is always set off by a comma.

This rule applies no matter how short that clause may be:

> <u>When the quartet finished performing its final concert of the year</u>, the audience stood and applauded for five minutes.

> <u>When the quartet finished performing</u>, the audience stood and applauded for five minutes.

When the adverbial clause closes the sentence, the punctuation will vary, depending on the relationship of the information in the dependent clause to that of the main clause. As a general rule, when the idea in the main clause is conditional upon or dependent upon the idea in the adverbial clause, there is no comma. For example, the idea of the main clause—the opening clause—in the following sentence will be realized only if the idea in the adverbial clause is carried out; thus, the main clause depends on the *when*-clause:

> Pat went to parties only when he knew everyone who had been invited.

In other words, Pat went to parties only under certain conditions. But in the next sentence the dependent clause does not affect Pat's behavior. The comma confirms that lack of effect.

> Pat went to the party, <u>although</u> she didn't know everyone who had been invited.

Here's another pair of sentences that illustrates this distinction:

> Shawn didn't compete, because he hates competition. He prefers activities that call for cooperation.
>
> Shawn didn't compete because he hates competition. He just didn't feel well enough to race.

In the first sentence, the *because* clause states a reason; in the second clause, it refers to a cause.

The use of the comma with a final adverbial clause is probably one of the least standardized of our punctuation rules. It is one situation where you can use your voice to help you decide about the punctuation: If you put extra stress on the last word in the main clause, or if you detect a slight change in the pitch of your voice at the end of the main clause, you probably need a comma.

....

The Movability of Adverbial Clauses

The movability of adverbial clauses is especially important from a rhetorical point of view. As a sentence opener, the clause often supplies the transition from the previous sentence or paragraph, usually with a cohesive link of known information. The old standard rule of putting subordinate ideas in dependent clauses and main ideas in main clauses is probably more accurately stated as "known information in the opening clause, new information in the closing clause." And certainly that closing clause could be an adverbial clause, depending on the context. For example, the reason for an action or decision as stated in a *because* clause could easily be the new information.

Although most adverbial clauses occupy either the opening or closing positions in the sentence, they can also occur in the middle, between the subject and predicate or between the verb and complement. In this position the clause will be set off by commas, one before and one after:

> I learn later that night, <u>when ties are loosened during a coffee break</u>, that I am wrong.
>
> —James R. Chiles, *Smithsonian*

> My brother, <u>when he was only four years old</u>, actually drove the family car for about a block.

That interruption in the usual flow of the sentence slows the reader down. Notice also that it adds stress and length to the word just preceding the clause, and it changes the rhythm pattern. We saw the same principle at work in Chapter 6, when we manipulated the rhythm of the sentence by shifting word order and changing the punctuation. Ordinarily the subject is unstressed; it is old information. But a parenthetical comment following it, a word or a phrase or a clause set off by commas, as in our example, puts the subject in a position of stress; the reader will give it extra length and emphasis. Compare the stress given to *brother* in the previous example with the following revisions, where the adverbial clause either opens or closes the sentence:

> When he was only four years old, my brother actually drove the family car for about a block.
>
> My brother actually drove the family car for about a block when he was four years old.

And it's not only a difference in the stress on *brother* that makes the inserted *when*-clause noteworthy. That internal positioning of the adverbial clause is unusual; it sends a message to the reader that says, "Pay attention. I did this on purpose."

The Because-*Clause Myth*

Because a dependent clause looks so much like a full sentence (remember, it consists of a sentence preceded by a subordinator), it is often criticized for being a fragment—that is, a part of a sentence punctuated as a full sentence. One of the most common such fragments is, apparently, the *because*-clause:

> Everyone agreed that the call was unfair. Because the replay showed that the player had not been fouled.

It appears that some teachers have discovered a surefire way to prevent such fragments: Ban *because* as a sentence opener. As a result, many student writers don't understand that *because* can, indeed, open a sentence, just as all the other subordinating conjunctions can; however, if that *because*-clause is new information, it belongs at the end of the sentence. In the previous example, the *because*-clause should be added to the previous sentence:

> Everyone agreed that the call was unfair because the replay showed that the player had not been fouled.

It's possible that the *because*-clause is frequently punctuated as a full sentence on the basis of speech. In answer to a spoken question of cause, the natural answer is a dependent clause:

> Why are you late? Because I missed the bus.

In this speech situation, the respondent has simply omitted the known information, the information in the question. The response in the following exchange, which includes the known information, is much less likely to occur:

> Why are you late? I'm late because I missed the bus.

EXERCISE 26

Combine each of the following groups of sentences into a single sentence, using coordination and subordination. In some cases you may have to reword the sentence to make it sound natural. You can probably come up with more than one possibility for each.

1. The famous Gateway Arch is located in St. Louis.
   Kansas City claims the title "Gateway to the West."

2. Our spring semester doesn't end until the second week of June.
   Many students have a hard time finding summer jobs.

3. Thomas Jefferson acquired the Ozark Mountains for the United States in 1803.
   That was the year of the Louisiana Purchase.
   We bought the Louisiana Territory from Napoleon.

4. Auto companies offered enticing cash rebates to buyers of new cars last January.
   Car sales increased dramatically.

5. The neighbors added a pit bull to their pet population, which now numbers three unfriendly four-legged creatures.
   We have decided to fence in our backyard.

6. The human circulatory system is a marvel of efficiency.
   It is still subject to a wide variety of degenerative diseases.

The Elliptical Adverbial Clause

One common variation of the adverbial clause is the **elliptical clause**, one in which something is deleted. Elliptical clauses introduced by the time connectors *while* and *when* are especially common:

> <u>While waiting for the bus</u>, we saw the police arrest a pickpocket at the edge of the crowd.
> <u>When stripped of its trees</u>, the land becomes inhospitable.

Here the deletions of the subject and part of the verb have produced tighter structures, and there is certainly no problem in interpreting the meaning. The understood subject in the elliptical clause is also the subject of the main clause:

> While <u>we</u> were waiting for the bus
>
> When <u>the land</u> is stripped of its trees

This feature of elliptical clauses—let's call it a rule—is an important one for the writer to recognize:

The subject of the main clause is always the understood subject of the elliptical clause as well.

This rule simply reflects the interpretation that the reader expects. Unfortunately, it is not always followed. Note what has happened in the following sentence:

> *While waiting for the bus, the police arrested a pickpocket at the edge of the crowd.

This sentence reports—no doubt inadvertently—that it is the police who were waiting for the bus. We call that a *dangling elliptical clause*. The writer should not expect the reader to give the sentence any other interpretation.

FOR GROUP DISCUSSION

Discuss the following sentences with your classmates. Does each have a subject in the main clause that is also the subject of the elliptical clause? If you find a sentence that is problematic, suggest a revision.

1. When descending a cliff, rappelling is sometimes the easiest way down.
2. When descending a cliff, mountain climbers sometimes decide to rappel.
3. When descending a cliff, consider rappelling only if you have had training.

EXERCISE 27

A. Underline all of the adverbial structures in the following sentences. When structures are embedded within others, you will have to underline them twice.

B. Identify the form of each: adverb, noun phrase, prepositional phrase, infinitive phrase, or dependent clause.

C. Identify the kind of information it provides: time, frequency, duration, place, purpose, reason, manner, condition, direction.

1. To save money, I often eat lunch at my desk.

2. After my dad came home from abroad, he started his own business.

3. The ceremony started late that night.

4. While the wind howled, we prepared to leave.

5. The legislature held a special session last week to consider a new tax bill.

6. Because the weather was unseasonably warm, people flocked to the beaches.

7. If the team moves to another city, the stadium will be demolished.

8. The crew departed late Monday night and arrived early Tuesday morning.

D. For further practice with adverbials, change the form of the adverbial.

FOR GROUP DISCUSSION

In *Notes Toward a New Rhetoric,* Francis Christensen describes a study undertaken by his students in an English class to discover how professional writers open their sentences. They selected works (ten fiction, ten nonfiction) of twenty American authors and counted the first 200 sentences. (They omitted from the count quotations, dialogue, fragments, questions, and sentences with postponed subjects—that is, cleft sentences and *there*-transformations). Here are the findings, based on the 4,000 sentences counted:

979 (24.5%) had a sentence opener other than subject;

919—in other words, all but 60—were adverbials, including adverbs, prepositional phrases, clauses, and nouns (adverbial infinitives were counted with the verbal group, listed next);

47 were verbal phrases (including infinitives and *-ing* verbs); and

13 were other constructions, including adjective phrases and inverted subjects and predicates.

In addition to the 979 sentence openers, there were 266 sentences (6.65%) that opened with coordinating conjunctions (*and, but, or, nor, so, yet, for*).

Examine the sentence openers in your own writing; then compare your percentages with those of your classmates and with the professionals.

(***Note:*** One of the works included in the study was Rachel Carson's *The Sea Around Us*, quoted on page 142. Her numbers were the highest among the twenty writers: 79 nonsubject openers in her 200 sentences, 74 of which were adverbials; and 29 conjunctions as sentence openers.)

KEY TERMS

Adverb	Infinitive phrase	Redundancy
Adverbial	Manner adverb	Sentence modifier
Adverbial clause	Movability	Subordinating
Dependent clause	Noun phrase	conjunction
Elliptical clause	Prepositional phrase	

RHETORICAL REMINDERS

Placement of Adverbials

Have I considered transition and cohesion and the known–new contract in using adverbials?

Proliferating Prepositional Phrases

Have I avoided strings of prepositional phrases that obscure the focus of the sentence and add no new information?

Understood Subjects

Is the understood subject in every elliptical clause also the subject of the main clause?

Is the subject of every adverbial infinitive also the subject of the main clause?

PUNCTUATION REMINDERS

Have I used a comma to set off an adverbial clause that opens the sentence?

Have I used a comma to set off an infinitive phrase that opens the sentence?

Choosing Adjectivals

CHAPTER PREVIEW

Opportunities abound for writers to enhance their prose with adjectivals. Determiners, adjectives, and modifying nouns can be inserted before the noun headword; prepositional phrases, adjective phrases, participial phrases, and relative clauses can be placed after the noun. This chapter will help you to

- identify and discuss the use of adjectivals by other writers;
- make noun phrases more precise;
- improve cohesion by placing adjectivals purposefully; and
- use punctuation to enhance clarity.

THE NOUN PHRASE

Adjectivals are words, phrases, and clauses that modify nouns. **Adjectives**, of course, are the prototypical adjectivals. As you've seen on the Form-and-Function chart on page 140, there are also other forms that function as adjectivals. It will be useful to put these in the context of the noun phrase, to picture them in relation to the noun **headword**. Each of the forms has its designated place, with the headword noun occupying the central position; the single-word modifiers—determiners, adjectives, and nouns—come before the noun headword; the phrases and clauses follow:

Determiner   Adjective   Noun   HEADWORD   Phrase   Clause

We will take up each of these positions, beginning with the determiners.

PREHEADWORD MODIFIERS

Determiners

Most nouns require a **determiner**, the noun signaler that occupies the opening position in the noun phrase. As you learned in Chapter 1, the determiner class includes articles, possessive nouns, possessive pronouns, demonstrative pronouns, and numbers, as well as a variety of other common words. As the first word in the noun phrase, and thus frequently the first word of the sentence and even of the paragraph, the determiner can provide a bridge between ideas. The selection of that bridge can make subtle but important differences in emphasis, providing transition for the reader—and it can certainly change the rhythm of the sentence:

> The decision that Ben made was the right one.
>
> That decision of Ben's was the right one.
>
> Ben's decision was the right one.
>
> Every such decision Ben made …
>
> His decision …
>
> Such a decision might have been questionable …
>
> A decision like that …

In selecting determiners, then, writers have the opportunity to make subtle distinctions and to help their readers move easily from one idea to the next in a meaningful way.

FOR GROUP DISCUSSION

In Chapter 12 we look briefly at the semantic features of nouns that regulate our selection of determiners. For example, the indefinite article *a* signals only countable nouns, while the definite *the* can signal both countables and noncountables.

All the determiners are missing from the following passages. Add them to all the nouns that need them. You'll discover, when you compare your versions with those of your classmates, that for some nouns there are choices—not only a choice of determiner but in some cases a choice of whether or not to use a determiner.

> A. Dorothy was little girl who lived on farm in Kansas. Tornado struck farm and carried her over rainbow to land of Munchkins. Soon afterwards she met scarecrow who wanted brain, tin man who wanted heart, and lion who wanted courage. On way to Emerald City four friends met wicked witch who cast spell on them in field of flowers. Witch wanted

magic shoes that Dorothy was wearing. When they reached city, as you recall, they met wizard. Story has happy ending.

B. Planet has wrong name. Ancestors named it Earth, after land they found all around them. So far as they thought about planet as whole, they believed for centuries that surface consisted almost entirely of rocks and soil, except for smallish bodies of water like Mediterranean Sea and Black Sea. They knew about Atlantic, of course, but they regarded it as relatively narrow river running around rim of world. If ancients had known what earth was really like they undoubtedly would have named it Ocean after tremendous areas of water that cover 70.8 percent of surface.

—adapted from *The Sea*, Time-Life Books

There were several nouns in those passages that you left bare, without determiners. Why? How do they differ from the nouns that needed them? In how many cases did you have a choice of adding a determiner or not?

Did you notice a relationship between your use of the articles (*a* vs. *the*) and information—that is, whether known or new information? Which article did you use when a noun was mentioned for the first time? Which for subsequent mentions? What conclusions can you draw about the indefinite *a* and the definite *the?*

Adjectives and Nouns

Adjectives and nouns fill the position between the determiner and the headword. When the noun phrase includes both, they appear in the following order:

Determiner	Adjective	Noun	Headword
a	dismal	weather	forecast
the	new	pizza	shop
your	important	career	decision

Although we rarely use more than one noun as a modifier, we frequently use more than one adjective:

a recent covert military operation

an unusual financial arrangement

You'll notice that there are no commas in the preceding noun phrases, even though there are several modifiers in a row. But sometimes commas are called for. A good general rule is to use a comma if it's possible to insert *and* between the modifiers. We would not say *a recent and covert and military operation* or *an unusual and financial arrangement.* However, we would say *an exciting and innovative concept,* so in writing that phrase without *and,* we would use a comma: *an exciting, innovative concept.*

In general, our punctuation system calls for a comma between two adjectives when they are of the same class—for instance, when they are both subjective qualities like *festive* and *exciting* and *innovative.* However, in the noun phrases we saw no commas—*covert military operation* and *unusual financial arrangement*—the two adjectives in each pair are different kinds of qualities. The easiest way to decide on punctuation is to remember *and:*

Use a comma between prenoun modifiers if *and* can be used between them.

Sometimes prenoun modifiers are themselves modified or qualified:

When the first modifier is an *-ly* adverb, as in this example, we do not connect it with a hyphen. With compound modifiers, however, we do use a hyphen:

the English-speaking world   a four-door minivan

Here the hyphen makes clear that *English* modifies *speaking* rather than *world* and that *four* modifies *door,* not *minivan.*

Here are some other examples of hyphens with prenoun modifiers:

a problem-solving approach   a bases-loaded home run

a poor inner-city neighborhood   a small-town high school teacher

Another occasion for hyphens in preheadword position occurs when we use a complete phrase as a modifier:

an off-the-wall idea   the end-of-the-term party

Use a hyphen to link the words in a prenoun compound modifier; omit the hyphen when an -ly adverb precedes an adjective.

Modifier Noun Proliferation. There's a pitfall for writers in this system of prenoun modifiers: the temptation to string together too many adjectives or nouns. It's easy to do. For example, the curriculum committee of the faculty is known as the "faculty curriculum committee." And when the committee meets, it has a "faculty curriculum committee meeting." The minutes of that meeting then become the "faculty curriculum committee meeting minutes." And so on. Such strings are not ungrammatical, but they easily become unreadable.

You can make such noun phrases somewhat easier to read by using an *of* phrase in place of the last modifier in the string:

> a meeting of the faculty curriculum committee
>
> the minutes of the faculty curriculum committee meeting

EXERCISE 28

Punctuate the following sentences, paying particular attention to commas and hyphens that might be needed in prenoun position. Remember the rule about those commas: If you can add *and,* you probably need a comma.

1. The president's recent clean air proposals have been criticized as inadequate by highly placed government officials.

2. The stock market reached an all time high last week and will probably keep going up.

3. There was a splendid old table for sale at the auction.

4. I found an expensive looking copper colored bracelet in the locker room and immediately turned it in to the coach.

5. I had back to back exams on Wednesday.

6. The highly publicized paper recycling program has finally become a reality on our campus this fall after a year long surprisingly acrimonious discussion.

POSTHEADWORD MODIFIERS

Prepositional Phrases

The adjectival **prepositional phrase**, which follows the headword noun, is our most frequently occurring postnoun modifier. It is identical in form to the adverbial prepositional phrase we saw in Chapter 8; only its function is different. It's there to add a distinguishing feature to the noun, often answering the question *which one:*

The security guard <u>in our building</u> knows every tenant personally.

The meeting <u>during our lunch hour</u> was a waste of time.

In place of certain adjectival prepositional phrases, the writer may have the option of using a prenoun modifier:

an elderly lady with white hair = an elderly white-haired lady

guests for dinner = dinner guests

the soliloquy in the second act = the second-act soliloquy

the problems with the budget = the budget problems

And sometimes revision may be just a matter of choosing a more precise word:

a bunch of flowers = a bouquet

birds that fly south in the winter = migratory birds

Adjective Phrases

We've described the usual position for an adjective: between the determiner and the noun headword. However, when the adjective is linked to another adjective (that is, compounded) or is expanded into a phrase with qualifiers, it can also occupy a position following the headword, where it will be set off by commas:

The hot, tired hikers trudged the last mile to their campsite.

The hikers, <u>hot and tired</u>, trudged the last mile to their campsite.

This highly unusual banking crisis calls for extraordinary measures.

This banking crisis, <u>highly unusual</u>, calls for extraordinary measures.

And in one of the weasel sentences in Chapter 2, we saw an opening adjective phrase when the subject was a personal pronoun:

Obedient to instinct, he bites his prey at the neck.

In this case, the opening position is the only one that sounds natural; personal pronouns rarely have modifiers in postheadword position.

Unlike the previous examples of adjective phrases, which simply comment on the subject, in the following sentence the adjective phrase in postnoun position clarifies the referent of the noun:

The students <u>unable to attend the audition</u> will have to make special arrangements with the director.

Here the modifier tells which students will have to make arrangements.

The punctuation of postnoun modifiers is taken up later in this chapter.

Participial Phrases

In Chapter 3 you saw the verb forms labeled participles: the **present participle** (*filming, driving*) and the **past participle** (*filmed, driven*). (For a quick review, return to the verb chart on page 37.) One of our most versatile adjectivals is the **participial phrase**, a verb phrase headed by the present or past participle form of the verb.

> The helicopter <u>hovering over the roof</u> frightened the dogs.
>
> The travelers <u>lined up in front of airport security</u> did not look happy.

You'll notice that the noun phrases modified by the participial phrases resemble sentences; the only thing missing is an auxiliary:

> the helicopter [is] hovering over the roof
>
> the travelers [are] lined up in front of airport security

In these examples, the noun and the participle that modifies it have a subject–predicate relationship. This is an important feature of participial phrases, as you'll see later in the discussion of dangling participles.

Although the majority of participial phrases are formed without an auxiliary, sometimes *have* or *be* will be used. To indicate the perfect form, *having* combines with the past participle: *having waited.* To signal the perfect-progressive, *having* combines with both *been* and the present participle: *having been waiting.*

Active Voice

General form	waiting
Perfect form	having waited
Perfect-progressive form	having been waiting

There are also three possibilities in the passive voice. The general form is the past participle: *offered.* The progressive form is a combination of the auxiliary verb *be* and the past participle: *being offered.* The perfect form is a combination of *having been* and the past participle: *having been offered.*

Passive Voice

General form	offered
Progressive form	being offered
Perfect form	having been offered

Why do we use participles? Like adjectives and prepositional phrases, participles add information about the noun headword; and because they are verb phrases in form, they add a whole verbal idea, just as the predicate does. In the first example, the subject, *helicopter,* is the subject of two verb phrases: *hovering over the roof* and *frightened the dogs.* The two verb phrases could have been expressed with a compound predicate:

> The helicopter hovered over the roof and frightened the dogs.

or with a main clause and a dependent clause:

> The helicopter frightened the dogs as it hovered over the roof.

The participial phrase, however, allows the writer to include both verbal ideas in a more concise way. Even more important than conciseness is the clear focus of the sentence with a single predicating verb.

The Prenoun Participle. When the participle is a single word—the verb with no complements or modifiers—it usually occupies the adjective pre-headword position:

> Our <u>snoring</u> visitor kept the household awake.
>
> The old hound growled at every <u>passing</u> stranger.

And, as we saw in the earlier discussion of hyphens, an adverb sometimes modifies the participle:

> a <u>well-developed</u> paragraph

Remember, too, that if the adverb in that prenoun modifier is an *-ly* adverb, there will be no hyphen:

> a carefully conceived plan

The Movable Participial Phrase. We can think of the position following the headword in the noun phrase as the home base of the participial phrase, as it is of the adjectival prepositional phrase. However, the participial phrase can be moved to the beginning of the sentence—*but only if it modifies the subject and if it is set off by commas:*

> <u>Looking out the window,</u> my mother waved to me.
>
> <u>Carrying all their supplies,</u> the Boy Scouts trudged up the mountain in search of a campsite.
>
> <u>Pressured by Congress,</u> the president agreed to support an increase in the minimum wage.

Only those participial phrases that are set off by commas can undergo this shift—that is, only those that are nonrestrictive. (Punctuation of phrases and clauses is discussed on pages 173–176.)

While the single-word participle generally fills the preheadword adjective position, it too can sometimes open the sentence—and with considerable drama:

> <u>Exasperated,</u> she made the decision to leave immediately.
>
> <u>Outraged,</u> the entire committee resigned.

You'll note that both of these openers are past participles, rather than the *-ing* present participle form; they are, in fact, the passive voice. The last participial phrase in the previous set of examples, *"Pressured by Congress,"* is also passive. There the *by* phrase offers a clue. (Underlying it is the sentence *"Congress pressured the president."*) In the case of the single-word participles here, the *by* phrase is understood.

That same participial phrase—the nonrestrictive phrase that modifies the subject—frequently comes at the end of the sentence:

> The Boy Scouts trudged up the mountain in search of a campsite, <u>carrying all their supplies on their backs.</u>

The reason for choosing one position over another has to do with sentence rhythm and focus. At the end of the sentence the participle gets much more attention than it would at the beginning or in the home-base position. At sentence end, participial phrases have great flexibility; there's room to spread out and expand, so it's not unusual to see more than one and to see them with embedded modifiers of their own. In opening and closing position they are sometimes called **free modifiers**.

The first example is from Jeff Shaara's Civil War story *The Last Full Measure*:

> He [Grant]'d been up front again this morning, <u>correcting one officer's mistake, adjusting lines of infantry that had dug in too close to the mouths of their own big guns.</u>

The following passage is from J. M. Coetzee's *Waiting for the Barbarians*:

> They live in settlements of two or three families along the banks of the river, <u>fishing and trapping for most of the year, paddling to the remote southern shores of the lake in the autumn to catch redworms and dry them, building flimsy reed shelters, groaning with cold through the winter, dressing in skins.</u>

And many of the details we learned about weasels in Chapter 2 came by way of participial phrases:

> Outside, he stalks rabbits, mice, muskrats, and birds, <u>killing more bodies than he can eat warm, and often dragging the carcasses home</u>. Obedient to instinct he bites his prey at the neck, <u>either splitting the jugular vein at the throat or crunching the brain at the base of the skull</u>, and he does not let go.

The Dangling Participle. The participial phrase provides a good way to change the focus of the sentence, as we've seen in these variations—but it carries an important restriction:

The participle can open or close the sentence *only* if it modifies the subject—that is, when the subject of the participle is also the subject of the sentence and is in regular subject position. Otherwise, the participle will dangle.

Remember, a participle modifies its own subject. Simply stated, a dangling participle is a verb without a subject:

> *Having slept little on the plane, the thought of a meeting was unwelcome.
>
> *Furiously filling in the bubbles on the answer sheet, the time was up before I could finish the test.

The thought, of course, did not do the sleeping; and I was the one filling in those bubbles, not "the time." You can fix such sentences (and avoid them in the first place) by making sure that the subject of the sentence is also the subject of the participle:

> Having slept little on the plane, *Anne* did not want to think about the meeting.
>
> Furiously filling in the bubbles on the answer sheet, *I* still wasn't able to finish the test before time was up.

Another common source of the dangling participle, and other dangling modifiers as well, is the sentence with a delayed subject—a *there*-transformation, for example, or an *it*-cleft:

> *Having moved all the outdoor furniture into the garage, there was no room left for the car.
>
> *Knowing how much work I had to do, it was kind of you to come and help.

In the second sentence, *you* is the subject of the participle, so it's there in the sentence, but it's not in the usual subject position. Sometimes the most efficient way to revise such sentences is to expand the participial phrase into a complete clause. That expansion adds the missing subject:

> After we moved all the outdoor furniture into the garage, there was no room left for the car.

> It was good of you to come and help when you learned how much work I had to do.

However, if your rhetorical situation calls for avoiding the use of expletives such as *there* and *it,* consider recasting your sentence with different words:

> Knowing how much work I had to do, you were kind to come and help.

Even though there is often no problem of communication with dangling and misplaced modifiers—that is, the reader probably knows what you mean—you may in fact be communicating something you hadn't intended: You may be sending a message that says, "Fuzzy thinking."

Our language includes a few participial phrases that we use in sentence-opening position that are not dangling, even though the subject of the sentence is not their subject. They function as sentence modifiers rather than as noun modifiers. The most common are the "speaking of" phrases:

> <u>Speaking of</u> silent movies, have you seen *The Artist?*

> <u>Speaking of</u> the weather, we should probably cancel the picnic.

There are other *-ing* words that have the status of prepositions. They often open a sentence in order to set up the topic:

> <u>Regarding</u> your job interview, the supervisor called to change the time.

> <u>Concerning</u> the recent book about the Kennedys, several reviewers have doubted its credibility.

Because of their common use, such expressions have achieved the status of set phrases. Nevertheless, they may be regarded by some readers as too casual or informal for certain writing situations.

EXERCISE 29

Rewrite the following sentences to eliminate the dangling participles. In some cases you may want to expand the participles into full clauses.

1. Having endured rain all week, the miserable weather on Saturday didn't surprise us.

2. Hoping for the sixth win in a row, there was great excitement in the stands when the band finally played "The Star Spangled Banner."

3. Known for her conservative views on taxes and the role of government, we were not at all surprised when the county commissioner announced her candidacy for the General Assembly.

4. Exhausted by the heat and humidity, it was wonderful to do nothing but lie in the shade and drink iced tea.

5. Having spent nearly all day in the kitchen, everyone agreed that my superb gourmet meal was worth the effort.

6. Feeling pressure from the environmentalists, the Clean Air Act was immediately put on the committee's agenda.

Relative Clauses

Another modifier in the noun phrase following the noun is the adjectival dependent clause called the **relative clause**, also called the *adjectival clause*. Because it is a clause—that is, a structure with a subject and a predicate—this adjectival modifier is a powerful tool; it enables the writer to embed a complete subject–predicate idea into a noun phrase.

In many respects, the relative clause and the participial phrase are alike. The participial phrase, in fact, is actually a shortened version of the relative clause. All of the examples we saw earlier could easily be expanded into clauses with no change in their meaning:

> The helicopter <u>that is hovering over the roof</u> frightened the dogs.
>
> The travelers <u>who are lined up in front of airport security</u> did not look happy.

One feature the participial phrase has that the clause does not is its movability: The clause rarely moves out of the noun phrase; it almost always follows the noun it modifies.

The Relatives. The relative clause is introduced by either a **relative pronoun** (*that, who,* or *which*) or a **relative adverb** (*where, when,* or *why*); the relative plays a part in the clause it introduces. In the case of the relative pronoun (the most common introducer), the part will be that of a noun: a subject, direct object, indirect object, subject complement, object of the preposition, or, as possessive nouns generally function, a determiner.

The relative pronoun *who* has different forms depending on its **case**, its role in the clause—*who* (**subjective**), *whose* (**possessive**), and *whom* (**objective**):

> The man <u>who called that night</u> turned out to be my uncle.

Here *who* is the subject in its clause.

> The student <u>whose notes I borrowed</u> never returned to class.

Here the possessive relative, *whose,* is the determiner for *notes.* (You'll recall that *determiner* is a common role for possessive pronouns.) The clause, in normal left-to-right fashion, is *I borrowed whose notes.*

> Josh Lee, <u>whom the manager traded</u>, later became rookie of the year.

Here the objective relative pronoun, *whom,* is the direct object in its clause: *The manager traded whom.*

When the relative pronoun is an object in its clause, it can be deleted if the clause is **restrictive**—that is, if the clause is not set off by commas. In the previous example, the clause is **nonrestrictive**, so the relative *whom* cannot be deleted. And you'll notice also that *whom* makes the sentence sound formal, not like something you would say. But in the following example, the *whom* can be omitted, and in speech it certainly would be. Most writers too would probably omit it.

> King Edward VIII gave up the throne of England for the woman <u>(whom) he loved</u>.

The relative pronoun *that* always introduces restrictive clauses; in other words, *that* relative clauses are never set off by commas:

> Angie chose the color <u>that she liked best</u>.
> Someone <u>that I knew in junior high</u> called me last week.

In these two sentences, *that* can be omitted. Some writers, in fact, would insist on leaving it out in the second one because it refers to a person; other writers insist on *who* and *whom* in reference to people—not *that.* The easiest and smoothest solution is simply to omit the relative pronoun:

> Someone <u>I knew in junior high</u> called me last week.

However, the relative pronoun *cannot* be omitted when it functions as the subject in its clause:

> The cell phone <u>that rang in class</u> belonged to the teacher.

Nor can it be omitted if the clause is nonrestrictive—no matter what role the pronoun fills:

> Rob Miller, <u>whom I knew in junior high,</u> called me last week.

We should note, too, that in speaking this sentence we're more likely to say *who,* even though the objective case of the pronoun is called for; most listeners wouldn't notice the difference. (*Who* actually sounds correct because it's at the beginning of the clause, where the subjective case is found.)

The relative pronoun *which* is generally reserved for nonrestrictive clauses—those set off by commas:

> My roommate's financial problems, <u>which he finally told me about</u>, have caused him a lot of stress this semester.

The relative adverbs *where, when,* and *why* also introduce relative clauses, modifiers of nouns denoting place (*where*-clauses), time (*when*-clauses), and the noun *reason* (*why*-clauses):

> Newsworthy events rarely happen in the small *town* <u>where I lived as a child.</u>
> We will all feel nervous until next *Tuesday,* <u>when results of the auditions will be posted.</u>
> I understand the *reason* <u>why I got the ticket.</u>

In the past, *reason why* was considered redundant, but today many reputable writers use this form. However, note that the final example could be rewritten as *I understand why I got the ticket* or *I understand the reason I got the ticket.* Both of these versions are more concise.

THE BROAD-REFERENCE CLAUSE

As we've seen, the relative clause is part of a noun phrase—and the **antecedent** of the relative pronoun that introduces it is the headword of that noun phrase:

> That red Ferrari, which Joe is so proud of, is actually a gas guzzler.

However, the relative clause introduced by *which,* instead of referring to a particular noun, sometimes has what is called **broad reference:**

> Joe bought a gas guzzler, <u>which surprised me</u>.
>
> Tom showed up without being invited, <u>which made me suspect that he wanted to talk about something</u>.

Here the antecedent of *which* in both cases is the idea of the entire main clause, not a specific noun.

One way to revise this vague broad-reference clause is to furnish a noun that sums up the idea of the main clause, so that the clause will have specific, rather than broad, reference. Note in the revisions that the relative *that* has replaced *which,* and the clauses now have nouns to modify:

> Joe bought a gas guzzler, <u>a decision</u> that surprised me.
>
> Tom showed up without being invited, <u>a rare event</u> that made me suspect he wanted to talk about something.

This solution to the vague antecedent is sometimes called a **summative modifier**. It is also referred to as a *sentence appositive,* which you will learn about in the next chapter.

There are other solutions to the broad-reference *which*-clause besides the summative modifier. For example, we could revise the previous example sentence in at least two ways:

> When Tom showed up without being invited, I suspected that he wanted to talk about something.
>
> Tom's showing up uninvited made me suspect he wanted to talk about something.

While it's true that broad-reference clauses often have a vague quality, sending a message of carelessness, there are times when a *which* in reference to the whole clause makes the point clearly—and, in fact, may be preferred:

> The men my two sisters married are brothers, which makes their children double cousins.

EXERCISE 30

Revise the following sentences to eliminate any instances of the broad-reference *which*.

1. The first snowstorm of the season in Denver was both early and severe, which was not what the weather service had predicted.

2. The president had some harsh words for Congress in his recent press conference, which some observers considered quite inappropriate.

3. We have overspent our budget three times this week, which means eating hotdogs for the rest of the month.

4. The Brazilian government has grudgingly agreed to consider new policies regarding the rain forests, which should come as good news to everyone concerned about the environment.

5. As state governments decrease funding for college, tuition invariable increases, which makes an education difficult for many students to afford.

PUNCTUATION OF PHRASES AND CLAUSES

Does this modifier need to be set off by commas? That's the question to be answered about the punctuation of participial phrases and relative clauses in the noun phrase. The question also comes up in the case of certain appositives, which are discussed in Chapter 10.

The answer to the question has to do with the purpose of the modifier: Is it there to identify the referent of the noun being modified—that is, to restrict its meaning—or simply to comment on it? (The traditional terms for the difference are *restrictive* and *nonrestrictive*.)

You may recall that in Chapter 2 you saw the word *referent* in the discussion of sentence patterns: When the subject complement in the *be*-pattern or the linking-verb pattern is a noun or noun phrase, it has the same **referent** as the subject (*Mary* is *my sister*). *Referent* means the thing (or person, event, concept, and so on) that the noun or noun phrase stands for: *Mary* and *my sister* refer to the same person. The term *referent* is useful here, too, in thinking about the purpose of the modifier as well as the knowledge of the reader: Is the referent of the noun clear to the reader without the modifier?

In the following sentence, with no other context, the relative clause is needed to identify the referent of the noun phrase *the president*:

The president <u>who was elected in 1932</u> faced problems that would have overwhelmed the average person.

Ordinarily we would say that the noun phrase *the president* has many possible referents; the *who*-clause is needed to make the referent clear; it defines and restricts *the president* to a particular man, the one elected in

1932. But what if the reader already knows the referent from previous context?

> Franklin Delano Roosevelt took office at a time when the outlook for the nation was bleak indeed. The president, <u>who was elected in 1932</u>, faced decisions that would have overwhelmed the average person.

In this context the referent of *the president* is already defined by the time the reader gets to it: The clause is simply commenting, so it needs to be set off by commas. In other words, the commas are sending the message that the *who*-clause is extra information, just a comment. You don't need this information to know who is being discussed here. In contrast, the lack of commas in the earlier sentence without context sends the message that the *who*-clause is needed to identify the referent of *president*. In other words,

> Restrictive (no commas) = identifying or defining
>
> Nonrestrictive (commas) = commenting[1]

Punctuation of participial phrases works the same way. When the participial phrase provides information for identifying, or defining the referent, there are no commas:

> The merchants <u>holding the sidewalk sales</u> hoped for good weather.

This lack of commas, then, implies that not all merchants were concerned about the weather—only those who were holding the sidewalk sales. The *holding* phrase is there to tell which merchants are hoping for good weather. In other words, there's another group of merchants who may or may not be concerned about the weather. The lack of commas identifies a particular subgroup of merchants—in this case, those concerned about the weather.

Use commas to set off commenting (nonrestrictive) modifiers—when the reader already knows the referent or if there is only one possible referent.

In the punctuation of relative clauses, the relative pronoun provides clues:

1. The *that*-clause is always restrictive; it is never set off by commas.
2. The *which*-clause is generally nonrestrictive; it is set off by commas. If you want to figure out if your *which*-clause needs

---

[1]*Comment* and *identify* are terms that Francis Christensen introduced in his book *Notes Toward a New Rhetoric.*

commas, try substituting *that*. If you can do so without changing the meaning, then the commas can, and perhaps should, be omitted. Note, however, that some writers use *which* in restrictive clauses.

3. If the relative pronoun can be deleted, the clause is restrictive:

> The bus (that) I ride to work is always late.
> The woman (whom) I work with is always early.

The next two general rules apply to both clauses and phrases:

4. After any proper noun, the modifier is nonrestrictive:

> Willamette University, which was established seven years before the Gold Rush of 1849, is within walking distance of Oregon's capitol.

> In Alaska, where the distance between some cities is vast, many businesses and individuals own private planes.

5. After any common noun that has only one possible referent, the modifier will be nonrestrictive:

> The highest mountain in the world, which resisted the efforts of climbers until 1953, looks truly forbidding from the air.

> Mike's twin brother, who lives in Austin, has a personality just like Mike's.

> My mother, sitting by the window, is talking to herself.

EXERCISE 31

Decide whether the modifiers in the following sentences are participial phrases or relative clauses. Then note whether they are restrictive (defining) or nonrestrictive (commenting) and punctuate them accordingly.

1. Many coal miners who work in West Virginia refused to approve two sections of the contract offered by management. They maintain that the sections covering wages and safety represent no improvement over their present contract which expires on Friday at midnight.

2. A group of students held a protest rally in front of the administration building yesterday. The students hoping for a meeting with the provost were demonstrating against the tuition hike

recently approved by the trustees. The increase which is expected to take effect in September will raise tuition almost 15 percent.

3. The senator and her husband who was sitting next to her on the speaker's platform both looked calm as they waited for the mayor to finish the introduction. Then the mayor turning to look directly at the senator shocked both the audience and the listeners on the platform.

....

EXERCISE 32

Combine the following groups of sentences into single sentences by embedding some of the ideas as modifiers. You'll probably want to use both adverbial and adjectival modifiers. In some cases you may have to make other changes in the wording as well.

1. Fingerprints have been used for criminal identification since 1891.

   A police officer in Argentina introduced the method.
   The computer has revolutionized the storage and retrieval of fingerprints.

2. The leaning tower of Pisa is 179 feet high.

   It is over 800 years old.
   It leans 17 feet off the perpendicular.

3. The highest incidence of colon cancer in the United States occurs in the Northeast.

   The Northeast also has the highest levels of acid rain.
   Cancer researchers suspect that there is a causal link between the two.

4. The rate of colon cancer is related to the amount of carbon dioxide in the air.

   Carbon dioxide absorbs ultraviolet light.
   Ultraviolet light fuels the body's production of vitamin D.

5. Influenza, or flu, is a viral infection.

   It begins as an upper respiratory infection and then spreads to other parts of the body.
   Flu causes aches and pains in the joints.

6. Flu viruses mutate constantly.

> We cannot build up our immunity.
> New varieties spread from person to person and from
>   place to place.

....

A Punctuation Rule Revisited

The very first punctuation lesson you learned in this book, back in
Chapter 2, concerned the boundaries between parts of the sentence:

> Do not use a single comma to separate the required units in the
>   basic sentence.

The punctuation lessons in this chapter perhaps explain why the word
single was included in that rule. In this chapter you've seen sentences
in which a modifier that falls between two units is set off with two
commas:

> My mother, sitting by the window, is talking to herself.

You may be tempted to think that here the subject and predicate are separated by a single comma, the comma after *window.* But they are not. It's
important to recognize that the second comma has a partner and that the
purpose of these commas is to allow the participial phrase into the noun
phrase as a modifier. *That particular phrase wouldn't be allowed without its
two commas.* In other words, that comma is not *between* sentence units; it
is part of the subject.
   You've learned a great many punctuation rules so far in this book—
and there are more to come in the next chapter! Learning those rules
in connection with the expansion of sentences, as you're doing, should
help you recognize their purposes. And you can be sure that using
punctuation well—using it to help the reader and doing so according
to the standard conventions—will go a long way in establishing your
authority.

KEY TERMS

Adjectival	Case	Headword
Adjective	Clause	Nonrestrictive
Adjective phrase	Dangling modifier	(commenting)
Antecedent	Determiner	modifier
Broad reference	Free modifier	Noun phrase

Participial phrase
Past participle
Prepositional phrase
Present participle

Referent
Relative adverb
Relative clause
Relative pronoun

Restrictive (defining)
 modifier
Summative modifier

RHETORICAL REMINDERS

Prenoun Modifiers
Have I paid attention to commas and hyphens in the noun phrase?

Have I avoided strings of nouns as modifiers?

Postnoun Modifiers
Do opening and closing participles modify the subject of the sentence?

Have I thought about sentence focus in placing participles and participial phrases?

Have I avoided fuzzy broad-reference *which*-clauses?

PUNCTUATION REMINDERS

Have I used a comma between prenoun modifiers when it's possible to use *and* between them?

Have I used commas around a nonrestrictive modifier when the modifier is only commenting on the noun rather than defining it—when the reader already knows its referent or if it has only one possible referent?

Have I used a comma to set off a participial phrase that opens the sentence? And have I made sure that the subject of the sentence is also the subject of the participle in that phrase?

Choosing Nominals

CHAPTER PREVIEW

Nominals are structures that function as nouns. This chapter includes information about the nominal functions of gerunds, infinitives, and dependent clauses, as well as a special nominal function called the appositive. By studying these forms and functions closely, you'll learn to

- identify and discuss the use of nominals by other writers;
- use nominals to make your writing more succinct;
- place nominals so that readers will focus on important information; and
- punctuate nominals appropriately.

APPOSITIVES

We'll begin with some examples of **appositives**:

> Our neighbor, <u>the deli manager at Giant Foods</u>, used to own a restaurant.
>
> <u>An ex-Marine who once played professional football</u>, the security guard at our school makes us feel very secure indeed.
>
> Jack London's novel *The Call of the Wild* was serialized in *The Saturday Evening Post* in the summer of 1903.

Can you see how the appositive and the subject are related in each of these sentences? If you put a form of the linking verb *be* between them, they would be Pattern 2 sentences ("something is something"). Note that sometimes the appositive can open the sentence, as the second example illustrates. Here's another appositive you saw in the previous chapter:

> Most nouns require a determiner, <u>the noun signaler that occupies the opening position in the noun phrase</u>.

You might be tempted to label these underlined structures as adjectivals rather than nominals. While they are noun phrases in form, they do appear to function like other noun modifiers. But there is one important difference: The appositive not only adds information about the subject or object but *renames* it in a way. The appositive could, in fact, take the place of the subject or object in the sentences we've been examining:

> The deli manager at Giant Foods used to own a restaurant.
>
> An ex-Marine who once played professional football makes us feel very secure indeed.
>
> *The Call of the Wild* was serialized in *The Saturday Evening Post* in the summer of 1903.
>
> Most nouns require the noun signaler that occupies the opening position in the noun phrase.

Clearly, we've lost some information in these revisions; but as you can see, the appositive could fill the noun phrase position on its own.

Often the appositive is simply a name:

> (1) Our friend <u>Blane</u> works as an EMT in the mountains.

Sometimes that name is set off by commas:

> (2) The judge's husband, <u>Morrie</u>, stays home with the kids.

Because the judge has only one husband (she wouldn't have been elected otherwise!), the purpose of adding the name in sentence (2) is different from the purpose in (1): We would know who stays home with the kids even if the sentence didn't include the husband's name. But in sentence (1), without a name, the reader doesn't know who the EMT is: The appositive is there to identify, to define, the referent of the noun phrase *our friend*. As you can see, the distinction between restrictive (identifying) and nonrestrictive (commenting) modifiers that you studied in connection with adjectivals applies to appositives as well. In other words, *Blane* restricts the meaning of "our friend." In (2), however, *Morrie* simply comments; the noun phrase, *the judge's husband,* needs no restriction: It has only one possible referent.

There's another important attribute of the appositive to consider: Not all appositives are noun phrases.

For example, here's one we used in the discussion of commas and sentence rhythm:

> This role for the comma, <u>to shift the peak of stress</u>, is probably one you hadn't thought about before.

This appositive is an infinitive phrase in form. While appositives are nominals in function, they need not be noun phrases in form. As you'll see later in this chapter, phrases with verb forms commonly fill nominal roles—and that includes the role of appositive.

FOR GROUP DISCUSSION

The relationship between the appositive and the noun it renames is very much like the relationship between the two NP (nominal) positions in Pattern 2 sentences where "something is something" type:

> Our neighbor **is** the deli manager at Giant Foods.
>
> The security guard at our school **is** an ex-Marine.
>
> The determiner **is** a noun signaler.

As you can see, we have turned these appositive examples into linking-*be* sentences. But like most writers, you probably don't need instruction for adding *be* to your prose. However, you might want to perform the opposite kind of revision: turning the subject complement of a Pattern 2 sentence into an appositive. This kind of sentence-combining technique can often solve the problem of choppy sentences, as well as the overuse of *be*.

You and your classmates will undoubtedly come up with more than one way to revise the following passages to eliminate the "something is something" opener:

1. *The Lost Colony* is an outdoor symphonic drama that tells the story of the British settlement on Roanoke Island. It has been performed in Manteo, North Carolina, every summer since 1937.

2. Alan B. Shepard was the first American to fly in space. He was launched on a 302-mile suborbital shot over the Atlantic in 1961.

3. The Gateway Arch in St. Louis is the nation's tallest memorial. It commemorates the westward expansion of the United States. It was designed by architect Eero Saarinen. It is made of stainless steel and rises 630 feet high from its foundation.

Colons and Dashes with Appositives

In Chapter 4 we saw the colon in its role as a connector of clauses in compound sentences. Here we see it in its more common role, as a signal for an appositive:

> I'll never forget the birthday present my dad bought me when I was ten: a new mountain bike.

This sentence can also be written with a dash instead of a colon:

> I'll never forget the birthday present my dad bought me when I was ten—a new mountain bike.

The colon is a strong signal, putting emphasis on the appositive. You could think of the dash as an informal colon. (If you don't want to emphasize the appositive, use a comma instead.)

One of the most common uses of the colon is to signal a list:

> Three committees were set up to plan the convention: program, finance, and local arrangements.

Here the list is actually a list of appositives specifying what types of committees. The colon is a way of saying, "Here it comes, the list I promised." Sometimes the separate structures in the list have internal commas of their own, in which case inserting semicolons makes the separation clear:

> The study of our grammar system includes three areas: phonology, the study of sounds; morphology, the study of meaningful combinations of sounds; and syntax, the study of sentence structure.

In this example each of the three noun phrases in the list has a modifier of its own, set off by a comma; the semicolons signal the reader that the series has three items, not six. This is one of the two occasions that call for the semicolon. The other, you'll recall, is the semicolon that joins the clauses in a compound sentence.

When an appositive series is in the middle of the sentence, we use a pair of dashes to set it off:

> Three committees—program, finance, and local arrangements— were set up to plan the convention.

> All three areas of our grammar system—phonology, morphology, and syntax—will be covered in the grammar course.

If we had used commas instead of dashes, the reader might have been confused:

*All three areas of our grammar system, phonology, morphology, and syntax, will be covered in the grammar course.

We need the two different marks of punctuation—the dashes as well as the commas—to differentiate the two levels of boundaries we are marking.

> **Use dashes to set off an appositive that includes internal punctuation, such as a list with commas.**

Avoiding Punctuation Errors

The use of the colon with appositives is the source of a common punctuation error, but one simple rule can resolve it:

> **The colon that introduces an appositive is preceded by a complete independent clause.**

Notice in the earlier examples that the structure preceding the colon is a complete sentence pattern, with every position filled:

Three committees   were set up   to plan the convention.
SUBJECT   VERB   ADVERBIAL

The study of our grammar system   includes   three areas.
SUBJECT   VERB   DIRECT OBJECT

Because the colon so often precedes a list, the writer may assume that all lists require colons, but that's not the case. In the following sentences, the colons are misused:

*The committees that were set up to plan the convention are: program, finance, and local arrangements.

*The three areas of the grammar system are: phonology, morphology, and syntax.

Your understanding of the sentence patterns will tell you that a subject complement is needed to complete a sentence that has a form of *be* (here it's *are*) as the main verb. (You can review the patterns in Chapter 2.)

One common variation for the sentence with a list includes the noun phrase *the following:*

> The committees that were set up to plan the convention are the following: program, finance, and local arrangements.

That noun phrase *the following* functions as the subject complement, so the sentence is indeed grammatical. But it's not necessarily the most effective version of the sentence. When you read the sentence aloud, you'll hear yourself putting main stress on the word *following*—a word with no information. If you want to use a colon in such a sentence for purposes of emphasis, the earlier version is smoother and more efficient:

> Three committees were set up to plan the convention: program, finance, and local arrangements.

It certainly makes more sense for the word *convention* to be emphasized rather than *following.*

EXERCISE 33

Use appositives to combine the following sentences. Insert any necessary colons, dashes, or semicolons.

1. Families chose their three favorite board games. They listed Monopoly, Scrabble, and Trivial Pursuit.

2. Many languages are spoken in the United States. The top four are English, Spanish, Chinese, and French.

3. Three states have over thirty electoral votes. California has fifty-five, Texas has thirty-two, and New York has thirty-one.

4. The "Big Three" at the Yalta Conference in 1945 were Franklin D. Roosevelt, Winston Churchill, and Joseph Stalin. Franklin D. Roosevelt was the president of the United States. Winston Churchill was the prime minister of Great Britain. Joseph Stalin was the general secretary of the Soviet Union.

The Sentence Appositive

Another effective—and dramatic—stylistic device is the **sentence appositive**, a noun phrase that renames or, more accurately, encapsulates the idea in the sentence as a whole. It is usually punctuated with the dash:

> The musical opened to rave reviews and standing-room-only crowds—<u>a smashing success</u>.

Compare that tight sentence with a compound sentence that has the same information but not the vigor of the first:

> The musical opened to rave reviews and standing-room-only crowds; it was a smashing success.

Here are two other examples, in which the reader's attention will be focused on the final sentence appositive:

> A pair of cardinals has set up housekeeping in our pine tree—<u>an unexpected but welcome event</u>.
> In August of 2005 Hurricane Katrina hit the Gulf Coast with winds that clocked 150 mph—<u>the worst natural disaster in the nation's history in over 100 years</u>.

The sentence appositive is similar to the appositives we saw earlier, except that instead of simply identifying or defining the referent of a subject or object, the sentence appositive offers a conclusion about the sentence as a whole in the form of a noun phrase.

The sentence appositive is a kind of summative modifier, which you saw in Chapter 9. You may recall that the summative modifier serves as an alternative to the broad-reference *which*-clause:

> Joe bought a gas guzzler, a decision that surprised me.
> Tom showed up without being invited, a rare event that made me suspect he wanted to talk about something.

NOMINAL VERB PHRASES

Gerunds

In Chapter 9 you saw examples of an *-ing* verb functioning as a noun modifier, called the *participial phrase*:

> <u>Carrying all their supplies</u>, the Boy Scouts trudged up the mountain in search of a campsite.

In this chapter we use the same *-ing* form as a nominal, to fill a position usually held by a noun phrase. When a verb phrase functions this way, it is called a **gerund:**

> <u>Carrying all their supplies</u> took not only effort but patience as well.

Here the gerund phrase is the subject of the sentence. We can think of gerunds as names, the way we sometimes think of nouns. But rather than naming persons or places and such, gerunds name actions or behaviors. And like noun phrases, the gerund can be replaced by a pronoun:

> <u>It</u> took not only effort but patience as well.

Gerunds can fill all the sentence positions usually occupied by noun phrases:

> The worst part of the airport security system is <u>taking off your shoes</u>. (subject complement)
>
> I enjoy <u>jogging</u> early in the morning. (direct object)
>
> My biology professor often begins class by <u>telling weird jokes</u>. (object of preposition)
>
> My dad's hobby, <u>collecting stamps</u>, can be time consuming. (appositive)

Having gerunds in your toolbox can help you avoid overusing the expletive *it* when opening a sentence. If you decide to use this tool, though, be sure to note the change in focus:

> It is difficult for most writers to draft a ten-page paper in a single evening.
>
> Drafting a ten-page paper in a single evening is difficult for most writers.

The Dangling Gerund. You may recall from the discussions of infinitives and participles that when they open the sentence, the subject of the main clause in the sentence is also the subject of the verb in that opening phrase:

> <u>To prepare for a job interview</u>, **an applicant** should research the company beforehand.
>
> <u>Having finished his college degree</u>, **Jason** decided to travel abroad for a year.

Remember that an opening infinitive or participial phrase sets up an expectation in the reader that the subject of that verb will follow. When something else follows, the opening verb phrase dangles:

> *<u>Having finished his college degree</u>, the idea of traveling abroad appealed to Jason.

The problem of this dangling participle is obvious: It seems to be saying that the idea has a college degree. Remember that a participle modifies its own subject. In this sentence the participle has no subject.

This same kind of dangler, this thwarted expectation, can occur when the sentence opens with a prepositional phrase in which the object of the preposition is a gerund:

> *<u>After finishing his college degree</u>, the idea of traveling abroad appealed to Jason.
> *<u>Since planting new trees</u>, more songbirds visit our yard.

The rule about opening sentences with phrases that contain verb forms is straightforward:

> **When a phrase with a verb form opens the sentence (whether an infinitive, a participle, or a gerund in a prepositional phrase), the subject of that verb will be the subject of the sentence.**

Shifting the prepositional phrase to the end of the sentence does not solve the problem. The error may not seem quite as obvious, but the dangling nature of the phrase is still there:

> *The idea of traveling abroad appealed to Jason <u>after finishing his college degree</u>.
> *More songbirds visit our yard <u>since planting new trees</u>.

So whether that phrase opens the sentence or simply *could* open the sentence, the subject–verb relationship must be there. You can easily revise dangling gerunds by either changing the subject or by expanding the prepositional phrase into an adverbial clause:

> Since planting new trees, we have more songbirds in our yard.
> Since we planted new trees, more songbirds visit our yard.

The Subject of the Gerund.   Another feature of gerunds that you'll want to be aware of is the form that their subjects sometimes take. In many cases the subject of the gerund does not appear in the sentence, especially when the gerund names a general activity:

> <u>Jogging</u> is good exercise.
> <u>Raising orchids</u> requires patience.

However, when the subject of the gerund appears in the gerund phrase itself, it is usually in the possessive case, especially when the subject is a pronoun:

> I objected to **their** <u>arriving</u> in the middle of the meeting.
> **My** <u>objecting</u> didn't make any difference.
> There is no point in **your** <u>coming</u> if you're going to be so late.

When the subject is a simple noun, such as a person's name, it too is possessive:

> I was surprised at **Terry's** refusing the job offer.

The possessive noun or pronoun fills the role of determiner. However, when the noun has modifiers, or when it is compound, then the possessive is generally not used:

> I was surprised at **Bill and Terry** turning down that beautiful apartment.

An alternative structure, which may sound more natural, is the use of a clause instead of the gerund:

> I was surprised when Bill and Terry turned down that beautiful apartment.

Infinitives

Another form of the verb that functions as a nominal is the **infinitive**—the base form of the verb with *to*. Like the gerund, the nominal infinitive names an action or behavior or state of being. In fact, the infinitive closely parallels the gerund and is often an alternative to it:

> *Gerund:*   Remaining neutral on this issue is unconscionable.
>
> *Infinitive:*   To remain neutral on this issue is unconscionable.

Like gerunds, the nominal infinitives can function in all the positions noun phrases generally hold:

> My cousin wants to be an underwater welder. (direct object)
> Tracy's ambition is to raise organic vegetables. (subject complement)
> She achieved her goal: to graduate in three years. (appositive)

EXERCISE 34

Underline the gerunds and infinitives in the following sentences. Identify the function of each nominal verb phrase. You might want to refer to the sentence patterns in Chapter 2 to refresh your memory.

1. The best thing would be to tell the truth.

2. By remaining silent, he was actually making the situation worse.

3. To ignore the doctor's advice would be foolhardy.

4. Ms. Graham chose to welcome the new investor into the company.

5. This invitation thwarted his latest plan, to buy up a controlling number of stocks.

6. Raising the company's national profile was the new owner's long-term goal.

7. I appreciate your proofreading this final version for me.

8. The baby's crying upset the rest of the passengers.

....

NOMINAL CLAUSES

One of the most common **nominal clauses** is the one introduced by *that*, known in this role as a **nominalizer**:

> He knew that I was right.
> The CEO announced that he was retiring.

You can see in these examples that we have taken a complete sentence and used it as the direct object in another sentence:

> I was right.
> He was retiring.

In the following sentence, the *that* clause fills the subject position:

> That the common cold is caused by a virus has been clearly established by science.

Any declarative sentence can be turned into a nominal clause in this way. And you'll discover that sometimes we don't even need *that*:

> He knew [_____] I was right.
> The CEO announced [_____] he was retiring.

In some cases, however, the *that* may be necessary as a signal to the reader that a clause is coming; its omission may cause the reader momentary confusion:

> *Last week I suspected my friend Kim, who never goes to class, was getting into academic trouble.
> *My uncle knows the stockbroker handling his retirement funds never takes unnecessary risks.

In both of these sentences, the addition of *that* would be helpful to signal the reader that *my friend* and *the stockbroker* are subjects, not objects.

When the *that* clause functions as the subject, the nominalizer cannot be omitted:

> *The common cold is caused by a virus has been clearly established by science.

The nominalizer *that* also allows us to turn a direct quotation into indirect discourse:

> *Direct:* He said, "For the past two years the economy has experienced a serious recession."
>
> *Indirect:* He said that for the past two years the economy had experienced a serious recession.

Many of our nominal clauses are introduced by **interrogatives,** the same words we use for questions:

> The scholar visiting from China wondered why the students were protesting.
>
> Who was responsible for the broken window remained a mystery.

Nominal clauses introduced by interrogatives can also function as objects of prepositions and as appositives:

> *Object of preposition:* The boy was curious about <u>what was in the box</u>.
>
> *Appositive:* The students' question, <u>why the summer schedule had been changed</u>, was not answered.

Unlike the nominalizer *that,* the interrogatives cannot be omitted from the clauses they introduce; these clauses are essentially questions under discussion.

Nominal clauses, as well as the clauses functioning as adjectivals and adverbials, are all **dependent clauses**. Any sentence with a dependent clause is called a **complex sentence**.

NOMINALS AS DELAYED SUBJECTS

The nominal *that* clauses functioning as subjects have a formal quality more characteristic of writing than speech; in fact, such sentences are uncommon in speech:

> That the common cold is caused by a virus has been clearly established.
>
> That Marie dropped out of school was a shock to us all.

In conversation we are more likely to delay the information in the opening clause by substituting the pronoun *it* for the subject—called the **anticipatory *it*:**

> It has been clearly established that the common cold is caused by a virus.
>
> It was a shock to us all that Marie dropped out of school.

The infinitive phrase as subject can also be delayed in this way:

> To remain neutral on this issue is unconscionable.
>
> It is unconscionable to remain neutral on this issue.

As you can see, the anticipatory *it* allows us to change the rhythm and stress of the sentence in much the same way that we saw with the *it*-cleft in the discussion of rhythm in Chapter 6 (pages 105–106).

EXERCISE 35

Underline the nominal clauses in the following sentences. Identify the function that each performs in its sentence.

1. The neighbors never suspected that we had a pet boa constrictor in our house.

2. The guest speaker's e-mail message informed us when he would arrive.

3. That the term *First Lady* wasn't used until 1849 is a little-known fact.

4. When I saw the exam questions, I realized I had studied the wrong chapters.

5. The suggestion that we reform our spelling system had little support.

6. Why reality shows are so popular mystified the whole staff.

EXERCISE 36

A. Continue your style inventory. This time count the kinds of sentences you have used in your essay, whether simple, compound, or complex. Compare your essay with one written by a professional—perhaps an essay that you've read in your English class or one that your instructor suggests.

	Your Essay	Professional
1. Total number of simple sentences	_____	_____
2. Total number of compound sentences	_____	_____
a. number connected with *and*	_____	_____
b. number connected with *but*	_____	_____
c. number connected with other conjunctions	_____	_____
d. number connected with semicolons	_____	_____
3. Number of complex sentences	_____	_____
4. Number with nominal clauses	_____	_____
5. Number with adjectival clauses	_____	_____
6. Number with participial phrases	_____	_____
a. at sentence opening	_____	_____
b. at sentence end	_____	_____
7. Number of opening adverbial clauses	_____	_____
8. Number of other adverbial openers	_____	_____

B. Now that you have studied the style of another writer in depth, write a paragraph in which you imitate that style.

KEY TERMS

Anticipatory *it*	Dependent clause	Nominal
Appositive	Gerund	Nominal clause
Complex sentence	Infinitive	Nominalizer
Dangling gerund	Interrogative	Sentence appositive

RHETORICAL REMINDERS

Have I taken advantage of appositives to tighten my prose, especially where I have used the linking-*be?*

Have I made sure that when opening prepositional phrases have gerunds as objects, the subject of the gerund is also the subject of the sentence?

PUNCTUATION REMINDERS

Have I remembered that a complete independent clause precedes a colon?

Have I set off with commas an appositive that simply comments on, rather than identifies or defines, the referent of the noun it renames?

Other Stylistic Variations

CHAPTER PREVIEW

We use the word *style* to refer to a writer's manner of expression—not only the words chosen but also the ordering of those words. By discussing variations of the patterns you've learned so far, we hope to encourage you to make the kinds of stylistic choice that will engage your readers. This chapter will provide you with the opportunity to

- identify and discuss the use of stylistic devices by other writers;
- use stylistic devices to improve the rhythm of and call attention to particular structures within a sentence;
- vary sentence structures to increase the dramatic impact of a passage; and
- punctuate stylistic variations appropriately.

STYLE

Everything we say, we say "with style," in one sense of the word—when the word refers simply to an individual's way of writing. You have your own style of writing, just as you have your own style of walking and whistling and wearing your hair. The word *style* also characterizes the overall impression of a piece of writing, such as the plain style, the pompous style, the grand style, the official style. When you follow advice about being brief and using simple words, the outcome will be a plain style; words that are too fancy will probably result in a pompous style.

We also use *style* in connection with variations in sentence structure, with the structural and punctuation choices that you as a writer can use to advantage. For example, in the second sentence of the previous paragraph, three verb phrases in a series are connected with two *and*s and no commas:

> walking and whistling and wearing your hair

It could have been written with two commas and only one *and:*

> walking, whistling, and wearing your hair

Or only commas:

> walking, whistling, wearing your hair

Such stylistic variations have traditionally occupied an important place in the study of rhetoric. In fact, the Greeks had names for every deviation from ordinary word order or usage, and Greek orators practiced using them. Some of the more common ones, you're familiar with, such **figures of speech** as simile, metaphor, and personification. But many of them, you probably don't even notice—such as the shift, in both this sentence and the previous one, of the direct object to opening position. The Greeks called this inversion of usual word order **anastrophe** (pronounced a-NAS-tro-fee).

In studying this chapter you'll look more closely at a number of variations. For some of these you'll learn the term the Greeks used. But is that important—to learn their labels? Yes and no. Yes, it's important to know that they have labels, to know that stylistic choices like these are used deliberately by good speakers and writers. But no, it's not really important that you remember their names. It's enough that you make their acquaintance, that you recognize them when you see them again, and feel comfortable using them.

ABSOLUTE PHRASES

We begin our discussion of stylistic variations with the **absolute phrase**, a structure you saw way back on the first page of Chapter 2 in our familiar weasel paragraph:

> A weasel is wild. Who knows what he thinks? He sleeps in his underground den, <u>his tail draped over his nose</u>.... One naturalist refused to kill a weasel who was socketed into his hand deeply as a rattlesnake. The man could in no way pry the tiny weasel off, and he had to walk half a mile to water, <u>the weasel dangling from his palm</u>, and soak him off like a stubborn label.

These two examples illustrate one of the two styles of absolutes, the phrase that adds a detail or point of focus to the idea stated in the main clause. Notice in the third sentence of the passage how the main clause describes the overall scene, the weasel asleep in his underground den; the absolute phrase moves the reader in for a close-up view, focusing on a detail, just as a filmmaker uses a camera. The example in the last sentence works the same way: The main clause gives us the long shot of the man walking; the absolute focuses on the weasel dangling from his palm.

With only one small addition, these absolutes become full clauses:

> His tail (is) draped over his nose.
> The weasel (is) dangling from his palm.

In other words, the absolute actually adds a subject–predicate relationship to its sentence, but does so without actually adding another clause. That third sentence,

> The weasel sleeps in his underground den, his tail draped over his nose,

is neither compound nor complex; in fact, it would be classified as simple in traditional grammar, since it has only one complete clause. However, you can see that it has the impact of a complex sentence, given that it includes what is essentially a subordinate subject–predicate construction, the absolute.

As you read the sentences containing these two examples, you can probably hear your voice giving emphasis to the noun headword of the absolute phrase. The absolute invariably calls attention to itself, sending a "Pay attention!" message to the reader. For that reason, writers often reserve the absolute for important details. It also sends a more subtle message: "I have crafted this sentence carefully; I know what I'm doing." Even though a reader may not be able to name, perhaps not even to consciously recognize, the absolute phrase, that reader will certainly recognize a writer in control. The well-chosen absolute can add to the writer's authority.

The absolute phrase that adds a focusing detail is especially common in fiction writing, much more common than in expository writing—such as the prose in this textbook and probably your texts for other classes. In the following passages, all from works of fiction, some have participial phrases, just as Annie Dillard has in her weasel description; however, you'll also see some with noun phrases, others with prepositional phrases.

> There was no bus in sight and Julian, <u>his hands still jammed in his pockets and his head thrust forward</u>, scowled down the empty street.
> —Flannery O'Connor, "Everything That Rises Must Converge"

He smiled a little to himself as he ran, holding the ball lightly in front of him with his two hands, <u>his knees pumping high, his hips twisting in the almost girlish run of a back in a broken field</u>.

       —Irwin Shaw, "The Eighty-Yard Run"

In the following series of three absolutes, the first and third have noun phrases: *tiny ribbons of light; a purple hollow* ...:

He saw the city spread below like a glittering golden ocean, <u>the streets tiny ribbons of light, the planet curving away at the edges, the sky a purple hollow extending to infinity</u>.

       —Anne Tyler, *The Accidental Tourist*

And these two examples have prepositional phrases:

Silently they ambled down Tenth Street until they reached a stone bench that jutted from the sidewalk near the curb. They stopped there and sat down, <u>their backs to the eyes of the two men in white smocks who were watching them</u>.

       —Toni Morrison, *Song of Solomon*

The man stood laughing, <u>his weapons at his hips</u>.

     —Stephen Crane, "The Bride Comes to Yellow Sky"

A second style of absolute phrase, rather than focusing on a detail, explains a cause or condition:

<u>Our car having developed engine trouble</u>, we stopped for the night at a roadside rest area.

We decided to have our picnic, <u>the weather being warm and clear</u>.

<u>Victory assured</u>, the fans stood and cheered during the last five minutes of the game.

The first example could be rewritten as a *because-* or *when*-clause:

When our car developed engine trouble, we stopped ...

       or

Because our car developed engine trouble, we stopped ...

The absolute allows the writer to include the information without the explicitness of the complete clause; the absolute, then, can be thought of as containing both meanings, both *when* and *because*. The absolute about the weather in the second example suggests an attendant condition rather than a cause.

Here's a familiar (and hotly debated) absolute of this style:

> A well-regulated militia being necessary to the security of a free state, the right of the people to keep and bear arms shall not be infringed.

As you can probably hear, this second style of absolute adds a formal tone to the sentence, formal almost to the point of stiffness. It's certainly not a structure that's used in speech. In fact, neither of these two styles of absolute phrases is used in speech—in speeches, perhaps, but certainly not in everyday speech.

FOR GROUP DISCUSSION

We could add *with* to most, if not all, of the examples, thus turning the absolute phrases into prepositional phrases:

> The man stood laughing, <u>with his weapons at his hips</u>.

> There was no bus in sight and Julian, <u>with his hands still jammed in his pockets and his head thrust forward</u>, scowled down the empty street.

Try the other examples as well, with the added *with*.

How would you characterize the difference in the two styles? Has the meaning changed at all?

EXERCISE 37

Expand the following sentences by adding the modifiers called for. (You might want to review participial phrases and relative clauses in Chapter 9.)

1. *My cousin [aunt, uncle, sister, etc.] who _____ surprised everyone at the family reunion.*

   A. Add a *who*-clause that describes one of your relatives.

   B. Now add a dependent clause that explains what your relative did that was so surprising.

   C. Finally, add an absolute phrase at the end of the sentence—a close-up detail.

2. *From the window we watched the cyclists.*

   A. Add a series of participial phrases that tell what the cyclists were doing.

   B. Now add an appositive at the end of the sentence as a comment on the whole scene.

3. *At the far end of the counter sat a trucker.*

    A. Add an appositive to describe the trucker.

    B. Now add two prenoun modifiers to explain what sort of counter it is so that the reader will be better able to picture the scene.

    C. Add an appositive at the end that provides a close-up detail.

4. *Endless cars jammed the freeway.*

    A. Open this sentence with an adverbial clause or phrase that tells *when*.

    B. Now add a series of absolute phrases that describe the cars.

THE COORDINATE SERIES

Many of the variations that writers use for special effects occur in connection with coordinate structures—pairs and series of sentences and their parts. One of those changes is a deviation in the use of conjunctions. You'll recall from the discussion of the serial comma in Chapter 4 that the usual punctuation for the series includes commas until the final *and:*

> You have your own style of writing, just as you have your own style of walking, whistling, and wearing your hair.

Here's a variation with an extra *and,* which was labeled **polysyndeton** by the Greek Rhetoricians:

> walking and whistling, and wearing your hair

Opposite of the extra *and* is the series with no conjunction at all, just commas, a style called **asyndeton:**

> walking and whistling and wearing your hair

The differences are subtle but meaningful. Polysyndeton puts emphasis on each element of the series with a fairly equal beat: _____ and _____ and _____. As Arthur Quinn notes in *Figures of Speech* (see the Bibliography), polysyndeton slows us down, perhaps adds a sense of formality, while asyndeton speeds us up. And asyndeton, the variation with no *and*s, also suggests that the list is open ended. It seems to suggest, "I could go on and on; I could tell you much more."

    In the following passage, Winston Churchill describes Stonewall Jackson using asyndeton in both series; he has embedded one such series within another:

> His character was stern, his manner reserved and unusually forbidding, his temper Calvinistic, his mode of life strict, frugal, austere.

The omission of the conjunctions contributes to the strictness and frugality of style that echo the words themselves. With conjunctions, the sentence would lose that echo:

His mode of life was strict and frugal and austere.

In the following sentence from *A Not Entirely Benign Procedure: Four Years as a Medical Student*, Perri Klass uses asyndeton to help convey the pressure of medical school:

The general pressure in medical school is to push yourself ahead into professionalism, to start feeling at home in the hospital, in the operating room, to make medical jargon your native tongue—it's all part of becoming efficient, knowledgeable, competent.

Perhaps the series is not a feature of language that you've thought much about in your writing. But as these examples illustrate, a well-constructed series can add a great deal of stylistic flair. And while it's not important that you remember their labels, now that you know about polysyndeton and asyndeton, you can add these devices to your collection of writers' tools with the assurance that using them will make the reader pay attention and, what's even more important, recognize your competence and authority as a writer.

REPETITION

Repetition has come up before in these pages—in both a positive and a negative sense. On the positive side, repetition gives our sentences cohesion: The known–new contract calls for the repetition, if not of words, then of ideas. It is part of the glue that holds paragraphs together. But, as you'll recall, we also have a negative label for repetition when it has no purpose, when it gets in the reader's way: Then we call it **redundancy**.

We confine our discussion to repetition in coordinate structures that make the reader sit up and take notice. Again, to emphasize their importance as tools, we use their ancient labels. Consider the Gettysburg Address. Which of Lincoln's words, other than "Fourscore and seven years ago," do you remember? Probably "government of the people, by the people, and for the people." It's hard to imagine those words without the repetition: "Of, by, and for the people" just wouldn't have the same effect. Lincoln's repetition of the same grammatical form is called **isocolon**. And think about President Kennedy's stirring words, with his repetition of *any* to signal five noun phrases:

[We] shall pay any price, bear any burden, meet any hardship, support any friend, oppose any foe to assure the survival and the success of liberty.

Notice, too, Kennedy's use of asyndeton. He seems to be saying, "I could go on and on with my list."

You don't have to be a president to use that kind of repetition, nor do you have to reserve it for formal occasions. Whenever you use a coordinate structure, there's an opportunity for you to add to its impact with repetition, simply by including words that wouldn't have to be included. The following sentence, from an essay in *Time* by Charles Krauthammer, could have been more concise, but it would have lost its drama:

> There is not a single Western standard, there are two: what we demand of Western countries at peace and what we demand of Western countries at war.

The following sentence by Terrence Rafferty is from a review of the movie *Mountains of the Moon,* which appeared in the *New Yorker.* Here too the repetition helps to persuade the reader of the accuracy of the description "an intellectual adventurer":

> He [Sir Richard Burton] <u>had travelled</u> widely, in Europe, Asia, and Africa; <u>he had mastered</u> a couple of dozen languages; <u>he had written</u> seven books; and <u>he had made</u> a reputation as an intellectual adventurer, a man whose joy was to immerse himself in other cultures, to experience everything—even (or perhaps especially) things that his countrymen loathed and feared.

The Greeks called this repetition of clause openings **anaphora**.

The repetitions we have seen so far are contained within sentences, in compound structures—verb phrases in Kennedy's speech and clauses in the Krauthammer and Rafferty sentences. But whole sentences with obvious repeated elements not only add a stylistic flair beyond the sentence level, they contribute a great deal to the cohesion of a paragraph and beyond.

FOR GROUP DISCUSSION

Shakespeare, of course, was a master of all kinds of stylistic variations. If you've read *The Merchant of Venice,* you may remember these well-known words, spoken by Shylock in Act III, Scene I:

> He hath disgrac'd me, and hind'red me half a million, laugh'd at my losses, mock'd at my gains, scorn'd my nation, thwarted my bargains, cool'd my friends, heated mine enemies; and what's his reason? I am a Jew. Hath not a Jew eyes? Hath not a Jew hands, organs, dimensions, senses, affections, passions?

Fed with the same food, hurt with the same weapons, subject to the same diseases, heal'd by the same means, warm'd and cool'd by the same winter and summer, as a Christian is? If you prick us, do we not bleed? If you tickle us, do we not laugh? If you poison us, do we not die? And if you wrong us, shall we not revenge?

A. Identify the various rhetorical figures that Shakespeare has used here. In what ways does the sentence style enhance the meaning of Shylock's words?

B. Examine your own use of compound structures or those in a classmate's paper. Look for places where one or more of the stylistic variations you have read about here—polysyndeton, asyndeton, isocolon, and anaphora—would enhance the effectiveness of the writing.

WORD-ORDER VARIATION

A number of the classical rhetorical schemes have to do with variation in normal subject–verb–complement word order, as we saw in the examples of *anastrophe* in the introductory pages. Such deviations are especially common in poetry. In reading poetry, we're always on the lookout for subjects and predicates in unexpected places. Here, for example, is the opening of Robert Frost's famous poem "Stopping by Woods on a Snowy Evening":

Whose woods these are, I think I know.

In this line the opening clause is the direct object of *know:*

I think I know *something.*

This inversion of word order can also be effective in prose, mainly because we're not looking for it. It can put stress on the verb, just as it did in Frost's line. In one of the earlier examples cited from this chapter,

But many of them, you probably don't even notice,

the verb is in line for end focus. And in the following sentence, Charles Dickens made sure that the reader would hear the contrast between *has* and *has not:*

Talent, Mr. Micawber has; money, Mr. Micawber has not.

Another variation in word order occurs with certain adverbs in opening position, when a shift of subject and auxiliary is required:

> Never before <u>had I seen</u> such an eerie glow in the night sky.
>
> Rarely <u>do I hear</u> such words of praise.

You'll notice that the opening adverbial is a peak of stress. The reader will focus on that opening negative—and will pay attention.

The following sentence, written by Winston Churchill, illustrates yet another kind of shift in word order. Here the very last noun phrase in the sentence is the grammatical subject:

> Against Lee and his great Lieutenant [Stonewall Jackson], united for a year of intense action in a comradeship which recalls that of Marlborough and Eugene, were now to be marshalled the overwhelming forces of the Union.

When you read this sentence aloud, you can hear your voice building to a crescendo on *overwhelming forces,* just as Churchill planned. In fact, it's hard to read the sentence without sounding Churchillian. The sentence leaves the reader in suspense until the end.

The inversion in this passage, from *The Templars* by Piers Paul Read, produces something of that same Churchillian effect:

> The conversion of Constantine was of momentous consequence for Christianity. Equally significant for the future of the Empire was his decision to move its capital from Rome to Byzantium on the Bosphorus.

In Chapter 9 we saw another variation in the expected word order when we shifted adjective phrases from their usual preheadword position:

> <u>Hot and tired</u>, the hikers trudged the last mile to their campsite.
>
> The hikers, <u>hot and tired</u>, trudged the last mile to their campsite.
>
> <u>Highly unusual</u>, the situation called for extraordinary measures.
>
> The situation, <u>highly unusual</u>, called for extraordinary measures.

These shifts are less dramatic than Churchill's, but they do change the emphasis and call attention to themselves. In both versions, they put the strong stress on the subject, rather than on the predicate, its usual place.

All these variations in word order change the rhythm patterns and thus the messages that the reader will get. As a writer, you will want to construct your sentences with the reader's expectations in mind.

FOR GROUP DISCUSSION

In the following paragraph, the opening paragraph of Chapter 5 in Daniel J. Boorstin's *The Discoverers,* you'll find two sentences that illustrate anastrophe:

> While man allowed his time to be parsed by the changing cycles of daylight, he remained a slave to the sun. To become the master of his time, to assimilate night into the day, to slice his life into neat, usable portions, he had to find a way to mark off precise small portions—not only equal hours, but even minutes and seconds and parts of seconds. He would have to make a machine. It is surprising that machines to measure time were so long in coming. Not until the fourteenth century did Europeans devise mechanical timepieces. Until then, as we have seen, the measuring of time was left to the shadow clock, the water clock, the sandglass, and the miscellaneous candle clocks and scent clocks. While there was remarkable progress five thousand years ago in measuring the year, and useful week clusters of days were long in use, the subdivided day was another matter. Only in modern times did we begin to live by the hour, much less by the minute.

A. You'll notice that the two sentences illustrating anastrophe also include the shift of the subject and the auxiliary verb. What do they have in common with those examples with *never before* and *rarely* in the discussion? Note as well other figures of speech that Boorstin uses here.

B. Note the variation in sentence length. Where do you find the topic sentence in this paragraph?

C. In Chapter 7 you read about metadiscourse; you'll find two examples in this paragraph. What effect do they have on you as a reader?

ELLIPSIS

Another fairly common stylistic variation—another that the Greeks used in their oratory—is **ellipsis**, which refers to a sentence in which a part is simply left out, or understood. As you might expect, they had many names for this variation, depending on the kind of structure deleted. We use the umbrella term *ellipsis* for all of them.

One example we've already seen is Churchill's description of Stonewall Jackson:

> His character was stern, his manner reserved and unusually forbidding, his temper Calvinistic, his mode of life strict, frugal, and austere.

And you saw this sentence as an illustration of the series without conjunctions, asyndeton; however, it's also a good example of ellipsis, where all the clauses except the first are missing the verb: "his manner [was] reserved ... his temper [was] Calvinistic," and so on. Here are some other, similar, examples, where part of the second clause or phrase is left out to avoid repetition:

> The first day of our vacation was wonderful; the second, miserable.
>
> For breakfast we had eggs; for lunch, eggs; and for dinner, eggs again.

Note that within the sentence a comma sometimes signals the omission, depending on the rhythm, where the pause produced by the comma may be needed to help the reader. As you can hear when you read these sentences, this use of ellipsis gives them a tight, controlled quality that would be missing if the clauses were complete.

In some clauses of comparison, the ellipsis is required by our grammar:

> I'm a week older than Terry [is old].
>
> My sister isn't as tall as I [am tall].
>
> > or
>
> I'm a week older than Terry is [old].
>
> My sister isn't as tall as I am [tall].

These structures are not a problem for native English speakers; we use them automatically.

We should note that *ellipsis* is also the term we use to refer to the string of periods, or *ellipsis points,* that indicate to the reader that we have left something out of quoted material. You can read more about this punctuation convention on page 251 in the Glossary of Punctuation.

ANTITHESIS

In his book on classical rhetoric, referred to in an earlier chapter (also listed in the Bibliography), Edward P. J. Corbett defines **antithesis** as "the juxtaposition of contrasting ideas, often in parallel" (464); among his examples illustrating this figure of speech are the words of Neil Armstrong as he stepped on the moon in 1969:

> That's one <u>small step for a man</u>, one <u>giant leap for mankind</u>.

This example is from George W. Bush's second inaugural address:

> Across the generations we have proclaimed the imperative of self-government because <u>no one is fit to be a master</u> and <u>no one deserves to be a slave</u>.

Benjamin Franklin included this example of antithesis in a letter he wrote in 1783:

> There never was <u>a good war</u>, or <u>a bad peace</u>.

Don't get the idea that world-changing events and presidential speeches are the only occasions for antithesis. Advertisers often use the same kind of juxtaposition of contrasting ideas. Here are some headlines from magazine ads published in *Atlantic* and *Harper's:*

> Before our <u>engineers design our cars</u>, our <u>racing programs design our engineers</u>.
>
> <u>Felt</u> but <u>not seen.</u> Because our miracle is on the inside … [mattress ad]
>
> We only <u>live once</u>. But we <u>sit many, many times</u>. [chair ad]
>
> You <u>can't see</u> the innovative technology. But you <u>can certainly hear</u> it. [sound system]

The first one is a clever play on words; in the last three, the negative comment is there to contrast with, and thus enhance, the positive quality being promoted. Earlier we saw an example of antithesis in a quotation from Dickens used to illustrate word-order variation:

> Talent, Mr. Micawber <u>has;</u> money, Mr. Micawber <u>has not</u>.

The following example is a portion of the paragraph that follows the paragraph about clocks quoted in the Group Discussion activity on page 204. It includes the kind of antithesis that you are likely to see in works you are reading—and also to use—where contrasts are included to emphasize the point:

> The first steps toward the mechanical measurement of time, the beginnings of the modern clock in Europe, <u>came not from</u> farmers or shepherds, <u>nor from</u> merchants or craftsmen, <u>but from</u> religious persons anxious to perform promptly and regularly their duties to God. Monks needed to know the times for their appointed prayers. In Europe the first mechanical clocks were designed <u>not to</u> *show* the time <u>but to</u> *sound* it…. [author's emphasis]

In his autobiography, *Long Walk to Freedom,* Nelson Mandela uses antithesis to explain the importance of education:

> Education is the great engine of personal development. It is through education that <u>the daughter of a peasant can become</u>

a doctor, that <u>the son of a mineworker can become the head of the mine</u>, that <u>a child of farmworkers can become the president of a great nation</u>. It is what we make out of <u>what we have, not what we are given</u>, that separates one person from another.

THE DELIBERATE FRAGMENT

The sentence **fragments** used for their stylistic effect are not the kind that teachers mark with a marginal *frag*; those are usually the result of punctuation errors, often a dependent clause punctuated as a full sentence. But experienced writers know how to use fragments deliberately and effectively—noun phrases or verb phrases that add a detail without a full sentence and invariably call attention to themselves. Here is an example from a novel by John le Carré:

> Our Candidate begins speaking. <u>A deliberate, unimpressive opening</u>.
>
> —A Perfect Spy

Barack Obama opens Chapter 5 of his memoir, *Dreams from My Father,* with three sentence fragments in two sentences:

> Three o'clock in the morning. The moon-washed streets empty, the growl of a car picking up speed down a distant road.

In the following passage from *The Shipping News,* E. Annie Proulx conveys a tentative quality of the characters' feelings:

> Wavey came down the steps pulling at the sleeves of her homemade coat, the color of slushy snow. She got in, glanced at him. <u>A slight smile. Looked away.</u>
>   <u>Their silence comfortable. Something unfolding</u>. But what? <u>Not love, which wrenched and wounded. Not love, which came only once.</u>

Both ellipsis and sentence fragments contribute to that tentativeness.

FOR GROUP DISCUSSION

The writers of the following passages have used a great many stylistic tools to good advantage. Identify the places where they have sent that special message to the reader: "Pay attention! I've crafted this sentence carefully."

[George Caleb] Bingham's greatest paintings depend upon an open rhetoric, an uncannily frank relation to their audience. We view his subjects from a perspective that includes us within the painting, and the direct looks we meet there usually recall the openness of Bingham's own disposition, itself characteristically American. Looking at *Fur Traders Descending the Missouri* as if from a canoe or from the Missouri's bank, we are obliged to remember that rivers have mouths and sources. *Fur Traders* can certainly be read as a painting in which the wilderness is brought into the frame of civilization, tending ever downriver. But it is more ambiguous than that, and ambiguity is an important source of its effect. Backlit by the diffuse light of the rising sun, offset by an island still in shadow, barely accented by a line of ducks wheeling over the far shore, these exotic figures are just as redolent of where they have been as of where they are going. And as time moves the viewer farther and farther downstream from the wilderness, it seems more and more as if this painting leads us upstream in imagination to the wilder country from which this man and boy have just descended.

—Verlyn Klinkenborg, *Smithsonian*

The general pressure in medical school is to push yourself ahead into professionalism, to start feeling at home in the hospital, in the operating room, to make medical jargon your native tongue—it's all part of becoming efficient, knowledgeable, competent. You want to leave behind that green, terrified medical student who stood awkwardly on the edge of the action, terrified of revealing limitless ignorance, terrified of killing a patient. You want to identify with the people ahead of you, the ones who know what they're doing. And instead, I have found it necessary to retain some of the greenness, so I could explain the hospital to people for whom it was not familiar turf.

—Perri Klass, *A Not Entirely Benign Procedure*

It is so known through the length and breadth of its watershed. The Bay. There is no possible confusion with any other body of water, no need for more precise description. It is, after all, the continent's largest estuary. Its waters are rich, the main supply of oysters, crabs, clams and other seafoods for much of the Atlantic seaboard. Its shorelines cradled our first settlements. It is the Chesapeake.

—William W. Warner, *Beautiful Swimmers*

(**Note:** This paragraph opens the book's first chapter, "The Bay.")

On two occasions, the contractor hired a group of Mexican aliens. They were employed to cut down some trees and haul off debris. In all, there were six men of varying age. The youngest in his late twenties; the oldest (his father?) perhaps sixty years old. They came and they left in a single old truck. Anonymous men. They were never introduced to the other men at the site. Immediately upon their arrival they would follow the contractor's directions, starting working—rarely resting—seemingly driven by a fatalistic sense that work which had to be done was best done as quickly as possible.

I watched them sometimes. Perhaps they watched me. The only time I saw them pay me much notice was one day at lunchtime when I was laughing with the other men. The Mexicans sat apart when they ate, just as they worked by themselves. Quiet. I rarely heard them say much to each other. All I could hear were their voices calling out sharply to one another, giving directions. Otherwise, when they stood briefly resting, they talked among themselves in voices too hard to overhear.

—Richard Rodriguez, *Hunger of Memory*

Thornton's command cracked out like a pistol shot. Buck threw himself forward, tightening the traces with a jarring lunge. His whole body was gathered compactly together in the tremendous effort, the muscles writhing and knotting like live things under the silky fur. His great chest was low to the ground, his head forward and down, while his feet were flying like mad, the claws scarring the hard-packed snow in parallel grooves. The sled swayed and trembled, half-started forward. One of his feet slipped, and one man groaned aloud. The sled lurched ahead in what appeared a rapid succession of jerks, though it never really came to a dead stop again ... half an inch ... an inch ... two inches.... The jerks perceptibly diminished; as the sled gained momentum, he caught them up, till it was moving steadily along.

—Jack London, *The Call of the Wild*

YOUR TURN

You've had two opportunities so far, at the end of Chapter 4 and at the end of Chapter 7, to look closely at your own writing and that of a published author, maybe your favorite. Now that you've studied stylistic variations and three types of clauses in Chapters 8, 9, and 10, you're prepared to continue your examination of writing. If you need to reread the directions for this activity, return to pages 75 and 135. The following is another student example to help you get started:

Original: Over the years the unrealized (or half-realized) dreams began to pile up, and reality began to set in.

Revision: Over the years the unrealized (or half-realized) dreams began to pile up, reality setting in.

Reason for the revision: I changed the second independent clause in the sentence into an absolute because it is more concise, and there are lots of compound sentences in my essay already.

KEY TERMS

Absolute phrase	Ellipsis	Redundancy
Anaphora	Figure of speech	Repetition
Anastrophe	Fragment	Style
Antithesis	Isocolon	Word-order variation
Asyndeton	Polysyndeton	

RHETORICAL REMINDERS

Have I taken advantage of the stylistic possibilities of absolute phrases and of various kinds of repetition, word-order variation, antithesis, and ellipsis to heighten the drama and/or call attention to particular passages?

In my series of three or more structures, have I considered order of importance and/or length? (Note: See the section on "Climax" in Chapter 4.)

PUNCTUATION REMINDERS

Have I used any punctuation variations for any series, such as asyndeton or polysyndeton?

Do my punctuation choices help the reader, especially in long sentences with internal punctuation?

PART IV

Your Way with Words

Whate'er you think, good words, I think, were best.
—WILLIAM SHAKESPEARE

Your intuitive understanding of sentences in your native language is more than matched by your remarkable way with words. The sentences that you automatically generate whenever the need arises are, of course, strings of individual words, which you select from an inventory, or **lexicon**, of many thousands of entries—an internal dictionary of sorts.

In reality, however, individual entries in our lexicon and their definitions are quite different from those in a standard dictionary. Our definitions are bound up with experience and memory, so they include all the associations that the word holds for us, negative and positive. For example, think about your own personal definition of *mother* and *kindergarten* and *picnic* and *summer;* it's obvious that no dictionary can describe the pictures that those words conjure up for you. But despite the differences in our mental word pictures, our desire to communicate demands that the words of our lexicon have referents in common with those of the larger community.

Although *knowing a word* may seem straightforward, it involves more than understanding a dictionary definition of that word. To know a word, we must of course know what it means, but we must also know how it is spelled, how it is pronounced, what part of speech it is, which words it goes with, what positions it takes in a sentence, and what its denotations and connotations are. To truly know a word, we must be able to use it effectively.

Words and Word Classes

CHAPTER PREVIEW

Like the grammatical choices we make, the words we choose contribute greatly to the rhetorical effect of our prose. In this chapter we'll look more closely at our lexical choices. By the end of the chapter, you should be able to

- select words with precise meanings;
- describe words in terms of their lexical features;
- identify word classes and parts of speech; and
- revise sentences according to the rules governing words and word order.

YOUR LEXICON

The number of words and their associations stored in your **lexicon** (the inventory of words in your memory) are indeed impressive; equally impressive are the grammatical rules and restrictions that determine how you put your words together into sentences. The following pairs of sentences illustrate how those subconscious rules and restrictions work—or fail to work:

> Kevin sometimes had some trouble with his homework.
>
> *Paul sometimes had a trouble with his homeworks.

> Sue was always being funny.
>
> *Rob was always being tall.

> Pam walked to school.
>
> *Kate walked to home.

You probably recognized that in each case the second sentence is not a sentence that a native speaker would say. A comparison of the two sentences in each pair illuminates the kinds of **lexical features** that affect the way we use words.

The first pair illustrates the restriction that prevents us from saying *homeworks,* a distinction we make between the **countable** and **noncountable nouns** in our lexicon: *Homework* is noncountable; it's a kind of **mass noun;** others in the class are *sugar, water, oil,* and *cotton.* Another noncountable class is that of **abstract nouns,** such as *happiness* and *peace.* The first pair of sentences also demonstrates the restriction built into the **indefinite article,** *a* (or *an*), one of our determiners, or noun signalers. Noncountable nouns, such as *homework* and *happiness,* cannot be signaled by *a,* nor do they have a plural form.

The second pair of sentences illustrates the semantic qualities of adjectives: *Tall* describes an unchanging condition, or state, so it cannot be used with the progressive *is being,* which suggests a dynamic quality. The adjective *funny* includes both possible meanings: *Sue is funny* suggests a permanent characteristic of Sue's personality; *Sue is being funny* suggests a condition of the present moment. The two sentences with *walked* in the list of pairs illustrate how arbitrary, or unsystematic, some of our rules are. Although we do not use the preposition *to* with *home,* we do, of course, use it before most other nouns signaling location, such as *school* or *church.*

The grammar rules illustrated here are obviously not the kind that you studied in your grammar classes; chances are, you were not even aware that you follow rules like these when you speak and write. And certainly you don't want to worry about such rules—or even try to remember them. We are looking at these rules simply to illustrate the kinds of information that our internal lexicon includes and to help you recognize and appreciate that your way with words is truly remarkable.

It is obvious that for a native speaker the restrictions illustrated by these pairs of sentences have somehow become internalized. Linguists sometimes describe such features as a built-in hierarchy, much like the

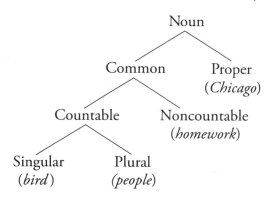

taxonomy that scientists use in classifying plants and animals. Each level—phylum, class, order, family, genus, and species—includes features that differentiate it from the other levels. The farther down the hierarchy, the more specific the details that distinguish the classes. The scheme shown on the previous page illustrates certain features of nouns:

The restrictions built into a word determine its place in the hierarchy: *Homework* is a noncountable, **common noun;** *bird* is a singular, countable, common noun.

Many words in our lexicon can appear in both branches of a node, depending on their context. For example, some nouns can be both countable and noncountable:

> I had <u>a</u> strange <u>experience</u> that day.
>
> I've had <u>experience</u> working with animals.

The countable/noncountable feature applies also to certain signalers of nouns, such as *less/fewer, amount of/number of,* and *much/many.* The commercial that advertises a certain brand of soft drink as having "less calories" than another brand has failed to make the countable/noncountable distinction: *Calories* is a countable noun; the fact that it's plural tells us that. We generally reserve *less* for noncountables; the description of that soft drink should be "*fewer* calories." We would also talk about the "number of calories," not the "amount of calories," just as we would say "many calories," not "much calories." Such noncountables as *water, soccer, love,* and *work* pattern with *amount of* and *much; calories* does not.

FOR GROUP DISCUSSION

A careful writer would avoid writing sentences like these two:

> *There have been less bicycle accidents in the county this year.
>
> *I have also noticed an increase in the amount of bicycles on the roads.

But there's no problem with these:

> There are fewer students enrolled in the advanced ceramics class this year.
>
> There is an increase in the number of students enrolled in the beginning course.

Think about where in the noun hierarchy you would find *accidents, bicycles,* and *students.* How would a careful writer revise those first two sentences? If you were helping a nonnative speaker revise those sentences, how would you explain the changes?

Would that careful writer avoid any of these?

1. There were less than a dozen bicycle accidents in the county this year.

2. We had fewer accidents than last year.

3. We have less dollars than we need.

4. We have less money than we need.

5. We have less than ten dollars to last until payday.

You probably gave that nonnative speaker some advice about the use of *less* and *fewer*. Should you revise your explanation? In what way?

PARTS OF SPEECH

Books about grammar commonly open with the classification of words into parts of speech. You perhaps remember your own language arts classes from junior high, where you began your study of grammar by defining **noun, verb, adjective, adverb,** and such. As you learned in the discussion of the lexicon, our internalized grammar includes rules and restrictions that determine how we use our words. In a sense, those rules constitute definitions of a sort for our word classes; so in this study of the parts of speech we look at those internalized definitions.

We begin by classifying the words of our lexicon into the two broad groups introduced in Chapter 1: **form classes** and **structure classes.** In general, the form classes—nouns, verbs, adjectives, and adverbs—provide the primary lexical content; the structure classes—determiners, pronouns, auxiliaries, qualifiers, prepositions, conjunctions—explain the grammatical or structural relationships. Using a metaphor, we can think of form-class words as the bricks of the language and structure words as the mortar that holds them together.

Although **pronouns** are commonly listed as members of the structure class, they actually straddle the line between the form and structure classes. Many pronouns are like the form classes, insofar as they have variations in form; and they function as nouns, as substitutes for nouns and noun phrases. But they also belong with the structure classes: The possessive and demonstrative pronouns also function as determiners (*my* house, *that* boat). Also, like the structure classes, pronouns are a small, closed class, admitting no new members.

Probably the most striking difference between the form classes and the structure classes is characterized by their numbers. Of the approximately half-million words in our language, the structure words number only in the hundreds. The form classes, however, are large, open classes; new nouns and verbs and adjectives and adverbs regularly enter the language as new technology and new ideas require them. They are sometimes abandoned, too, as the dictionary's *obsolete* and *archaic* labels testify. But with few exceptions, the structure classes remain constant—and limited. We have managed with the same small store of prepositions and conjunctions for generations, with few changes. It's true that we don't hear *whilst* and *betwixt* anymore, nor do we see them in modern prose and poetry, but most of our structure words are identical to those that Shakespeare and his contemporaries used.

THE FORM CLASSES

Nouns, verbs, adjectives, and adverbs are called the form classes because each class has specific forms, a set of inflectional endings, or **inflections,** that distinguishes it from all other classes. As we emphasized in Chapter 1, the feature of form is very useful in defining the class. For example, instead of defining *noun* in its traditional way, as "the name of a person, place, or thing," you can define it according to its form: "A noun is a word that can be made plural and/or possessive." And instead of defining *verb* as a word that shows action, which isn't very accurate, you can use the criterion of form, which applies to every verb, without exception: "A verb is a word that can take an *-s* or an *-ing* form." These are the definitions built into your internal grammar system.

Nouns

Recall from your study of Chapter 1 that **nouns** have an inflection for plural (*-s* or *-es*) and for **possessive case:**

Singular	Plural	Singular Possessive	Plural Possessive
cat	cats	cat's	cats'
treasure	treasures	treasure's	treasures'
fortress	fortresses	fortress's	fortresses'

Not every noun fits into the entire set. For example, noncountable nouns have no plural form. And some nouns have irregular plurals, an inflection other than *-s* or *-es: children, men, feet, mice, formulae.* But certainly the vast majority of our nouns are inflected in this regular way, with *-s* (or *-es*) for those that have a plural form, with *-'s* for singular possessive and *-s'* or (*-es'*) for plural possessive.

It's easy to make mistakes in writing the plural and possessive of some nouns; read aloud the three inflected forms in the set of nouns—*cats, cat's, cats'*—and you'll understand why. In speech we make no distinction; they sound identical. The apostrophe is strictly an orthographic signal, a signal in the written language.

As you may know, the apostrophe is easy to misuse. It's not unusual to see it used mistakenly in plurals, especially if the plural looks a bit strange:

*Fishing license's sold here.

This sign was spotted in the window of a sporting goods store; clearly, someone goofed. And the use of the apostrophe on this poster announcing the schedule of a musical group is also wrong:

>*Now playing Tuesday's at The Lounge.

We use the apostrophe with the *s* in the possessive case, not in the plural: *Joe's Bar & Grill, Tuesday's meeting.*

Probably the best rule to remember is that when you add an *s* sound, you add the letter *s*—in both plural and possessive: *cat, cat's, cats, cats'.* Words that end with an *s* (or an *s*-like sound), such as *fortress* or *church* or *dish,* require a whole syllable for the plural, an *-es: fortress/fortresses, church/churches, dish/dishes.* But we write the singular possessive just as we do with words like *cat:* We simply add *'s: fortress's, church's, dish's.* For the plural possessive, we simply add the apostrophe to the plural, as we do with *cats': fortresses', churches', dishes'.*

Even with nouns that already end in an *s* sound, we add another when we make it possessive. For example, the last name *Jones* ends in an *s* sound. To form the possessive, we add an apostrophe and another *s: Steve Jones's recent bestseller.* We should note two possible exceptions to this rule. Some editors recommend adding just an apostrophe when a name such as *Socrates* ends in the sound *eez: Socrates' reasons.* They also suggest using just an apostrophe after singular common nouns that end in *s: mathematics' contribution.*

Plural-Only Forms.   Some nouns, even when singular in meaning, are plural in form. One such group refers to things that are in two parts— that are bifurcated, or branching: *scissors, shears, clippers, pliers, pants, trousers, slacks, shorts, glasses, spectacles.* As subjects of sentences, these nouns present no problems with **subject–verb agreement:** They take the same verb form as other plural subjects do:

> The scissors were sharper than I had expected.

> The pencils were sharper than I had expected.

Collective Nouns.   Collective nouns such as *family, choir, team, majority, minority*—any noun that names a group of individual members—can be treated as either singular or plural, depending on context and meaning:

> The <u>family have</u> all gone their separate ways. (<u>they</u>)

> (It would sound strange to say, "The family *has* gone *its* separate way.")

> The whole <u>family is</u> celebrating Christmas at home this year. (<u>it</u>)
> The <u>majority</u> of our city council members <u>are</u> Republicans. (<u>they</u>)
> The <u>majority</u> always <u>rules</u>. (<u>it</u>)

Certain noncountable nouns take their number from the modifier that follows the headword:

> The remainder of the building <u>materials are</u> being donated to
>   Habitat for Humanity.
> The rest of the <u>books are</u> being donated to the library.

The headwords *remainder* and *rest* are noncountable nouns in this context; their plurality clearly derives from the modifier, which determines the form of the verb. A singular or noncountable noun in the modifier would change the verb:

> The rest of the <u>manuscript is</u> being donated to the library.
> The remainder of the <u>wood is</u> being donated to Habitat for
>   Humanity.

Some of our **indefinite pronouns,** among them *some, all,* and *enough,* work in the same way.

Proper Nouns.   In contrast to **common nouns,** which refer to general things, places, attributes, and so on, **proper nouns** are those with a specific referent: *Empire State Building, Grand Canyon, William Shakespeare, London, The CBS Evening News, Aunt Mildred, November, Thanksgiving.* Proper nouns name people, buildings, events, holidays, geographic regions and locations, months, and days of the week; they usually begin with capital letters. Most proper nouns are singular; exceptions occur with the names of mountain ranges (*the Rocky Mountains, the Rockies, the Andes*) and island groups (*the Falklands*), which are plural.

EXERCISE 38

Problems of subject–verb agreement sometimes occur when modifiers follow the headword of the subject noun phrase:

> *The <u>instructions</u> on the loan application <u>form was</u> very confusing.
> *This <u>collection of poems</u> by several well-known romantic poets
>   <u>were</u> published in 1910.

In these incorrect examples, the writer has forgotten that the headword determines the number of the noun phrase. To figure out the correct form of the verb, you can use the pronoun-substitution test:

> The instructions [<u>they</u>] <u>were</u> very confusing.
> This collection [<u>it</u>] <u>was</u> published in 1910.

Now test the following sentences to see if headwords and verbs agree:

1. The statement on the income tax form about deductions for children and other dependents were simply unreadable.

2. The type of career that many graduates are hoping to pursue pay high salaries and provide long vacations.

3. Apparently, the use of robots in factories have been responsible for a great deal of worker dissatisfaction.

4. The problems associated with government deregulation have been responsible for the economic plight of several major airlines in recent years.

5. The impact of computers on our lives is comparable to the impact of the industrial revolution.

6. The amount of money and time I spend on computer games is more than I can afford.

Verbs

Although traditional grammar books often describe **verbs** in ways that make them seem complicated, they are really quite simple and systematic, especially when compared with verbs in other languages. With one exception—*be*—English verbs have only five forms—the base and four inflected forms. The forms and uses of verbs are described in Chapter 1, page 7, and in Chapter 3, pages 36–38.

Adjectives

A third open class of words is that of **adjectives,** which can sometimes be recognized by their comparative and superlative inflections, a semantic feature known as **degree:**

<u>Positive</u>	<u>Comparative</u>	<u>Superlative</u>
big	bigger	biggest
silly	sillier	silliest
intelligent	more intelligent	most intelligent

Note that *more* and *most* are variations of the inflections *-er* and *-est.*

   A number of adjectives do not fit this set, for example, *principal* and *medical.* The adjectives that do not take the inflections of degree also do not fit into the adjective test frame:

   The _____ NOUN is very _____.

The adjective test frame is useful in identifying adjectives: A word that fits into both slots is an adjective—and most adjectives do fit:

> The clear example is very clear.
>
> The tough assignment is very tough.

The formula illustrates the two main positions that adjectives take; however, not all adjectives take both positions:

> *The principal reason is very principal.
>
> *The medical advice was very medical.

The test frame, then, can positively identify adjectives: Only an adjective can fit both slots. But it cannot rule them out—that is, just because a word doesn't fit, that doesn't mean it's *not* an adjective.

Adverbs

Our most recognizable **adverbs**—and the most common—are those that are formed by adding *-ly* to the adjective: *slowly, deliberately, exclusively, perfectly.* Most *-ly* adverbs are **adverbs of manner.** Some common adverbs have the same form as the adjective: *fast, far, near, hard, long, high, late.* These are sometimes called **flat adverbs.**

Like adjectives, the *-ly* adverbs and the flat adverbs have comparative and superlative forms:

Positive	Comparative	Superlative
slowly	more slowly	most slowly
fast	faster	fastest

The comparative form of *-ly* adverbs, usually formed by adding *more* rather than *-er,* is fairly common. However, the superlative degree of the *-ly* adverbs—*most suddenly, most slowly, most favorably*—is rare enough in both speech and writing to have impact when used; these forms invariably call attention to themselves and in most cases will carry the main stress:

> The committee was most favorably disposed to accept the plan.
>
> The crime was planned most ingeniously.

There are a number of adverbs, in addition to the flat adverbs, that have no endings to distinguish them as adverbs, nor are they used with *more* or *most.* Instead we recognize them by the information they provide, by their position in the sentence, and often by their movability, as we saw in Chapter 8.

Time: *now, today, nowadays, yesterday, then, already, soon*
Duration: *still*
Frequency: *often, seldom, never, sometimes, always*
Place: *here, there, everywhere, somewhere, elsewhere, upstairs*
Direction: *away*

There are also a number of words that can serve as either prepositions or adverbs: *above, around, behind, below, down, in, inside, out, outside, up.*

Derivational Affixes

Besides the inflectional endings that identify the form classes, we also have an extensive inventory of **derivational affixes,** suffixes and prefixes that provide great versatility to our lexicon by allowing us to shift words from one class to another and/or to alter their meanings. For example, the noun *beauty* becomes a verb with *-ify (beautify),* an adjective with *-ful (beautiful),* and an adverb with *-ly* added to the adjective *(beautifully).*

Some of our suffixes change the meaning rather than the class of the word: *boy/boyhood; citizen/citizenry; king/kingdom; terror/terrorism.* Prefixes, too, generally change the meaning of the word rather than the class: *un*deniable, *pro*-American, *inter*action, *intra*murals, *il*legal, *dis*enchanted. Some prefixes enable us to derive verbs from other classes: *en*chant, *en*courage, *en*able, *de*rail, *de*throne, *be*witch, *be*devil, *dis*able, *dis*agree.

This remarkable ability to expand our lexicon with uncountable new forms provides yet more evidence (if we needed more) for the idea of the inherent language expertise that native speakers possess. With this system of word expansion it's easy to understand why no one has yet come up with a definitive number of words in English. And although we follow certain rules in shifting words from one class to another, there is no real system: We can take a noun like *system,* turn it into an adjective *(systematic),* then a verb *(systematize),* then a noun again *(systematization).* There's also the adverb *systematically* in that set; and the same base, *system,* produces *systemic* and *systemically.* But we can't distinguish between those adjectives that pattern with *-ize* to form verbs *(systematize, legalize, realize, publicize)* and those that pattern with *-ify (simplify, amplify, electrify)* or another affix *(validate, belittle).*

EXERCISE 39

Fill in the blanks with variations of the words shown on the chart, changing or adding derivational affixes to change the word class. In some cases, you may think of more than one possibility.

	NOUN	VERB	ADJECTIVE	ADVERB
1.	grief	_____	_____	_____
2.	_____	vary	_____	_____
3.	_____	_____	_____	ably
4.	_____	defend	_____	_____
5.	_____	_____	_____	quickly
6.	_____	_____	pleasant	_____
7.	type	_____	_____	_____
8.	_____	prohibit	_____	_____
9.	_____	_____	_____	critically
10.	_____	_____	valid	_____
11.	_____	appreciate	_____	_____
12.	danger	_____	_____	_____
13.	_____	accept	_____	_____
14.	_____	_____	pure	_____
15.	_____	steal	_____	_____

THE STRUCTURE CLASSES

The structure classes—**determiners, auxiliaries, qualifiers, prepositions, particles, conjunctions,** and **pronouns**—are by no means new to you. Throughout the discussions of sentence structure, you have been working with these word categories: with the determiners that signal noun phrases, auxiliaries that alter the meaning of verbs, conjunctions that connect ideas, pronouns that serve in a variety of ways, including that of determiner. In some ways, the information you will find on the following pages will be a review of what you studied previously. However, by studying the structure classes in more detail, you will see how together they provide the mortar that holds the form-class bricks in place.

Determiners

You were introduced to the word *determiner* in Chapter 1, where you saw how our most common determiners—the indefinite articles *a, an,* and the **definite article** *the*—signal the noun phrase. You've also seen other word classes that function as determiners: the demonstrative pronouns (*this/that* car, *these/those* cars); possessive pronouns (*my, your, his, her, its, our, their* potential); possessive nouns and noun phrases (*Joe's* book; *our neighbor's* dog). Many of the indefinite pronouns you will read about later in this chapter also function as determiners (*every, each, any* person; *several, many, few, all* people). It's accurate to think of *determiner* as the name of a function rather than a specific word class.

Auxiliaries

When you read about verb tenses in Chapter 3, you learned about **auxiliary verbs.** *Be* is used in the progressive tense, *have* is used in the perfect tense, and both *have* and *be* are used in the present-progressive tense:

> **Progressive:**   *am, is, are, was, were* laughing
> **Perfect:**   *has, have, had* laughed
> **Perfect-Progressive:** *has, have, had been* laughing

The auxiliary *be* also plays a role in forming the passive voice. It joins with the past participle of the main verb: *am, is, are, was, were* intrigued.

   Do is another auxiliary verb, but it does not mark tense or voice. Instead, it is used for three special purposes—to form questions, negations, and emphatic sentences when there is no other auxiliary in the sentence:

> <u>Did</u> you finish your work?
> He <u>didn't</u> agree with the decision.
> I <u>did</u> pay my taxes!

Note that when the main verb is a form of *be, do*-support is not required.

   Another important class of auxiliaries is that of the **modals**—auxiliaries that add shades of meaning to the main verb. In Chapter 3 we listed ten modal auxiliaries: *can, could, will, would, shall, should, may, might, must,* and *ought to.* To this list, we are adding these common **semi-auxiliaries:**

> have (got) to   be going to

Like the modal auxiliary *must, have to* indicates obligation:

> Jeff had to work twenty hours a week.

The semi-auxiliary *be going to* is another way of indicating future time:

> Brook is going to law school next year.

224 Part IV Your Way with Words

Qualifiers

A **qualifier** is a word that modifies an adjective or adverb: It either amplifies or diminishes the meaning of the word it precedes.

> The air was <u>somewhat</u> cold that morning.
>
> The climber <u>very</u> cautiously set her route.

Among the most common words that qualify adjectives and adverbs are *very, quite, rather, too, still, even, much,* and *fairly.* Some adverbs of manner, the *-ly* adverbs, are themselves used as qualifiers with certain adjectives: *dangerously* close, *particularly* harmful, *absolutely* true. In the discussion of power words in Chapter 6, we saw the effect that qualifiers such as these can have on sentence rhythm.

As a rule, it's a good practice to let a single word do all the work it can. *Rushed* and *dashed* and *bolted* are stronger than *ran very fast;* leaves that *flickered* are more delicate in movement than leaves that *moved slightly.* The experienced writer, instead of describing a person as *really nice* or *very nice* or *very beautiful,* might say instead *cooperative* or *charming* or *stunning.* In most cases the difference is not a matter of knowing "big" words or unusual words. The difference is a matter of precision, of choosing words carefully. Such precision, even in small details, can make a difference in the overall effect on the reader.

One further caveat concerns the use of qualifiers with certain adjectives that have **absolute** meanings. Careful writers try to avoid *very* with *perfect* or *unique* or *round.* Although we might say *absolutely perfect* to emphasize the perfection, to say *very perfect* would probably have a negative effect on the reader. And certainly as careful users of language we should respect the meaning of *unique:* "one of a kind." *Round* and *square* have meanings in our lexicon other than their geometric absolutes, so it is possible for the shape of an object to be "nearly round" or "almost square." But qualifiers such as *very* or *quite* are best reserved for other kinds of qualities.

EXERCISE 40

As you read the following sentences, pay particular attention to the italicized words; replace them with words that are more precise.

1. The guest speaker's *really strong* denunciation of our foreign policy seemed *quite out of place* at the awards banquet.

2. The foreman gives his orders in a *very abrupt* manner.

3. It is usually *an absolute waste of time* to argue with radicals of any persuasion; they are unlikely to be influenced by mere reason.

4. The basketball players seemed *really tired* as they took the court for the second half.

5. The choir members were *really excited* about their summer trip to Europe.

6. The members of Congress were *really very surprised* at the extent of voter cynicism toward Washington.

....

Prepositions

Like many of the words you have studied in this chapter, **prepositions** are small words that have a large impact. To appreciate their contribution to meaning, try reading the following passage from Michael Chabon's novel *The Amazing Adventures of Kavalier and Klay* without the prepositions (shown in parentheses):

> (Atop) the thick concrete parapet (of) the eight-sixth floor, (like) a bright jagged hold punched (in) the clouds, balanced a smiling man (in) a mask and a gold-and-indigo suit. The suit clung (to) his lanky frame, dark blue (with) an iridescent glint (of) silk. He had (on) a pair (of) gold swim trunks, and (on) the front (of) his blue jersey was a thick gold appliqué, (like) the initial (on) a letterman's jacket, (in) the shape (of) a skeleton key.

You have probably discovered that without its prepositions the passage has lost not only its meaning but also its sense of rhythm.

The following are common one-word prepositions:

about	above	across	after
against	along	among	around
at	before	behind	below
beneath	beside	between	by
down	during	except	for
from	in	inside	into
of	on	over	past
since	through	to	toward
under	underneath	until	up
upon	with	within	without

Some prepositions consist of more than one word. Here is a list of common **phrasal prepositions:**

according to	because of	next to
ahead of	as for	instead of
in back of	in front of	in spite of

EXERCISE 41

Prepositions most frequently precede noun phrases, but they can precede other types of nominals as well. Locate the prepositions in the following sentences and identify the nominals that follow them (noun phrases, pronouns, gerunds, nominal clauses).

1. The canyon formed in a relatively short period of time.

2. We were interested in exploring the canyon, so we spoke to the guide about camping overnight.

3. We listened closely to what the guide told us about the trail leading into the canyon.

4. We trekked fifteen miles without really knowing where we were headed.

Particles

Particles join primarily one-syllable verbs such as *come, go, get,* and *take* to form **phrasal verbs.** The most common particles are words you've seen on the list of common one-word prepositions: *up, out, on, in, off,* and *down.* However, particles differ from prepositions: They combine with verbs to produce a new meaning.

> I <u>looked up</u> your phone number. (particle)
> I looked <u>up the narrow street</u>. (preposition)

Another distinguishing feature of some particles is their movability.

> I <u>looked</u> your number <u>up</u>.

Phrasal verbs can often be replaced by a single word, so if your rhetorical situation calls for a formal tone, consider replacing the phrasal verb with a single word.

> We have to ~~turn in~~ *submit* the report tomorrow.

For more information on this topic, review pages 125–126 in Chapter 7.

Conjunctions

In Chapter 4 you first learned about **coordinating conjunctions** (*and, but, or, nor, for, yet,* and *so*) and **subordinating conjunctions** (*when, before, if, because, although,* etc.). To writers, these words are particularly important because they indicate reasoning. They show how entities or ideas are related. The following list contains examples of conjunctions and the relationships they indicate.

Addition:	*and*
Alternate:	*or*
Cause or reason:	*for, because, since, as long as*
Contrast:	*but, yet, while, whereas*
Result:	*so, so that*

You'll also want to review the transitional phrases and the conjunctions with an adverbial meaning, the conjunctive adverbs, which you studied in Chapter 4.

PRONOUNS

We looked briefly at pronouns in earlier chapters when we substituted them for noun phrases in order to demonstrate whether the subject of the sentence was singular or plural and to figure out where the subject ended and the predicate began:

> Jenny *[she]* graduated from nursing school in 2011.
>
> The gymnasium *[it]* needs a new roof.

Those substitutions—*she* and *it*—are among the **personal pronouns,** the kind you probably recognize most readily. But there are many other classes of pronouns as well—**reflexive, demonstrative, relative, indefinite,** and others. In this discussion we look at all the pronouns, concentrating especially on those members of various classes that sometimes cause problems for writers.

Personal Pronouns

The easiest way to understand the system of personal pronouns is to first understand the concepts of **number, person,** and **case.** *Number* refers to the singular/plural distinction. *Person* is related to point of view, the relationship of the writer to the reader. The reference of the first person includes the writer; second person refers to the person or people addressed; third person refers to "third parties," someone or something other than the writer or the person addressed. (Notice that the form of the second person is the same regardless of number.) The choice of *case* is determined by the pronoun's function in the sentence—**subjective, objective,** or **possessive.**

Case	First-Person Singular	First-Person Plural	Second-Person Singular and Plural	Third-Person Singular	Third-Person Plural
Subjective	I	we	you	he, she, it	they
Objective	me	us	you	him, her, it	them
Possessive	my (mine)	our (ours)	your (yours)	his, her, its (his, hers, its)	their (theirs)

The Missing Pronoun. This set of personal pronouns may look complete—and, unfortunately, it does include all we have. But, in fact, it has a gap, one that is responsible for a great deal of the sexism in our language. The gap occurs in the third-person singular column, the column that already includes three pronouns representing masculine (*he*), feminine (*she*), and neuter (*it*). You'd think that those three would be up to the task of covering all contingencies, but they're not. For third-person singular we have no choice that is gender-neutral. In the past when writers needed a pronoun to refer to an unidentified person, such as *the teacher* or *a student,* they used the masculine:

A reporter should leave out <u>his</u> personal opinion.

But that usage is considered **sexist language** and so is no longer accepted practice. Times and attitudes change, and we have come to recognize the power of language in shaping those attitudes. So an important step in reshaping society's view of women has been to eliminate the automatic use of *he* and *his* and *him* when someone referred to could just as easily be female.

One common, but not necessarily effective, way to solve the problem of the pronoun gap is with *he or she, him or her,* or *his or her:*

A reporter should leave out <u>his or her</u> personal opinion.

The occasional use of both masculine and feminine pronouns works in many situations, but more than one in a paragraph will change the rhythm of the prose, slow the reader down, and call attention to itself when such attention is simply uncalled for.

Because we do have a gender-neutral pronoun in the plural, often the **antecedent** noun (the noun the pronoun stands for) can be changed to plural:

<u>Reporters</u> should leave out <u>their</u> personal opinions.

See also the section called "The *Everyone/Their* Issue" on pages 235–237.

Here, then, are some of the ways in which you can make up for the pronoun gap when you write and/or revise your own sentences:

1. USE THE PLURAL:

> Every writer should be aware of the power of language when <u>he</u> chooses <u>his</u> pronouns.
> *Revision:* Writers should be aware of the power of language when <u>they</u> choose <u>their</u> pronouns.

2. USE *HE OR SHE* IF YOU CAN USE IT ONLY ONCE:

> *Revision:* Every writer should be aware of the power of language when <u>he or she</u> chooses pronouns.

3. AVOID *HIS* AS A DETERMINER, EITHER BY SUBSTITUTING ANOTHER ONE OR, IN SOME CASES, DELETING THE DETERMINER:

> The writer of the news story should have kept <u>his</u> opinion out of it.
> *Revision:* The writer of the news story should have kept (<u>all</u>) opinion out of it.

4. TURN THE FULL CLAUSE INTO AN ELLIPTICAL CLAUSE OR A VERB PHRASE, THUS ELIMINATING THE PROBLEM SUBJECT:

> *Revision:* Every writer should be aware of the power of language when <u>choosing pronouns</u>.

This fourth method of revision is often a good possibility because the offending pronoun nearly always shows up in the second clause of a passage, often as part of the same sentence. In our example, we have turned the complete dependent clause into an elliptical clause—that is, a clause with something missing. In this case what's missing is the subject. (The elliptical clause, which may have hidden pitfalls, is discussed in Chapter 8.)

5. REWRITE THE ADVERBIAL CLAUSE AS A RELATIVE (WHO) CLAUSE:

> When <u>a person</u> buys a house, he should shop carefully for the lowest interest rate.
> *Revision:* <u>A person who</u> buys a house should shop carefully for the lowest interest rate.

The relative clause, with its neutral *who,* eliminates the necessity of a personal pronoun to rename *a person.*

6. CHANGE THE POINT OF VIEW:

> *Second person:* As a writer <u>you</u> should be aware of the power of language when you choose (<u>your</u>) pronouns.
> *First person:* As writers, <u>we</u> should be aware of the power of language when we choose (<u>our</u>) pronouns.

Case Errors. Among the most common pronoun errors that writers make are errors of case. As the chart on page 228 shows, case refers to the change that pronouns undergo on the basis of their function in the sentence. The subject of the sentence, of course, takes the **subjective case.**

> <u>I</u> finished the report on time.

When a pronoun is in the object position (as a direct object or an indirect object), we use the **objective case:**

> My roommate helped <u>me</u> with my math assignment. (direct object)
> Marie gave <u>him</u> a gift. (indirect object)

We also use the objective case for the object of the preposition:

> I walked to town <u>with him</u>.
> I walked to town <u>with Joe and him</u>.
> Joe walked to town <u>with him and me</u>.
> Marie walked <u>between Joe and me</u>.

Pronouns in the possessive case function as determiners. The alternative forms of the possessive case, shown on the chart in parentheses, are used when the headword of the noun phrase, the noun, is deleted:

> This is <u>my bicycle</u>. ⟶ This bicycle is <u>mine</u>.
> This is <u>her bicycle</u>. ⟶ This is <u>hers</u>.

We should note that nouns in the possessive case function in the same way:

> This is <u>Pete's bicycle</u>. ⟶ This is <u>Pete's</u>.

Most errors of case that writers make occur with the subjective and objective cases. And most of them probably occur as the result of **hypercorrection**—making a correction when one isn't called for:

> *There's no rivalry between <u>my brother and I</u>.
> *The supervisor told <u>Jenny and I</u> that we might get a raise.

In both cases, the noun/pronoun compound is functioning as an object, so the correct pronoun choice is *me,* not *I.* This is a common error, however, possibly made because people remember being corrected by their parents or teachers when they said such sentences as

> Me and Bill are going for a bike ride. ("No, dear. Bill and *I.*")
> Bill and me are going to be late. ("No, dear. Bill and *I.*")

As a consequence of those early lessons, some people simply find it hard to write *my brother and me* or *Jenny and me,* no matter what function the pronoun has in the sentence. The correct version of those sentences is as follows:

> There's no rivalry between <u>my brother and me</u>.
> The supervisor told <u>Jenny and me</u> that we might get a raise.

If we substituted pronouns for the complete noun phrases, the sentences would be written as follows:

> There's no rivalry <u>between us</u>.
> The supervisor told <u>us</u> that we might get a raise.

We wouldn't consider for a moment using *we.*

The Unwanted Apostrophe.   Another common pronoun error occurs with the pronoun *it:*

> *The cat caught it's tail in the door.

Here's the rule that's been broken with the word *it's:*

> **Personal pronouns have no apostrophes in the possessive case.**

If you check the chart showing the case of the personal pronouns on page 228, you'll see that there are no apostrophes. Notice that the rule also applies to other commonly confused pairs:

> *your* (possessive)/*you're (you are)*
> *their* (possessive)/*they're (they are)*

Here's what you have to remember—and check for: When you add *'s* to *it,* you're actually writing *it is* or *it has;* when you add *'re* to *you* or *they,* you're writing *you are* or *they are.* Unlike nouns, possessive pronouns have no apostrophe. The possessive *whose* is another word commonly confused with a contraction, in this case *who's* (*who is*). Because *it, you, they,* and *who* are such common words, and because the unwanted apostrophe is such an easy error to slip in, you should probably, during your final proofreading, make a point of double-checking all instances of *its* and *it's, whose* and *who's, your* and *you're,* and *their* and *they're*—and even *there!*

The Ambiguous Antecedent.   Another error that turns up with personal pronouns is the ambiguous **antecedent**—the pronoun that has more than one possible referent:

> When Bob accidentally backed the car into the toolshed, <u>it</u> was
>   wrecked beyond repair.

Here we can't be sure if the pronoun *it* refers to the car or to the toolshed.

> Just before they were scheduled to leave, Shelley told Ann that <u>she</u>
>   couldn't go after all.

Here we may suspect that *she* refers to Shelley—but we can't be sure. And the careful writer wouldn't make us guess.

> Uncle Dick and Aunt Teresa took the kids to <u>their</u> favorite restau-
>   rant for lunch.

Whose favorite restaurant?
   The ambiguous antecedent often gets resolved by the context; within a sentence or two the reader will very likely understand the writer's intention. But not always. And, of course, the reader shouldn't have to wait. It's the writer's responsibility to make sure antecedents are clear.

Reflexive Pronouns

Reflexive pronouns are those formed by adding *-self* or *-selves* to a form of the personal pronoun: *myself, ourselves, yourself, yourselves, himself, herself, itself, themselves.* The standard rule for using the reflexive is straightforward. We use it as an object in a clause when its antecedent is the subject:

> <u>I</u> glanced at <u>myself</u> in the mirror.
> <u>Jack</u> cooked an omelet for Barbara and <u>himself</u>.

The tendency toward hypercorrection occurs with the reflexives as well as with the personal pronouns. It's quite common to hear the reflexive where the standard rule calls for *me,* the straight objective case:

*Tony cooked dinner for Carmen and <u>myself</u>.

*The boss promised Pam and <u>myself</u> a year-end bonus.

Note that the antecedent of *myself* does not appear in either sentence. Another fairly common nonstandard usage occurs when speakers use *myself* in place of *I* as part of a compound subject:

*Ted and <u>myself</u> decided to go out and celebrate.

These nonstandard ways of using the reflexive are probably related to emphasis as well as to hypercorrection. Somehow the two-syllable *myself* sounds more emphatic than either *me* or *I*.

The nonstandard use of the reflexive occurs only with the first-person pronoun, *myself*, not with *himself* or *herself*. In the case of third person, the personal pronoun and the reflexive produce different meanings:

John cooked dinner for Jenny and <u>himself</u> (John).

John cooked dinner for Jenny and <u>him</u> (someone else).

This second interpretation assumes that another person, a known "someone else," is part of the situation, otherwise, *him* refers to *John*.

Intensive Pronouns

When we use the reflexive to add emphasis to a noun, we call it the **intensive reflexive pronoun.** It can appear in a number of positions:

I <u>myself</u> prefer classical music.

I prefer classical music <u>myself</u>.

<u>Myself</u>, I prefer classical music.

Each of these versions produces a different rhythm pattern. In the first version, the main stress falls on *myself*, whereas in the second it probably falls on *classical*. In the third, added stress is given to *I*.

EXERCISE 42

Edit the following passages, paying special attention to the pronoun problems.

1. Claire has always been interested in children and plans to make that her profession when she graduates. Both Claire and myself are majoring in early childhood education.

2. The goal of animal-rights activists is not just to prevent animal cruelty, as they advocated in earlier times, but also to promote the idea that they have intrinsic value, that they have a right to

live. As a result of their efforts, the Public Health Service has revised their policy regarding the treatment of laboratory animals.

3. When my sister Beth asked me to go to Salem with her to visit
   our grandmother, I had no idea that she was sick. We were almost
   there before she told me she had experienced stomach cramps
   since early morning. Our grandmother took one look at her,
   called the doctor, and drove her to the hospital, which turned out
   to be a good decision. It turned out to be appendicitis.

Reciprocal Pronouns

Each other and *one another* are known as the **reciprocal pronouns.** They
serve either as determiners (in the possessive case) or as objects, referring
to previously named nouns: *Each other* refers to two nouns; *one another*
refers to three or more, a distinction that careful writers generally observe.

> David and Ann help <u>each other</u>. They even do <u>each other's</u>
> laundry.
> All the students in my peer group help <u>one another</u> with their
> rough drafts.

Demonstrative Pronouns

As you recall from Chapter 5, a **demonstrative pronoun** (*this, that, these,*
or *those*) can be a substitute for a noun phrase (or other nominal structure)
as well as a signal for one (that is, when they function as a determiner):

<u>These old shoes and hats</u>	will be perfect for the costumes.
↓	
<u>These</u>	will be perfect for the costumes.

The role of demonstrative pronouns in cohesion is discussed on pages
91–93.

Indefinite Pronouns

The **indefinite pronouns** include a number of words that we use as
determiners:

Quantifiers:	*enough, few, fewer, less, little, many, much, several, more, most*
Universals:	*all, both, every, each*
Partitives:	*any, either, neither, none, some*

One is also commonly used as a pronoun (as are the other cardinal numbers—two, three, etc.) along with its negative, *none.* As a pronoun, *one* (or *ones*) often replaces only the headword, rather than the entire noun phrase:

> The blue shoes that I bought yesterday will be perfect for the trip.
>
> The blue ones that I bought yesterday will be perfect for the trip.

The personal pronoun, on the other hand, would replace the entire noun phrase:

> They will be perfect for the trip.

The universal *every* and the partitives *any, no,* and *some* can be expanded with *-body, -thing,* and *-one:*

$$
\text{some} \begin{cases} \text{body} \\ \text{thing} \\ \text{one} \end{cases}
\text{every} \begin{cases} \text{body} \\ \text{thing} \\ \text{one} \end{cases}
\text{any} \begin{cases} \text{body} \\ \text{thing} \\ \text{one} \end{cases}
\text{no} \begin{cases} \text{body} \\ \text{thing} \\ \text{one (two words)} \end{cases}
$$

These pronouns can take modifiers in the form of clauses:

> Anyone *who wanted extra credit* volunteered for the experiment.

They can also be modified by participles or participial phrases:

> Everyone *reporting late for practice* took fifteen laps.

And by prepositional phrases:

> Nothing *on the front page* interests me anymore.

And, unlike most nouns, they can be modified by adjectives that follow the headword:

> My grandfather couldn't eat anything *sweet.*

Notice the strong stress that you put on the adjective following the pronoun.

The *Everyone/Their* Issue. The question of number—that is, whether a word is singular or plural—often comes up in reference to the indefinite pronouns *everyone* and *everybody.* In form they are singular, so as subjects they take the *-s* form of the verb or auxiliary in the present tense:

> Everyone is leaving the room at once.

An illustration of the scene described by this sentence, however, would show more than one person—more than two or three, probably—leaving the room, even though the form of *everyone* is singular. In spite of this anomaly, the issue of subject–verb agreement is not a problem.

But often such a sentence calls for the possessive pronoun. And when it does, the traditional choice has been the singular masculine:

> Everyone picked up <u>his</u> books and left the room.

However, that makes no sense—even if the *everyone* refers to men only. And it certainly makes no sense if the group of people includes women. The only reasonable solution is the plural, in spite of the singular form of *everyone:*

> Everyone picked up <u>their</u> books and left the room.

Traditionally, this usage has been frowned upon. Recently, however, editors of *The American Heritage Dictionary* reported that a majority of their usage experts accept the use of *they, their,* or *them* with indefinite pronouns such as *everyone* and *anyone,* which are grammatically singular but notionally plural. The following sentence from President Obama's State of the Union address in 2012 accords with this new usage judgment:

> <u>Anyone</u> who says the United States is losing influence doesn't know what <u>they</u>'re talking about.

Nevertheless, some members of your audience may still expect you to follow the traditional rule. If you feel uneasy about using the plural, you can always avoid the problem by substituting a different subject:

> <u>All of the students</u> picked up their books and left the room.

English is such a versatile language that we nearly always have alternatives.

EXERCISE 43

Edit the following passages, paying particular attention to the nonstandard use of pronouns and to those with unclear referents.

1. I recall with great pleasure the good times that us children had at our annual family reunions when I was young. Our cousins and ourselves, along with some younger aunts and uncles, played volleyball and softball until dark. They were a lot of fun.

2. Aunt Yvonne and Uncle Bob always brought enough homemade ice cream for them and everyone else as well. There was great rivalry, I remember, between my brother and I over who could eat the most. Nearly everyone made a pig of himself.

3. It seemed to my cousin Terry and I that the grownups were different people at those family reunions. That may be true of family reunions everywhere.

4. The adults seemed to act like us kids. Once, in a water fight, my uncle started chasing my brother and myself with a huge bucket of water. Because him and I were faster, Uncle Bob couldn't catch us. When he wasn't looking, his own kids pelted him with water balloons. That always makes us laugh when we get together.

··

KEY TERMS

Absolute adjective
Abstract noun
Adjective
Adverb
Ambiguity
Antecedent
Auxiliary verb
Case
Collective noun
Common noun
Comparative degree
Conjunction
Coordinating
   conjunction
Countable noun
Definite article
Degree
Demonstrative
   pronoun
Derivational affix
Determiner

Flat adverb
Form classes
Hypercorrection
Indefinite article
Indefinite pronoun
Inflection
Intensive reflexive
   pronoun
Lexical feature
Lexicon
Manner adverb
Mass noun
Modal auxiliary
Noncountable noun
Noun
Number
Objective case
Particle
Person
Personal pronoun
Phrasal preposition

Phrasal verb
Plural-only form
Positive degree
Possessive case
Preposition
Pronoun
Proper noun
Qualifier
Reciprocal pronoun
Reflexive pronoun
Semi-auxiliary
Sexist language
Structure classes
Subjective case
Subject–verb
   agreement
Subordinating
   conjunction
Superlative degree
Verb

RHETORICAL REMINDERS

Word Choice

Have I selected words with clear and precise meanings?

Subject–Verb Agreement

Have I been careful to recognize the singular/plural meaning of the subject noun phrase, especially when collective nouns, plural-only forms, and indefinite pronouns are involved?

Sexist Language

Have I avoided sexism in my choice of pronouns?

Case

Have I used the objective case (*me, him, her*) for pronouns in the object positions (direct object, indirect object, object of the preposition)?

Have I resisted the urge to hypercorrect?

Antecedents

Have I avoided ambiguous antecedents? Does my reader understand the referent of every *he, his, him, she, they, it, this, that?*

Reflexives

Have I used the reflexive pronoun (*-self, -selves*) only in object positions and only when its referent precedes it in the clause?

Auxiliaries

Is my choice of modal auxiliary or semi-auxiliary effective?

Qualifiers

Have I used qualifiers sparingly, choosing instead precise adjectives, adverbs, or verbs whenever possible?

Conjunctions

Do the conjunctions in my paper accurately express my reasoning?

PUNCTUATION REMINDERS

Have I kept apostrophes out of possessive pronouns (*its, whose, yours, theirs*)?

Have I remembered that the apostrophe added to a noun turns it into the possessive case: *cat/cat's* (singular); *cats/cats'* (plural)?

PART V

Punctuation

Punctuation is a reasoned art.
—REBECCA BRITTENHAM AND HILDEGARD HOELLER

In the preceding chapters, you learned about the structure of sentences: their basic units and the options we have for expanding and combining them. An important consideration throughout the book has been the effect of those options on the reader—hence the word *rhetorical* in the title. Those rhetorical effects extend to punctuation, so in addition to the possibilities for constructing sentences, you have learned about both the required and the optional punctuation rules that apply.

As you might expect, the conventions of punctuation have changed through the centuries. Early punctuation practices, designed to assist in the oral reading of medieval manuscripts, eventually evolved into our modern system, based more on structural boundaries than on the oral reader's needs. By the nineteenth century, the system we know today was generally in place. However, even though our punctuation rules are well established, they still include a great deal of flexibility. Today we tend toward an "open" or "light" style—omitting commas, for example, where the boundaries are apparent without them.

In Chapter 13 we look more closely at the punctuation decisions that writers make and the rhetorical impact those decisions have. At the end of the chapter you will find a brief glossary of the punctuation rules described in the earlier chapters, covering commas, colons, dashes, semicolons, and parentheses, along with a few other concerns that writers must address in connection with these and other punctuation marks. This section should serve as a handy reference.

Punctuation: Its Purposes, Its Hierarchy, and Its Rhetorical Effects

---

CHAPTER PREVIEW

You've learned many punctuation rules so far. In this chapter we look more closely at the punctuation decisions that writers make and the rhetorical impact those decisions have. At the end of the chapter you'll find a brief glossary of all the rules described in earlier chapters, along with a few other concerns that writers often have to address. By reading this chapter and using the glossary as a reference, you'll be able to

- discuss the punctuation choices specific authors have made; and
- explain your own punctuation decisions.

THE PURPOSES OF PUNCTUATION MARKS

In *A Linguistic Study of American Punctuation,* Charles F. Meyer classifies the purposes of punctuation into three categories: syntactic, prosodic, and semantic. Although you may not recognize these three words, they do describe the punctuation principles you have been studying in the preceding chapters.

> **Syntax** refers to the structure of sentences—the main subject matter of this book. When you learned about the parts of the sentence and their relationships and their expansions, you were learning about syntax.
>
> **Prosody** is the study of rhythm and intonation.
>
> **Semantics** is the study of meaning.

Syntax

Linguists generally agree that the purpose underlying most of our punctuation rules is syntactic: In other words, the structure of the sentence determines the punctuation marks it will contain. A good example of a syntactically based punctuation rule is the one you learned in connection with the sentence patterns in Chapter 2: "Do not mark boundaries of the required sentence units with punctuation." This rule is clearly based on syntax, on sentence structure. In fact, syntax overrides all considerations of rhythm. Even though the reader may have to stop for breath between sentence units, that pause is not marked by a comma. Here's an example that requires an extra breath—but has no boundaries that take punctuation:

> The images and information sent back by *Voyager 2* have given space scientists here on Earth enough information about four of our distant planets to keep them busy for years to come.

The predicate contains an indirect object and a direct object with two postnoun modifiers, but not one of those boundaries calls for punctuation.

Prosody

We often revise a sentence in order to change the way that the reader will read it—to change its rhythm pattern. For example, the stress pattern of the sentence you just read would change if the first two words were reversed:

> Often we revise a sentence . . .

With this word order the reader will probably put more stress on *often*. To guarantee that emphasis, we can follow *often* with a comma. You'll recall from the discussion of sentence rhythm in Chapter 6 that the visual signal of a comma causes the reader to give added length and stress to the preceding word.

> Often, we revise a sentence . . .

This, then, is an example where the purpose of the punctuation mark can be attributed to prosody.

In Chapter 11 we saw another example in the discussion of the coordinate series, when we compared the rhythm patterns of two punctuation styles:

1. You have your own style of writing, just as you have your own style of walking and whistling and wearing your hair.
2. You have your own style of writing, just as you have your own style of walking, whistling, wearing your hair.

It is the rhythm of (2) that changes the message: It has an open-ended quality, as if to suggest, "I could go on and on with the list." Again, the purpose of the punctuation is to produce that rhythm. In this case, however, we would have to say that semantics is also involved: The punctuation affects both the rhythm and the meaning.

Semantics

One situation in which semantics, or meaning, determines the need for punctuation is that of the nonrestrictive phrase or clause, as we saw in the discussion of noun modifiers in Chapter 9. Syntax, of course, determines the boundaries of that modifier, but semantic considerations dictate the presence or absence of the commas: Does the modifier define the noun or simply comment on it?

This pair of sentences illustrates the distinction:

1. The man sitting by the window is talking to himself.
2. My mother, sitting by the window, is talking to herself.

We can assume in (1) that the scene includes at least one other man and that the purpose of the participial phrase is to identify the referent of the subject noun phrase, *the man.* That kind of identification is unnecessary in (2), where the subject noun phrase, *my mother,* has only one possible referent—no matter how many other women are present. Here the participial phrase merely comments.

The purpose of the punctuation is perhaps even more obviously a semantic one for the writer who has to decide between the following:

1. My sister Mary studied global health.
2. My sister, Mary, studied global health.

The sentence without commas implies that the writer has more than one sister. Clearly, it's the meaning that dictates the use of the comma.

Meyer cites the following pair of sentences to illustrate another situation where the comma changes the meaning:

1. Earlier negotiations were planned.
2. Earlier, negotiations were planned.

Here the punctuation has actually changed the class of the word *earlier.* In (1) it is an adjective, a modifier of the noun; in (2) it is an adverb, modifying the whole sentence.

In both of these examples, where the comma changes the meaning, it also alters the structure, the syntax, of the sentence. And it changes the rhythm. So these are probably good examples to illustrate the combination of all three punctuation purposes: syntactic, prosodic, and semantic.

THE HIERARCHY OF PUNCTUATION

If you were asked to place the parts of the sentence into a hierarchy, starting with *word,* the result would look like this:

> word
>
> phrase
>
> clause
>
> sentence

The hierarchy of punctuation works in much the same way, usually in reverse order, with *sentence* at the top.

In the study of punctuation cited earlier, Meyer describes the hierarchy, the levels of punctuation, according to the kinds of boundaries that a particular punctuation mark encloses. For example, occupying the top level are the period, the question mark, and the exclamation point, all of which define sentence boundaries—and only sentence boundaries.

At the next level are the colon, the dash, and parentheses, all of which can define not only the boundaries of independent clauses, but also the boundaries of words, phrases, and dependent clauses.

The semicolon occupies the next level. It also defines clause boundaries, but in a much more limited way than the other three; and it has only one other role—to separate items in the coordinate series.

At the bottom level of the hierarchy is the comma, which can define the boundaries of words, phrases, and dependent clauses, but not the boundaries of independent clauses (unless a coordinating conjunction precedes it).

Here then is the hierarchy of punctuation marks:

> period, question mark, exclamation point
>
> colon, dash, parentheses
>
> semicolon
>
> comma

The hierarchy is obviously not a measure of importance or of frequency. In fact, the comma, although it occupies the lowest level, is our most frequent punctuation mark; and the exclamation point, one of three marks at the highest level, is the least frequent. The purpose of this scheme, rather, is to recognize the level of the functions that these marks can perform. For example, in Chapter 10 we looked at the following sentence in connection with appositives:

> Three committees—program, finance, and local arrangements—
> were set up to plan the convention.

The word boundaries here, marked by commas, are subordinate to those of the phrase boundaries; in order to distinguish the two levels, then, we use two different punctuation marks. The dashes mark the higher, or superordinate, level. To use commas for both levels of punctuation would make the sentence difficult to read. In the following version of the sentence, where the word boundaries are taken care of by conjunctions rather than commas, we may use commas for the phrase boundaries:

> Three committees, program and finance and local arrangements,
> were set up to plan the convention.

However, we could have retained the dashes in this revision, even though the phrase has no internal commas. Dashes would make the series stand out more strongly.

Because commas play so many roles in the sentence—providing boundaries for words and phrases and clauses—a sentence, especially a long one, can sometimes become heavy with commas:

> During the second two-year stretch of a term in office, the presi-
> dent may have to be on defensive, even with the nominating
> party, and, when, as frequently happens, this party loses a num-
> ber of Senate and House seats in the midterm election, that sec-
> ond stretch can become even more defensive.

This sentence contains many levels of punctuation, with its coordinate independent clauses. The first clause contains opening and closing adverbial phrases, both of which are set off by commas. The other independent clause includes a dependent *as*-clause embedded in a dependent *when*-clause. Yet the only internal punctuation mark used for all of these levels is the comma.

One way to improve the sentence, to make it clearer for the reader, is to consider other punctuation marks that perform at some of these levels. One obvious boundary where we can use different punctuation is at the clause level—that is, to mark the two independent clauses—in place of the comma following *party*. We know that colons, dashes, and semicolons can all mark the boundary of an independent clause. In this case the best choice is the semicolon, because of its "and" meaning. (You'll recall that the colon generally connects two independent clauses with a "namely" or "here it comes" meaning—rather than "and.") Another choice is to begin a new sentence here. The semicolon, however, makes clear the close connection of the two independent clauses.

Next we should look at the comma following *and:* What is its function? It works with a partner, the comma after *election,* to set off the dependent *when*-clause. Is there any other mark that can do that job? In this position, the answer is probably "no." (On some occasions, dashes or parentheses can enclose dependent clauses, as we show later in this discussion.) But now that we've substituted a semicolon, it is possible to eliminate *and.* After all, the reason for the *and* was the comma, which we've deleted. (You'll recall the rule about connecting two independent clauses with a comma: It requires a conjunction.)

Already our sentence looks better—and reads much more easily:

> During the second two-year stretch of a term in office, the president may have to be on the defensive, even with the nominating party; when, as frequently happens, his party loses a number of Senate and House seats in the midterm election, that second stretch can become even more defensive.

We're also using a comma here to set off the opening prepositional phrase. There's nothing else that can do that job, so that one has to stay. And we're using commas to set off the *as*-clause within the *when*-clause. Have we any other choice? Well, yes. We could mark that boundary with dashes—if we think it deserves the extra attention that dashes provide:

> During the second two-year stretch of a term in office, the president may have to be on the defensive, even with the nominating party; when—as frequently happens—this party loses a number of Senate and House seats in the midterm election, that second stretch can become even more defensive.

You may have noticed another place where a dash would fit: in the first clause after *defensive,* to set off the adverbial *even* phrase—in this case, only one dash, not a pair. But we probably don't want dashes in both places: They lose their special quality when they're used too often. And twice in one sentence is probably too often. We'll want to try it out in that earlier spot, just to see the difference. But chances are we'll leave the dashes where we have them now, where they replace two commas.

Now compare the two versions of that sentence—the original and the last revision. They're both punctuated "correctly." But certainly the difference makes clear how important it is for the writer to understand the various boundaries that require punctuation, to know how the tools of punctuation work.

EXERCISE 44

Revise the following passages, turning some of the sentences into modifiers. Experiment with commas, colons, and dashes.

1. The cost of repairs to the nation's public transportation facilities is an expenditure that cannot be delayed much longer if the system is to survive. Roads, bridges, and railroads are all in need of repair.

2. To many people, the mushroom is a lowly fungus. It has little food value. To other people, it is a gourmet's delight.

3. The paper nautilus octopus is a rare marine animal. It normally lives in the coastal waters of Japan. It was found recently in the squid nets off Santa Catalina in California.

4. The ivory-billed woodpecker is one of North America's rarest birds. It is North America's largest woodpecker. There have been documented sightings of this woodpecker in recent years.

THE RHETORICAL EFFECTS OF PUNCTUATION

The subtitle of this book is *Grammatical Choices, Rhetorical Effects.* Those grammatical choices, of course, include punctuation choices, and such choices also have rhetorical effects. In Chapter 4 you studied a variety of ways to combine the clauses into a compound sentence with the comma, the semicolon, and the colon. These four variations offer as many choices as you will ever need in this situation for eliciting appropriate responses in your reader:

1. I loved the book, but I hated the movie.
2. I loved the book; I hated the movie.
3. I loved the book; however, I hated the movie.
4. I loved the book: It made me want to try to write my own memoir.

The first one we might think of as the basic compound sentence rule, with fairly equal emphasis on the two clauses. In (2) and (3), the greater pause that the semicolon provides puts more emphasis on the second clause. The addition of *however* in (3) adds a note of deliberation, a degree of thoughtfulness in coming to a decision about the movie. The colon in (4) commands special attention: The reader expects to learn why I loved the book.

How about using just the comma—in other words, a comma splice? The sentences are certainly short and closely connected:

> I loved the book, I hated the movie.

Yes, that choice could work. (After all, it's not always an error—at least, not when famous writers use it.) The comma splice gives both clauses a kind of flatness—especially the second one. As in the version with the bare semicolon, the reader will sense that same "no argument" tone. However—and this "however" is important—that comma splice will work best if you're one of those famous writers. Then the reader will recognize your choice as deliberate, not as an error: The reader will know that you know the rule. But in an essay for your English class, the teacher will probably mark the comma splice as an error and ask you to review the rule. On the job, your supervisor will probably fix the splice before handing your report on to the next level—and be on the lookout in your next report. And a prospective employer who spots a comma splice in your letter of application might see it as an error—and remain prospective.

Another commonly marked punctuation error is the omitted comma following an introductory element. This situation is covered in several of the highlighted rules you read in previous chapters: Where that introductory element is a verb phrase or contains a verb phrase and where the introductory element is an adverbial clause, the comma is required. Here are some examples:

> To understand the punctuation of compound sentences, you have to recognize independent clauses.
>
> Before studying the punctuation of compound sentences, you must learn to recognize independent clauses.
>
> If you can recognize independent clauses, you will find it easy to punctuate compound sentences.

Writers rarely deviate from this punctuation. However, when that opening structure is a prepositional phrase, you have a choice. If you want the reader to pause, to put strong stress on the opening element, particularly on its last word, then go ahead and use the comma:

> From the doorway, I can see the last of my students walking up the dirt road into the school grounds.
> —Frank Bures, "Test Day"

You might recall that the comma is recommended for the opening prepositional phrase if it exceeds five or six words. That recommendation is related to readability. If the comma would help the reader, you'll want to include it, no matter how many words in the opener.

The highlighted boxes throughout the book are reserved for those rules that constitute agreed-upon conventions. They are rules that you should know thoroughly. And while it's true that writers do deviate from them on occasion, you will want to consider the effect on your reader before doing so. Chances are, the reader will have more confidence in your ideas when you demonstrate your expertise of the standard punctuation conventions—even those situations where deviations from the standard may be common.

Not all of the punctuation rules in this book are highlighted. For example, there is no hard and fast rule about the serial comma (page 54–55). And certainly the use of conjunctions in the series rather than commas will produce quite different rhetorical effects. Other discussions that emphasize variation describe the choices we have with dashes and colons for special emphasis. With these two punctuation marks, you achieve different levels of formality. And using them well can affect the reader's judgment of your ability as a writer—and very likely the reader's judgment of your ideas.

If you had the notion, before studying *Rhetorical Grammar,* that punctuation is nothing more than a final, added-on step in the writing process, we hope you have learned otherwise. Many of the punctuation choices you make are determined by the rhetorical situation; those choices are an integral part of the composing and revision stages in all of your writing tasks.

Remember, punctuation can do in writing what your voice does in speech—not as well in many cases, but even better in some. Punctuation helps the reader hear your voice and understand your message.

FOR GROUP DISCUSSION

One of Robert Frost's most famous poems is "Stopping by Woods on a Snowy Evening." In some printed versions the last stanza begins like this:

> The woods are lovely, dark, and deep,
> But I have promises to keep

In others, the punctuation of the first line follows the poet's original:

> The woods are lovely, dark and deep,

Given what you know about the punctuation of the series and of the appositive, do you think that these two versions mean the same thing? If they do, why would anyone object to that extra comma?

EXERCISE 45

The following paragraphs are reproduced exactly as they were published—with one exception: *All internal punctuation has been removed; only the sentence-end marks have been retained.* Your job is to put the punctuation marks back into the sentences. (Don't forget hyphens and apostrophes!) As you know, punctuation rules are not carved in stone; consequently, in some places your version may differ from the original—and still be correct. You can check your version against that of the author in the Answers to the Exercises section.

> Management is still taught in most business schools as a bundle of techniques such as budgeting and personnel relations. To be sure management like any other work has its own tools and its own techniques. But just as the essence of medicine is not urinalysis important though that is the essence of management is not techniques and procedures. The essence of management is to make knowledge productive. Management in other words is a social function. And in its practice management is truly a liberal art.
>
> The old communities family village parish and so on have all but disappeared in the knowledge society. Their place has largely been taken by the new unit of social integration the organization. Where community was fate organization is voluntary membership. Where community claimed the entire person organization is a means to a person's ends a tool. For 200 years a hot debate has been raging especially in the West are communities organic or are they simply extensions of the people of which they are made? Nobody would claim that the new organization is organic. It is clearly an artifact a creation of man a social technology.
>
> —Peter F. Drucker, *The Atlantic Monthly*

FOR GROUP DISCUSSION

The following is an excerpt from *Willie Mays,* a biography written by James S. Hirsch. Find the rule for each of the punctuation marks in the Glossary of Punctuation.

1. On May 24, 1951, a young center fielder who had dazzled crowds in the minor leagues left Sioux City, Iowa, traveling light: a change of clothes and some toiletries, his glove, his spikes, and his two favorite thirty-four-ounce Adirondack bats.

2. The twenty-year-old Alabaman was driven to the airport in Omaha, Nebraska, where he bought a ticket from United Airlines for an all-night journey, landing in New York early the following day.

3. He had been there once before, three years earlier, to play in the Polo Grounds with the Birmingham Black Barons.

4. On that team the veterans had protected him, instructing the youngster on how to dress, act, and play ball; on how to represent his team, his city, and his race.

5. But now, on a sunny morning at La Guardia Airport, Willie Mays slid into the back seat of a taxi and pressed his face against the window, alone.

6. He had never seen so many people walk so fast in his life.

KEY TERMS

Colon	Parentheses	Question mark
Comma	Prosody	Semantics
Dash	Punctuation	Semicolon
Exclamation point	Punctuation hierarchy	Syntax

Glossary of Punctuation

Apostrophe

1. **Possessive Case**

    A. For Singular Nouns

    To show the possessive case, add *'s* to singular nouns, both common and proper:

    > Bob's friend   the ocean's blue color

    The rule also applies to indefinite pronouns:

    > someone's book   everyone's vote

    Note. Remember that possessive pronouns do not have apostrophes. Some pronouns are easily confused with contractions:

its (possessive)	it's (it is)
your (possessive)	you're (you are)
their (possessive)	they're (they are)
whose (possessive)	who's (who is)

    When a singular noun ends in *s*, the rule gets a bit fuzzy. Generally, we add an apostrophe and another *s: Brooks's poetry*. However, there are two possible exceptions to this rule. Some editors recommend adding just an apostrophe when a name such as *Achilles* ends in the sound *eez: Achilles' heel*. They also suggest using just an apostrophe after some singular common nouns that end in *s: physics' offering*.

    B. For Plural Nouns

    To make a regular plural noun possessive, add only the apostrophe:

    > the cats' tails   the students' complaints

    For irregular plurals (those formed without adding *s*), add *'s:*

    > the women's movement   children's books

2. **Plurals of Initials and Words Other Than Nouns**

    In making initials and non-nouns plural, when the addition of *s* alone would be misleading, include an apostrophe:

    > two B's (sometimes two Bs)   p's and q's   yes's and no's

3. **Contractions**

In writing contractions, use an apostrophe to replace the missing syllable or letter(s):

don't = do not	he'll = he will	Pat's = Pat is, Pat has
it's = it is, it has	can't = cannot	

Brackets

1. **Within Parentheses**

Use brackets for parenthetical material that is already within parentheses:

> Mount Washington is so dangerous because of its location amid three storm routes (reported by *National Geographic* staff writer Neil Shea in "Backyard Arctic" [February 2009]).

2. **In Quoted Material**

Use brackets for interpolations or explanations within quoted material—to show that it is not part of the quotation:

> According to Adam Gopnik, "He [William Cowper] was a wonderfully chatty poet."

Colon

1. **Appositives**

Use the colon to introduce an appositive or a list of appositives:

> The government had one priority: maintaining the status quo.

> The board appointed three committees to plan the convention: finance, program, and local arrangements.

Often such a list is introduced by *as follows* or *the following:*

> The three committees are as follows: finance, program, and local arrangements.

> The board appointed the following committees: finance, program, and local arrangements.

Remember that a complete sentence precedes the colon; what follows the colon is an appositive. *Do not* put a colon between a linking verb and the subject complement:

> *The committees that were appointed are: finance, program, and local arrangements.

2. **Coordination of Independent Clauses**

Use a colon to join the two independent clauses of a compound sentence, where the second completes the idea, or the promise, of the first. The connection often means "namely" or "that is":

> Only one obstacle lay between us and success: We had to find the money.

Note: The convention of capitalizing the first word of a complete sentence following the colon is on the fence: Some publishers always capitalize; others capitalize only when what follows is a direct quotation; others capitalize questions and direct quotations. Whichever method you follow, as with any optional convention, be sure to follow it consistently.

3. **Quotations**

Colons are sometimes used to introduce speech in a dialogue:

> Jeff: We'll drive all night. Tomorrow we'll be in El Paso.
> Lyn: In this car, we'll be lucky if we make it to Dallas.

They may also be used instead of commas to introduce a long quotation more formally, especially a quotation set off from the main text.

Comma

1. **Compound Sentences**

Use a comma along with a coordinating conjunction between the independent clauses in a compound sentence:

> I didn't believe a word Phil said, and I told him so.

Remember that the comma alone produces a comma splice.

2. **Series**

Use commas when listing a series of three or more sentence elements:

> We gossiped, laughed, and sang the old songs at our class reunion.
> We hunted in the basement, in the attic, and through all the storage rooms, to no avail.

The serial comma, the one before *and,* is optional; however, usage—either with or without it—must be consistent.

3. **Introductory Dependent Clauses**

Use a comma to set off an introductory dependent clause:

> When the riot started, the police fired tear gas into the crowd.

4. **Sentence-Ending Clauses**

Use a comma to set off a dependent adverbial clause following the main clause if the adverbial clause has no effect on the outcome of the main clause:

> Some people refused to leave, even though the hurricane winds had started.

Note that in the following sentences the idea in the main clause will not be realized without the adverbial clause; therefore, we do not use a comma:

> I'll pack up and leave if you tell me to.
> We left the area because we were afraid to stay.

Be aware that the rules regarding adverbial clauses are among the least standardized of our punctuation conventions.

5. **Introductory Verb Phrases (Infinitival and Participial)**

Use a comma to set off any introductory phrase that contains a verb form:

> After *studying* all weekend, I felt absolutely prepared for the midterm exam.
> *Having worked* at McDonald's for the past four summers, Max felt confident when he applied for the job of assistant manager.
> *To get* in shape for ski season, my roommate works out on the NordicTrack.

Note: In most cases the subject of the sentence must also be the subject of the verb in that introductory phrase; otherwise, the phrase dangles. Exceptions occur with set phrases:

> Speaking of the weather, let's have a picnic.
> To tell the truth, I have never read *Silas Marner.*

6. **Introductory Prepositional Phrases**
   Use a comma to set off adverbial prepositional phrases of approximately six or more words:

   > Toward the end of the semester, everyone in my dorm starts to study seriously.

   It is perfectly acceptable to set off shorter prepositional phrases, especially if you think the reader should pause. For example, information of specific dates is sometimes set off:

   > In 1990, the official dismantling of the Berlin Wall began.

   In making the decision about such commas, consider the punctuation in the rest of the sentence: Don't overload the sentence with commas. Set off any prepositional phrase that might cause a misreading:

   > During the summer, vacation plans are our main topic of conversation.

   See the next section for prepositional phrases that are parenthetical.

7. **Other Sentence Modifiers**
   Set off words and phrases that modify the whole sentence, serve as transitions, or have a parenthetical meaning—at both the beginning and the end of the sentence:

   A. Adverbs

   > Luckily, we escaped without a scratch.
   > We escaped without a scratch, luckily.
   > Meanwhile, there was nothing to do but wait.

   B. *Yes* and *no:*

   > Yes, he's the culprit.   No, I can't go out tonight.

   C. Transitional prepositional phrases

   > In fact, there was nothing I could do about her problem.
   > In the meantime, I listened to her sad tale.

   These parenthetical words and phrases often provide a transitional tie to the previous sentence, which the comma emphasizes. They are also used to slow the reader down or to shift the point of sentence stress.

   D. Absolute phrases

   > Money in our pockets, we headed to town.
   > Ginny relaxed before the fire, her feet propped on the footstool.

8. **Nonrestrictive Elements**
   Use commas to set off nonrestrictive (commenting) elements such as nonrestrictive appositives and adjectival clauses:

   > My oldest brother, a history major, spends every night in the library.

Now, in the twenty-first century, we have different challenges.
Steve Jobs, who co-founded Apple in the 1970s, was known for his entrepreneurial savvy.

9. Coordinate Adjectives

Use commas in the noun phrase between coordinate adjectives in preheadword position. Coordinate refers to adjectives of the same class—for example, subjective qualities:

a tender, delightful story   an easy, winning smile

If the adjectives are of different classes, no comma is necessary.

a tall young man   a huge red ball

A good general rule for making a decision about commas between these prenoun modifiers is this: If you could insert *and* or *but,* use a comma:

A tender and delightful love story

Notice that the two phrases without commas contain adjectives from different classes (height, age, size, color)—so they will not be separated:

*a tall and young man   *a huge and red ball

10. Nouns of Direct Address

Use a comma to set off vocatives in both opening and closing position:

Students, your time is up.   Put your pencils down, everyone.

11. Direct Quotations

Use commas to set off direct quotations after verbs such as *say* and *reply:*

The waiter said, "Good evening. My name is Pierre."
Harold replied, "I'm Harold, and this is Joyce."

Note: This is actually an exception to the punctuation rule you learned in Chapter 2: "Do not mark the boundaries of the basic sentence units with commas." When the direct object is a direct quotation, we do mark the boundary.

Direct quotations can also be introduced by colons:
Harold replied: "I'm Harold, and this is Joyce."

12. State and Year

Use commas to set off the name of a state when it follows the name of a city:

I was surprised to learn that Cheyenne, Wyoming, isn't a larger city.

Also set off the year in a complete date:

Born on August 13, 1899, Alfred Hitchcock was the youngest of three children.

Dash

1. Interruptions or Asides

Use a dash (or pair of dashes) to set off any interrupting structure within the sentence or at the end:

Tim quit his job—a brave decision, in my opinion—to look for something new.
Tim decided to quit his job and look for another—a brave decision.

When the interrupter is a complete sentence, it is punctuated as a phrase would be:

> Tim quit his job—he was always a rash young man—to follow Horace Greeley's advice and go West.

2. Appositives
Use dashes to call attention to an appositive:

> The microorganisms that seem to have it in for us in the worst way—the ones that really appear to wish us ill—turn out on close examination to be rather more like bystanders, strays, strangers in from the cold.
>
> —Lewis Thomas

Use a pair of dashes to set off a list of appositives that are themselves separated by commas:

> All the committees—finance, program, and local arrangements— went to work with real enthusiasm.

The list of appositives set off by a dash can also come at the beginning of the sentence when the subject is a pronoun referring to the list:

> The faculty, the students, the staff—all were opposed to the provost's decision to reinstate the old dormitory regulations.

Namely and *that is,* both of which are signalers of appositives, can be preceded by either a dash or a comma; the dash gives the appositive more emphasis:

> Some mammals have no hair—namely, the whales.
> The provost's decision brought out over 1,500 student protesters, that is, a third of the student body.

Ellipsis Points

1. Three periods, each preceded and followed by a space, are used to indicate the omission of one or more words within a quoted sentence. An omission at the end of a sentence is indicated by a period (preceded by no space) followed by three spaced periods. Here is an original sentence and the cut versions that illustrate these two styles:

   > A group of the West Oxfordshire local squires and the wealthier farmers, just like their opposite numbers in countless other towns and villages up and down the country, had decided to have the local fields apportioned privately, and farmed efficiently. A surveyor was needed, and Webb was brought over from Stow-on-the-Wold, ten miles away.
   >
   > —Simon Winchester, *The Map That Changed the World*

   > A group of the West Oxfordshire local squires and the wealthier farmers ... had decided to have the local fields apportioned privately, and farmed efficiently. A surveyor was needed ....

2. Four periods are also used for the omission of a complete sentence or more, even a complete paragraph. In poetry the omission of a line is indicated by a complete line of periods.

Exclamation Point

1. **Exclamatory Sentence**
   The exclamation point is the terminal punctuation for the exclamatory sentence, usually beginning with a *what* or *how:*

   > What a tough job that was!
   > How expectations have changed!

   The exclamation point is actually optional—and in some cases would be inappropriate:

   > How calm the ocean is today.   What a sweet child you have.

2. **Emphasis**
   The exclamation point is used in declarative and imperative sentences that call for added emotions; however, it should be used sparingly. It is rarely used in formal prose.

   > "Get out!" he shouted. "I never want to see you again!"

Hyphen

1. **Compound Words or Phrases**
   The hyphen expresses a compound word or phrase in prenoun position as a unit:

   > a two-inch board   a silver-plated teapot
   > a well-designed running shoe   an out-of-work carpenter

   Note that when they are not in prenoun position, the hyphens are not needed in most cases:

   > The board is two inches wide.   The shoe was well designed.

   When the modifier in prenoun position is an *-ly* adverb, the hyphen is not used:

   > a nicely designed running shoe   a clearly phrased message

Parentheses

1. **Interruptions or Asides**
   Parentheses, in many cases, function just as dashes and commas do—to set off explanatory information or, in some cases, the writer's digressions:

   > I stopped her and put a five-sou piece (a little more than a farthing) into her hand.

   > —George Orwell

   Unlike dashes, which call attention to a passage, the parentheses generally add the information as an aside: They say, "By the way," whereas the dash says, "Hey, listen to this!"

2. **Technical Information**
   Parentheses are also used for including technical information within a text:

   > For years I never missed an issue of *Astounding* (now published as *Analog*).

3. **Punctuation Notes**
A complete sentence added parenthetically within another sentence has neither an opening capital letter nor end punctuation:

> The long winters in North Dakota (newcomers quickly learn that March is a winter month) make spring a time of great joy.

However, when a complete sentence is enclosed in parentheses but it is not embedded in another sentence, the terminal punctuation is placed within the parentheses:

> I look forward to every month of the year. (February, I will admit, is short on saving graces, but at least it's short.)

Period

1. **Sentence End**
The period marks the end of a declarative or imperative sentence:

> It's raining. Close the window.

2. **Abbreviations**
Abbreviations with internal periods have no space after the internal period.

> U.S.   B.A.   a.m.

Initials of personal names, however, retain the space:

> J. F. Kennedy   H. L. Mencken

The period is omitted after an abbreviation at the end of a sentence that has a period of its own:

> My publisher is part of Pearson Education, Inc.

The abbreviating period is retained before other end punctuation:

> Did you remember to bring the pillows, blankets, towels, etc.?

Question Marks

1. **End of Question**
Use the question mark as terminal punctuation in all direct questions:

> Do you have anything to add?   He said what?

However, polite requests in the form of questions are often punctuated with the period:

> Would you mind opening the window.

2. **Quotations**
In punctuating quoted questions, include the question mark within the quotation marks:

> John asked, "Do you have anything to add?"

When a quoted statement is embedded at the end of a question, the question mark is outside the quotation marks:

> Who said, "Give me liberty or give me death"?

Note that the period is omitted from the quoted sentence.

When a quoted question is embedded in another question, only one question mark is used—and that one is inside the quotation marks:

Did he ask you straight out, "Are you a shoplifter?"

Quotation Marks

1. For Direct Quotations
Use double quotation marks to indicate another person's exact words, both spoken and written:

In 1943 Churchill told Stalin, "In war-time, truth is so precious that she should always be attended by a bodyguard of lies."

Notice that the quotation marks are outside the period. This system applies even when the quotation marks enclose a single word, such as a title:

My father's favorite poem is Rudyard Kipling's "If."

However, quotation marks are placed inside semicolons and colons:

She said, "Come to the party"; I had to turn her down.

Place parenthetical citations between the final set of quotation marks and the period.

2. Within Direct Quotations
Use single quotation marks when the quoted material is within a quoted passage:

Describing the degeneracy of the nation in a letter to Joshua F. Speed, Lincoln wrote that "as a nation we began by declaring that 'all men are created equal.' We now practically read it 'all men are created equal except Negroes.' "Notice that both the single and the double quotation marks are outside the period. For quotation marks with questions, see the preceding section under "Question Marks."

Semicolon

1. As a Conjunction
Use a semicolon to connect independent clauses in a compound sentence. You can think of the semicolon as having the connective force of the comma-plus-conjunction:

The use of the semicolon indicates a close relationship between clauses; it gives the sentence a tight, separate-but-equal bond.

2. In the Separation of a Series
Use semicolons to separate a series of structures that have internal punctuation:

In this chapter we looked at three purposes underlying our punctuation system: syntactic, related to structure; prosodic, related to sentence rhythm; and semantic, related to meaning.

Glossary of Terms

For further explanation of the terms listed here, check the index for page references.

Absolute adjective.   An adjective with a meaning that is generally not capable of being intensified or compared, such as *unique* or *perfect* or *square.* Careful writers avoid such usages as *very perfect* or *more unique.*

Absolute phrase.   A subject–predicate construction without a tense-carrying verb. The absolute phrase is related to the sentence as a whole, providing a detail or point of focus: "She sat quietly, *her hands folded in her lap.*"

Abstract noun.   A noun that refers to a quality, such as *peace* or *happiness,* rather than a concrete object, such as *cup* or *computer.*

Action verb.   A verb that refers to an action or event: "He *slipped* on the ice"; "The accident *happened* quickly." See also *Linking verb.*

Active voice.   A property of sentences in which the subject is generally the agent, the performer of the action indicated by the verb. Verb phrases in such sentence do *not* include a form of the *be* auxiliary combined with the past participle. See also *Passive voice.*

Adjectival.   Any structure, no matter what its form, that functions as a modifier of a noun—that is, that functions as an adjective normally functions. See Chapter 9.

Adjectival clause.   See *Relative clause.*

Adjective.   One of the four form classes, whose members act as modifiers of nouns; most adjectives can be inflected for comparative and superlative degree *(big, bigger, biggest)*; they can be qualified or intensified *(rather big, very big)*; they have characteristic derivational affixes such as *-ous (famous), -ish (childish),* and *-ful (graceful).*

Adjective phrase.   An adjective that includes a modifier: *very nice, afraid to fly.*

Adverb.   One of the four form classes, whose members act as modifiers of verbs, contributing information of time, place, reason, manner, and the like. Like adjectives, certain adverbs can be qualified *(very quickly, rather fast)*; some can be inflected for comparative and superlative degree *(more quickly, fastest)*; they have characteristic derivational endings such as *-ly (quickly), -wise (lengthwise), -ward (backward).*

Adverbial.   Any structure, no matter what its form, that functions as a modifier of a verb—that is, that functions as an adverb normally functions. See Chapter 8.

Adverbial of emphasis. An adverbial, generally a single word, that shifts emphasis to a particular structure: for example, *hardly, always, rarely, never.*

Agent. The initiator of the action in the sentence. Usually the agent is the subject in an active sentence: "*John* groomed the dog"; "*The committee* elected Pam." In a passive sentence the agent, if mentioned, will be the object of a preposition: "Pam was elected by *the committee.*"

Agreement. (1) Subject–verb. A third-person singular subject in the present tense takes the *-s* form of the verb: "*The dog barks* all night"; "He *bothers* the neighbors." A plural takes the base form: "*The dogs bark*"; "*They bother* the neighbors." (2) Pronoun–antecedent. The number of the pronoun (whether singular or plural) agrees with the number of its antecedent. "*The boys* did *their* chores"; "The *man who* works for us is on vacation." (Note that both *man* and *who* take the *-s* form of their verbs.)

Ambiguity. A condition in which a structure has more than one possible meaning. The source may be lexical ("She is *blue*") or structural ("*Visiting relatives* can be boring") or both ("The detective looked *hard*").

Anaphora. A figure of speech describing repetition at the beginning of successive sentences: "*Mad* world! *Mad* kings! *Mad* composition!" [Shakespeare]

Anastrophe. A figure of speech describing a reversal of the normal order of a sentence: "*The rest of the story you know.*"

Antecedent. The noun or nominal that a pronoun refers to: "*Max* said he would come."

Anticipatory *It*. The use of the pronoun *it* in subject position that puts the noun clause or verb phrase subject in predicate position: "Pleading with him is no use" → It's no use pleading with him.

Antithesis. The juxtaposition of contrasting ideas: "I come to bury Caesar, not to praise him." [Shakespeare]

Appositive. A structure, usually a noun phrase, that describes or further identifies a nominal structure, usually another noun phrase: "My neighbor, *a butcher at Weis Market,* recently lost his job."

Article. One of the determiner classes, including the indefinite *a,* or *an,* which signals only countable nouns, and the definite *the,* which can signal all classes of nouns.

Asyndeton. A figure of speech describing the omission of a conjunction: "*I came, I saw, I conquered.*" [Shakespeare]

Attributor. A metadiscourse signal that refers to the source of quoted information: *according to, cited in.*

Auxiliary verb. One of the structure-class words, a marker of verbs. Auxiliaries include forms of *have* and *be,* as well as the modals, such as *will, shall,* and *must.* See also Do-*support.*

Backgrounding. The process of placing known information, or perhaps less important information, in a subordinate role in the sentence rather than in a position of main focus. See also *Foregrounding.*

***Be* patterns.** Sentence Patterns 1 (Subject+*Be*+Adverbial) and 2 (Subject+*Be*+Subject Complement).

Broad reference. A pronoun that refers to a complete sentence rather than to a specific noun or nominal. The broad-reference clause is introduced by *which.* "Judd told jokes all evening, *which annoyed everyone after a while.*" The demonstrative pronouns *this* and *that* and the personal pronoun *it* are also sometimes used with broad reference: "Judd told jokes nonstop; *that* annoyed everyone after a while." Those sentences with demonstratives can be improved if the pronoun is turned into a determiner: "*That* crazy behavior of his annoyed everyone after a while."

Case. A feature of nouns and certain pronouns that denotes their function in the sentence. Pronouns have three case distinctions: subjective (*I, they, who,* etc.), possessive (*my, their, whose,* etc.), and objective (*me, them, whom,* etc.). Nouns have only one case inflection, the possessive *(John's, the cat's).* The case of nouns other than the possessive is sometimes referred to as common case.

Clause. A structure with a subject and a predicate. The sentence patterns are clause patterns.

Cleft sentence. A sentence variation using an *it*-clause or *what*-clause to shift the sentence focus: "Lightning caused the fire" → "It was lightning that caused the fire"; "What caused the fire was lightning."

Cliché. A worn-out word or phrase: "hard as nails"; "cute as a bug's ear."

Climax. The arrangement of a series of words, phrases, or clauses in order of scope, length, or importance.

Code gloss. A metadiscourse signal used to clarify the meaning of a word or phrase, often a parenthetical comment.

Cohesion. The connections between sentences. Cohesive ties are furnished by pronouns that have antecedents in previous sentences, by conjunctions and conjunctive adverb, by known information, and by knowledge shared by the reader.

Collective noun. A noun that refers to a collection of individuals: *group, team, family.* Collective nouns may be replaced by either singular or plural pronouns, depending on the meaning.

Comma splice. The connection of two independent clauses in a compound sentence with a comma alone. Conventional punctuation requires a conjunction with the comma.

Command. See *Imperative sentence.*

Common noun. A noun with general, rather than unique, reference (in contrast to proper nouns). Common nouns may be countable *(house, book)* or noncountable *(water, oil)*; they may be concrete *(house, water)* or abstract *(justice, indifference).*

Comparative degree. See *Degree.*

Complement. A structure that "completes" the sentence. The term includes those slots in the predicate that complete the verb: direct object, indirect object, subject complement, and object complement.

Complementizer. A word that enables the writer or speaker to embed one sentence in another: "He loves me" → "I know *that* he loves me."

Complex sentence. A sentence that includes a dependent clause.

Compound–complex sentence. A sentence with two or more independent clauses and at least one dependent clause.

Compound sentence. A sentence with two or more independent clauses.

Conjunction. One of the structure classes, which includes connectors that coordinate structures of many forms (e.g., *and, or, but*), subordinate sentences (e.g., *if, because, when*), and coordinate sentences with an adverbial emphasis (e.g., *however, therefore*).

Conjunctive adverb. A conjunction that connects two independent clauses with an adverbial emphasis, such as *however, therefore, moreover,* and *nevertheless.*

Connotation. The idea or feeling that a word evokes. See also *Denotation.*

Contraction. A combination of two words written or spoken as one, in which letters or sounds are omitted. In writing, the omission is marked by an apostrophe: *isn't, they're.*

Coordinating conjunction. A conjunction that connects two or more sentences or structures within a sentence as equals: *and, but, or, nor, for,* and *yet.*

Coordination. A way of expanding sentences in which two or more structures of the same form serve as a unit. All the sentence parts, as well as the sentence itself, can be coordinated.

Correlative conjunction. A two-part conjunction that expresses a relationship between the coordinated structures: *either–or, neither–nor, both–and, not only–but also.*

Countable noun. A noun whose referent can be identified as a separate entity; the countable noun can be signaled by the indefinite article, *a,* and by numbers: *a house; an experience; two eggs; three problems.* See also *Noncountable noun.*

Dangling modifier. A phrase with a verb form placed so that it has no clear relationship to its subject, which is the word it should modify. The dangling participial phrase occurs when the sentence subject is not also the subject of the sentence-opening or sentence-closing participle: *"Driving home at night,* fog made it hard to see down the road." Revised: "Driving home at night, we found it hard to see the road because the fog was quite dense." Sentences with dangling gerunds, infinitives, or elliptical clauses also require revision.

Declarative sentence. A sentence in the form of a statement (in contrast to a command, a question, or an exclamation).

Definite article. The determiner *the,* which generally marks a specific or previously mentioned noun: *"the* man at *the* airport"; *"the* point I made previously."

Degree. The variations in adjectives and some adverbs that indicate the simple quality of a noun, or positive degree ("Bill is a *big* boy"); its comparison to another, the comparative degree ("Bill is *bigger* than Tom"); or its comparison to two or more, the superlative degree ("Bill is the *biggest* person in the whole class"). In most adjectives of two or more syllables, the comparative and superlative degrees are marked by *more* and *most,* respectively.

Demonstrative pronoun. The pronouns *this* (plural *these*) and *that* (plural *those*), which function as nominal substitutes and as determiners. They include the feature of proximity: near *(this, these)* and distant *(that, those).*

Denotation. The primary or dictionary definition of a word. See also *Connotation.*

Dependent clause. A clause that functions as an adverbial, adjectival, or nominal (in contrast to an independent clause).

Derivational affix. A suffix or prefix that is added to a form-class word, either to change its class *(fame–famous)* or to change its meaning *(legal–illegal; boy–boyhood).*

Determiner. One of the structure-class words, a signaler of nouns. Determiners include articles *(a, the),* possessive nouns and pronouns (e.g., *Chuck's, his*), demonstrative pronouns *(this, that, these, those),* and indefinite pronouns (e.g., *many, each*).

Diction. The selection of words in terms of their meaning and their appropriateness for a specific audience and purpose.

Direct address. A noun or noun phrase addressing a person or group: "*Ladies and gentlemen,* may I have your attention"; "Tell me, *dear,* what you're thinking."

Direct object. A nominal in the predicate of the transitive sentence patterns. The direct object names the objective, goal, or receiver of the verb's action: "We ate *the peanuts*"; "The boy hit *the ball*"; "I enjoy *playing chess.*"

Do-support. The addition of the auxiliary *do* to a verb string that has no other auxiliary. The question, the negative, and the emphatic transformations all require an auxiliary. *Do* also substitutes for a repeated verb phrase in compound sentences: "Bryan liked the movie, and I *did* too."

Ellipsis. See *Elliptical clause.*

Elliptical clause. A clause in which a part has been left out but is "understood": "Chet is older *than I (am old)*"; "*When (you are) planning your essay,* be sure to consider the audience."

End focus. The common rhythm pattern in which the prominent stress falls on or near the final sentence unit.

Existential *there*. The use of *there* to signal the existence of something, often the signal of new information: "*There* is a community garden near the playground."

Expletive. A word that enables the writer or speaker to shift the stress in a sentence. "A fly is in my soup" → "*There* is a fly in my soup."

Figurative language. Language that expresses meaning in nonliteral terms, characterized by figures of speech, such as metaphors, similes, analogies, and personification.

Figure of speech. Stylistic variations, also called figurative language, including comparisons (metaphor, similes, analogy, personification) that help readers understand the message, along with structural variations (e.g., repetition, parallelism, and antithesis).

Flat adverb. A class of adverb that is the same in form as its corresponding adjective: *fast, high, early, late, hard, long,* and so on.

Foregrounding. The placement of important information in the position of prominent focus. See also *Backgrounding.*

Form classes. The classes of words that provide the lexical content of the language: nouns, verbs, adjectives, and adverbs. Each has characteristic derivational and inflectional affixes that distinguish its forms.

Fragment. A phrase or clause that is punctuated as a full sentence. Some are simply punctuation errors; others are used deliberately for special effects.

Free modifier. A modifying phrase or clause that opens or closes the sentence, generally expanding on the main idea. Participial phrases, absolute phrases, and resumptive modifiers are among common free modifiers.

Fused sentence. A compound sentence without appropriate connectors or punctuation between independent clauses. Also called a *run-on sentence.*

Gerund. An *-ing* verb functioning as a nominal: "I enjoy *jogging*"; "*Running* is good exercise"; "After *getting* my pilot's license, I hope to fly to Lake Tahoe."

Headword. The key noun in the noun phrase: "the little *boy* across the street"; the verb that heads the verb phrase: *plays,* was *written,* has been *playing.*

Hedge. One of the metadiscourse signals in which the writer expresses uncertainty or a qualification: *may, perhaps, under certain circumstances.*

Helping verb. See *Auxiliary verb*.

Hypercorrection. Making a correction when one isn't necessary. The tendency to hypercorrect usually stems from the misapplication of rules learned in childhood.

Idiom. A combination of words whose meaning cannot be predicted from the meaning of the individual words. Many phrasal verbs are idioms: *put out, back down, give in*.

Imperative sentence. The imperative sentence includes the base form of the verb and usually an understood subject *(you)*: "*Finish* your report as soon as possible."

Indefinite article. The determiner *a* or *an*, which marks an unspecified countable noun. See also *Definite article*.

Indefinite pronoun. A large category that includes quantifiers (e.g., *enough, several, many, much*), universals *(all, both, every, each)*, and partitives (e.g., *any, anyone, anybody, either, neither, no, nobody, some, someone*). Many of the indefinite pronouns can function as determiners.

Independent clause. A sequence of words that includes a subject and a predicate and can stand alone. A sentence must have at least one independent clause.

Indirect object. The nominal following verbs like *give or send*. The indirect object is the recipient; the direct object is what is given, sent, etc.: "We gave *our friends* a ride home."

Infinitive. The base form of the verb, usually expressed with *to*, which is called *the infinitive marker*.

Infinitive phrase. A phrase headed by the infinitive. The infinitive phrase can function adverbially ("I stayed up all night *to study for the exam*"); adjectivally ("That is no way *to study*"); and nominally ("*To study all night* is unproductive in the long run").

Inflection. A suffix that is added to the form classes (nouns, verbs, adjectives, and adverbs) to change their grammatical role in some way. Nouns have two inflectional suffixes (*-s* plural and *'s* possessive); verbs have four (*-s, -ing, -ed,* and *-en*); adjectives and some adverbs have two (*-er* and *-est*).

Intensive reflexive pronoun. The function of the reflexive pronoun when it emphasizes a noun or pronoun: "I *myself* prefer chocolate." See also *Reflexive pronoun*.

Interrogative sentence. A sentence that is a question in form: "Are you leaving now?" "When are you leaving?"

Intransitive verb. A verb that requires no complement to be complete: "Everyone *applauded*."

Irregular verb. Any verb in which the *-ed* and *-en* forms are not that of a regular verb; in other words, a verb in which the *-ed* and *-en* forms are not simply the addition of *-d, -ed,* or *-t* to the base form.

Isocolon. A figure of speech describing the repetition of grammatical forms: "government *of the people, by the people, and for the people*."

It-cleft. See *Cleft sentence*.

Known–new contract. The common feature of sentences in which old, or known, information (information that is repeated from an earlier sentence or paragraph to provide cohesion, often in the form of a pronoun or related word) will appear in the subject position, with the new information in the predicate.

Lexical cohesion. The continuity of text created by the use of repeated or related words.

Lexical feature. A characteristic of a word that serves to distinguish it from similar words; for example, only countable nouns can be signaled by the indefinite article, *a*, or by numbers.

Lexicon. The store of words—the internalized dictionary—that every speaker of the language has.

Linking-*be*. The use of the verb *be* to link the subject to an adverbial (Pattern 1) or to link the subject to a subject complement (Pattern 2).

Linking verb. A verb that requires a subjective complement to be complete. *Be* is commonly used as a linking verb: "She *is* a senior"; "She *seems* nice." See also *Action verb*.

Main clause. See *Independent clause*.

Manner adverb. An adverb that answers the question of "how" or "in what manner" about the verb. Most manner adverbs are derived from adjectives with the addition of *-ly: quickly, merrily, candidly*.

Mass noun. See *Noncountable noun*.

Metadiscourse. Certain signals, such as connectors and hedges, that communicate and clarify the writer's attitude or help the reader understand the direction and purpose of the passage: *for example, in the first place, next*.

Metaphor. The nonliteral use of a word that allows the speaker or writer to attribute qualities of one thing to another for purposes of explanation or persuasion: the *war* on drugs, the *engine* of government, *sunset* legislation, *food* for thought.

Modal auxiliary. The auxiliaries *may/might, can/could, will/would, shall/should,* and *must*. A modal auxiliary adds nuances of meaning to the main verb, referring to probability, possibility, obligation, and the like. Other modal-like verbs include *have (got) to* and *be+going to*.

Modifier. A word, phrase, or clause that adds information to another structure, thereby changing, or modifying, its meaning: "The *small* town *in Oregon where I was born*."

Nominal. Any structure that functions as a noun phrase normally functions—as subject, direct object, indirect object, object complement, subject complement, object of preposition, appositive.

Nominal clause. A dependent clause that functions as a noun phrase normally functions. See Chapter 10.

Nominalization. The process of producing a noun by adding derivational affixes to another word class: *legalize–legalization; friendly–friendliness*. Often a sentence will be more effective when the verb is allowed to function as a verb rather than being turned into a noun.

Nominalized verb. See *Nominalization*.

Noncountable noun. A noun referring to what might be called an undifferentiated mass—such as *wood, water, sugar, glass*—or an abstraction—*justice, love, indifference*.

Nonrestrictive modifier. A modifier in the noun phrase that comments about the noun rather than defines it. Nonrestrictive modifiers following the noun are set off by commas. See also *Restrictive modifier*.

Noun. One of the four form classes, whose members fill the headword position in the noun phrase. Most nouns can be inflected for plural and possessive *(boy, boys, boy's, boys')*. Nouns have characteristic derivational endings, such as *-ion (action, compensation), -ment (contentment),* and *-ness (happiness)*.

Noun phrase. The noun headword with all of its attendant pre- and postnoun modifiers. See Chapter 9.

Number. A feature of nouns and pronouns, referring to singular and plural.

Object complement. The unit following the direct object in Pattern 7 sentences, filled by an adjectival or a nominal. The object complement has two functions: (1) It completes the idea of the verb; and (2) it modifies (if an adjectival) or renames (if a nominal) the direct object: "I found the play *exciting*"; "We consider Pete *a good friend.*"

Object of the preposition. The nominal position—usually filled by a noun phrase—that follows the preposition to form a prepositional phrase.

Objective case. The role in the sentence of a noun phrase or pronoun when it functions as an object—direct object, indirect object, object complement, or object of a preposition. Although nouns do not have a special form for objective case, many of the pronouns do. Personal pronouns and the relative pronoun *who* have separate forms when they function as objects: *me, you, him, her, it, us, them, whom.*

Parallelism. See *Parallel structure.*

Parallel structure. A coordinate structure in which all the coordinate parts are of the same grammatical form: "I'll take either *a bus* or *a taxi*" (parallel noun phrases).

Participial phrase. A verb phrase containing a present or past participle and functioning as an adjectival, the modifier of a noun: "*the students organizing the march.*"

Participle. The *present participle* is the -*ing* form of the verb used in the progressive tense (*writing*). The *past participle* (*written*) is the form of the verb used with the auxiliary *have* to form the perfect tenses in the active voice and with *be* to form the passive voice. The term *participle* refers both to these forms of the verb and to their function as adjectivals: *laughing* children; stories *written* by J. K. Rowling.

Particle. Words such as *in* and *out* that join verbs to create phrasal verbs. See *Phrasal verb.*

Passive voice. A property of sentences in which the subject is generally the recipient of the action indicated by the verb. If an agent is included in the sentence, it is usually found after the preposition *by*. Verb phrases in such sentences include a form of the *be* auxiliary combined with the past participle: "The editorial *was written* by Jon." See also *Active voice.*

Past participle. See *Participle.*

Past tense. The form of the verb usually denoting a specific past action. Regular verbs take an -*ed* ending (*talked, raced*); irregular verbs vary in spelling (*were, wrote*).

Person. A feature of personal pronouns relating to point of view, the relationship of the writer or speaker to the reader or listener: It can refer to writer or speaker (first person), the person addressed (second person), and the person or thing spoken about (third person).

Personal pronoun. A pronoun referring to a specific person or thing: In the subjective case the personal pronouns are *I, you, he, she, we, you, they,* and *it.* The personal pronouns have different forms for objective and possessive case.

Personal voice. The unique identity created through choosing words and arranging them on the page, usually indicating familiarity with the topic and with the language used to discuss the topic.

Phrasal preposition. A preposition consisting of two or three words: *according to, in front of.*

Phrasal verb. A verb combined with a particle (a preposition-like word); the combination produces a unique meaning, often idiomatic: *bring about, come across, make up.*

Phrase. A word or combination of words that constitutes a unit of the sentence.

Plural-only noun. A noun that has no singular form: *shorts, jeans, scissors, clothes.*

Point of view. The relationship of the writer to the reader, as shown by the use of pronouns: first, second, and/or third person.

Polysyndeton. A figure of speech describing the addition of conjunctions in a series: "I took exams in biology *and* psychology *and* history—all in one day."

Positive degree. See *Degree.*

Possessive case. The inflected form of nouns *(John's, the dog's)* and pronouns *(my, his, your, her, their, whose,* etc.), usually indicating possession or ownership.

Power words. Words that have the power to make a difference in the emphasis and rhythm of a sentence, often affecting reader expectation as well.

Predicate. One of the two principal parts of the sentence, the comment made about the subject. The predicate includes the verb, together with its complements and modifiers.

Preposition. A structure-class word found in pre-position to—that is, preceding—a nominal. Prepositions can be classed according to their form as simple, or single-word *(above, at, in, with, of,* etc.), or phrasal *(according to, along with, instead of,* etc.).

Prepositional phrase. The combination of a preposition and its object. In form, the object of the preposition is usually a noun phrase ("After *class,* he worked at a clinic"), but it can be a phrase with a gerund ("After *graduating,* he'll go to med school").

Present participle. The *-ing* form of the verb.

Present tense. The base form and the *-s* form of the verb: *help, helps.* The present tense denotes a present point in time ("I *understand* your position"), a habitual action ("I *swim* every day"), or the "timeless" present ("Shakespeare *helps* us understand ourselves").

Pronoun. A word that carries little meaning outside of a specific context. A pronoun takes the position of a nominal. See also *Case.*

Proper noun. A noun with individual reference to a person, building, holiday, historical event, work of art or literature, or geographic region or location, and other such names. Proper nouns are capitalized.

Prosody. The study of the rhythm and intonation of language, which are determined by pitch, stress (loudness), and juncture (pauses).

Qualifier. A structure-class word that qualifies or intensifies an adjective or adverb: "We worked *rather* slowly"; "We worked *very* hard."

Question. A sentence that elicits information. See Interrogative sentence.

Reader expectation. An awareness by the writer of what the reader is expecting to read.

Reciprocal pronoun. The pronouns *each other* and *one another,* which refer to previously named nouns.

Redundancy. Unnecessary repetition.

Referent. The thing (or person, event, concept, action, etc.)—in other words, the reality—that a word stands for.

Reflexive pronoun. A pronoun formed by adding *-self* or *-selves* to a form of the personal pronoun, used as an object in the sentence to refer to a previously named noun or pronoun.

Regular verb. A verb in which the past tense and the past participle are formed by adding *-ed* (or, in some cases, *-d* or *-t*) to the base. These two forms of a regular verb are always identical: "I *lived* in Boston"; "I have *lived* in Boston since 2010."

Relative adverb. The adverbs *where, when,* and *why,* which introduce adjectival (relative) clauses: "The town *where* I was born has only one traffic light."

Relative clause. A clause modifying a noun phrase, introduced by a relative pronoun *(who, which, that)* or a relative adverb *(when, where, why)*: "The car *that Joe bought* is a lemon." See Chapter 9.

Relative pronoun. The pronouns *who (whose, whom), which,* and *that* in their role as introducers of relative (adjectival) clauses.

Repetition. A technique for strengthening the continuity of text with key words. Repetition is especially important in parallel structures.

Restrictive modifier. A modifier in the noun phrase whose function is to restrict, or define, the meaning of the noun. A modifier is restrictive when it is needed to identify the referent of the headword. The restrictive modifier is not set off by commas. See also *Nonrestrictive modifier.*

Rhythm. The pattern of stresses in the spoken language.

Run-on sentence. See *Fused sentence.*

Second person. See *Person.*

Semantics. The study of the meaning of words and sentences.

Sentence. A word or group of words based on one or more subject–predicate, or clause, patterns. The written sentence begins with a capital letter and ends with terminal punctuation—a period, a question mark, or an exclamation point.

Sentence fragment. See *Fragment.*

Sentence modifier. A word or phrase or clause that modifies the sentence as a whole (see Glossary of Punctuation, pp. 254).

Sentence patterns. The simple skeletal sentences, made up of two or three or four required elements, that underlie our sentences, even the most complex among them. The seven patterns listed in Chapter 2 account for almost all the possible sentences of English.

Serial comma. The comma that is used before the conjunction in a series: "On our fishing trip to Alaska, we caught salmon, halibut, *and* the elusive Arctic grayling." Some publications, as a matter of policy, omit the serial comma.

Series. Three or more words, phrases, or clauses joined together.

Sexist language. The use of the masculine pronoun in a general sense, to include the feminine; and the word *man* is used to mean "human being" or "people": "All *men* are created equal."

Showing. The demonstration of emotion or evaluation in writing by providing sensory details and action: "*The runner grinned as she crossed the finish line*" (instead of "*The runner was happy to win the race*").

Simile. A comparison that uses *like* or *as:* "My love is *like a red, red rose*" [Robert Burns].

Split infinitive. An infinitive phrase in which an adverbial modifier comes between to and the base form of the verb: "I was happy to *finally* finish my science project."

Stress. See *Prosody.*

Structure classes. The small, closed classes of words that explain the grammatical or structural relationships of the form classes. The major ones are determiners, auxiliaries, qualifiers, prepositions, and conjunctions.

Style. A writer's manner of expression, influenced by word choice, sentence length and complexity, figurative language, tone, and other sentence features.

Subject. The opening position in the sentence patterns, usually a noun phrase or other nominal structure, that functions as the topic of the sentence.

Subject complement. The nominal or adjectival that follows a linking verb, renaming or describing the subject ("Pam is *the president*"). In the passive voice the transitive sentence with an object complement (Pattern 7) will have a subject complement: "We elected Pam president" → "Pam was elected *president.*"

Subject–verb agreement. See *Agreement.*

Subjective case. The role in the sentence of a noun phrase or a pronoun when it functions as the subject of the sentence. Personal pronouns have distinctive inflected forms for subjective case: *I, he, she, they,* and so on. And as the subject complement, a pronoun will be in the subjective case. The relative pronoun *who* is also subjective case—*whose* (possessive), *whom* (objective).

Subjunctive mood. An expression of the verb in which the base form, rather than the inflected form, is used (1) in certain *that* clauses conveying strong suggestions, resolutions, or commands ("My father always suggests that Mary *go* with us"; "I move that the meeting *be* adjourned"; "I demanded that the company *increase* its charitable contributions") and (2) in the expression of wishes or conditions contrary to fact ("If I *were* you, I'd be careful"; "I wish it *were* summer").

Subordinate clause. See *Dependent clause.*

Subordinating conjunction. A conjunction that introduces a dependent clause and expresses the relationship of the clause to the main clause. Among the most common are *after, although, as, as long as, as soon as, because, before, even though, if, provided that, since, so that, though, till, until, when, whenever, whereas, while.*

Subordination. The placement of information in a dependent clause that functions adverbially or adjectivally.

Summative modifier. A modifier—usually a noun phrase—at the end of the sentence that sums up the idea of the main clause: The teacher canceled class on the Friday before spring break, *a decision that was greeted with unanimous enthusiasm.*

Superlative degree. See *Degree.*

Syntax. The way in which the words of the language are put together to form the structural units, the phrases and clauses, of the sentence.

Telling. Description that lacks the kind of sensory details, action, and dialog that would allow readers to evaluate and/or picture the scene. See *Showing.*

Tense. A grammatical feature of verbs and auxiliaries relating to time. Tense is designated by an inflectional change *(walked),* by an auxiliary *(will walk),* or both *(am walking, have walked).*

There-**transformation.** A variation of a basic sentence in which the expletive *there* is added at the beginning and the subject is shifted to a position following *be:* "A fly is in my soup" → "*There is a fly in my soup.*"

Third person. See *Person.*

Time frame. The part of the verb-tense label indicating time: *present, past,* or *future.*

Tone. The writer's attitude toward the reader and the text: serious, formal, tongue-in-cheek, sarcastic, casual, and so on.

Transitional phrase. A prepositional phrase used to relate ideas in adjacent sentences.

Transitive verb. The verbs of Patterns 5, 6, and 7, which require at least one complement, the direct object, to be complete. With only a few exceptions, transitive verbs are those that can be transformed into the passive voice.

Triplet. A three-item series: "Residents of the park include *elk, bison, and grizzly bears.*"

Verb. One of the four form classes, traditionally thought of as the action word in the sentence. Every verb, without exception, has an *-s* and an *-ing* form (present participle); every verb also has a past-tense form and a past-participle form, although in the case of some irregular verbs these forms are not readily apparent. And every verb, without exception, can be marked by auxiliaries. Many verbs also have characteristic derivational forms, such as *-ify (typify), -ize (criticize),* and *-ate (activate)*. See Chapter 3.

Verb phrase. A verb together with its complements and modifiers; the predicate of the sentence is a verb phrase. Some verb phrases have verb forms that do not carry tense: gerunds, infinitives, and participles.

Voice. The relationship of the subject to the verb. See also *Active voice* and *Passive voice.*

What-cleft. See *Cleft sentence.*

Writer's voice. The identity the writer creates through word choice and word arrangement.

Bibliography

In the following books and articles, you can find further information about some of the topics you have studied here.

Cohesion
Fahnestock, Jeanne. "Semantic and Lexical Coherence." *College Composition and Communication* 34:4 (1983): 400–416.

Halliday, M. A. K., and Ruqaiya Hasan. *Cohesion in English.* London: Longman, 1976.

Vande Kopple, William J. "Functional Sentence Perspective, Composition, and Reading." *College Composition and Communication* 33:1 (1982): 50–63.

Comprehensive Grammar
Biber, Douglas, Stig Johansson, Geoffrey Leech, Susan Conrad, and Edward Finegan. *Longman Grammar of Spoken and Written English.* New York: Longman, 1999.

Huddleston, Rodney, and Geoffrey K. Pullum. *The Cambridge Grammar of the English Language.* Cambridge: Cambridge UP, 2002.

Quirk, Randolph, Sidney Greenbaum, Geoffrey Leech, and Jan Svartvik. *A Comprehensive Grammar of the English Language.* New York: Longman, 1985.

Figures of Speech
Corbett, Edward P. J. *Classical Rhetoric for the Modern Student,* 2nd ed. New York: Oxford, 1971.

Quinn, Arthur. *Figures of Speech: 60 Ways to Turn a Phrase.* Davis, CA: Hermagoras Press, 1993.

Grammar and Writing Instruction
English Journal (three grammar issues). May 2006, January 2003, November 1996.

Hunter, Susan, and Ray Wallace, eds. *The Place of Grammar in Writing Instruction: Past, Present, Future.* Portsmouth, NH: Boynton/Cook, 1995.

Noguchi, Rei. *Grammar and the Teaching of Writing: Limits and Possibilities.* Urbana, IL: National Council of Teachers of English, 1991.

Weaver, Constance. *Grammar to Enhance Writing.* Portsmouth, NH: Heinemann, 2008.

Grammar Rules
Cameron, Deborah. *Verbal Hygiene.* London: Routledge, 1995.

Haussamen, Brock. *Revising the Rules: Traditional Grammar and Modern Linguistics*, 2nd ed. Dubuque, IA: Kendall/Hunt, 1997.

Schuster, Edgar H. *Breaking the Rules: Liberating Writers Through Innovative Grammar Instruction*. Portsmouth, NH: Heinemann, 2003.

Language Development

Gleason, Jean Berko, and Nan Bernstein Ratner. *The Development of Language*, 7th ed. Boston: Allyn & Bacon, 2009.

Nippold, Marilyn. *Later Language Development: School-Age Children, Adolescents, and Young Adults*. Austin, TX: PRO-ED, 2007.

Metadiscourse

Cheng, Xiaoguang, and Margaret S. Steffensen. "Metadiscourse: A Technique for Improving Student Writing." *Research in the Teaching of English* 30:2 (1996): 149–181.

Crismore, Avon. *Talking to Readers: Metadiscourse as Rhetorical Act*. New York: Peter Lang, 1989.

Hyland, Ken. *Metadiscourse*. London: Continuum, 2005.

Vande Kopple, William J. "Some Exploratory Discourse on Metadiscourse." *College Composition and Communication* 36:1 (1985): 82–93.

Pedagogical Grammar

Celce-Murcia, Marianne, and Diane Larsen-Freeman. *The Grammar Book*. Boston: Heinle & Heinle, 1999.

Hancock, Craig. *Meaning-Centered Grammar: An Introductory Text*. London: Equinox, 2005.

Kolln, Martha, and Robert Funk. *Understanding English Grammar*, 9th ed. New York: Longman, 2012.

Punctuation

Christensen, Francis. *Notes Toward a New Rhetoric: Six Essays for Teachers*. New York: Harper & Row, 1967.

Lunsford, Andrea A., and Karen J. Lunsford. "'Mistakes Are a Fact of Life': A National Comparative Study." *College Composition and Communication* 59:4 (2008): 781–806.

Meyer, Charles F. *A Linguistic Study of American Punctuation*. New York: Peter Lang, 1987.

Rhetoric and Style

Corbett (cited under "Figures of Speech").

Holcomb, Chris, and M. Jimmie Killingsworth. *Performing Prose: The Study and Practice of Style in Composition*. Carbondale: Southern Illinois Press, 2010.

Williams, Joseph M., and Gregory G. Colomb. *Style: Lessons in Clarity and Grace*, 10th ed. New York: Longman, 2010.

Sentence Appreciation

Fish, Stanley. *How to Write a Sentence: And How to Read One*. New York: HarperCollins, 2011.

Tufte, Virginia. *Artful Sentences: Syntax as Style*. Cheshire, CT: Graphics Press, 2006.

Text Analysis

Dillon, George L. *Constructing Texts*. Bloomington, IN: IUP, 1981.

Answers to the Exercises

Chapter 1

Exercise 1, page 10.

 1. The(d) guitar(H)   a(d) instrument(H)
 3. This(d) innovation(H)   the(d) world(H)
 5. Experience Music Project(H)   an(d) exhibit(H)
    guitars(H)

Exercise 2, page 11.

 1. Our county commissioners (They)
 3. The mayor (She)
 5. This new law (It)

Exercise 3, page 15.

 1. at special parties—adverbial
 3. in ancient Rome—adjectival
 5. to the top of the birthday cake—adverbial, of the birthday cake—adjectival

Chapter 2

Exercise 4, page 22.

 1. AD / is / a ... nature. (P 2)
 3. His excuse / sounded / plausible. (P 3)
 5. The bus from Flagstaff / arrived / at two o'clock. (P 4)
 7. The public ... area / is / unreliable. (P 2)

Exercise 5, page 28.

 A1. Many people / now / consider (trans) / the penny / a nuisance coin.
 A3. During World War II / the government / required (trans) / large amounts of
     copper / for war production.
 A5. The Philadelphia Mint / unwittingly / produced (trans) / twelve copper pennies /
     that year / in addition to the new model.
 A7. Those twelve 1943 copper pennies / soon / became (linking) / valuable
     collectors' items.

Here are some possible revisions of the sentences in the first part:

 B1. Now many people consider ....
 B3. The government required large amounts of copper for war production during
     World War II.

B5. Unwittingly, the Philadelphia Mint ....

B7. Soon those twelve 1943 copper pennies ....

Exercise 6, page 31.

1. In 1747 / a physician in the British Navy / conducted / an experiment / to discover a cure for scurvy. (P 5)
3. Dr. James Lind / fed / six groups of scurvy victims / six different remedies. (P 6)
5. Although ... findings, / a daily dose ... juice / became / a requirement. (P 3)
7. In the eighteenth century / the British / called / lemons / limes. (P 7)
9. This word / is / in the dictionary / though ... "derogatory." (P1)

Exercise 7, page 31.

1. No comma between the subject and the verb
3. No comma between the direct object and the object complement

Chapter 3

Exercise 8, page 40.

1. Okay
3. convinced

Exercise 9, page 44.

Active to Passive:

A1. The lead article in today's *Collegian* was penned by my roommate.

A3. A new tax-collection system is being proposed by the county commissioners this year.

Passive to Active:

B1. A committee chose this year's cheerleading squad last spring.

B3. You should change your car's oil on a regular basis.

Either:

C1. The next six chapters should be read before Monday. (A to P)

C3. A new vacation schedule is being tried out this year by our company. (A to P)

Exercise 10, page 47.

Answers will vary.

Chapter 4

Exercise 11, page 58.

Answers may vary.

1. Both tea and coffee contain caffeine.
3. Some people drink either coffee or tea, but not both.

Exercise 12, page 60.

1. go
3. go
5. finds

Exercise 13, page 70.

1. The Smithsonian Institution comprises nineteen museums, nine research centers, and the National Zoo.
3. No extra punctuation necessary.
5. The museum ... in 1976; however, its collection ... Airport.
7. Together ... air- and spacecraft; they also sponsor vital research into aviation and related technologies.

Exercise 14, page 73.
Answers will vary.

Exercise 15, page 76.
Here are some of the problems:
1. Unparallel verb phrases: *to lift* and *swimming*
3. Unparallel complements: introduced+noun phrase and said+nominal clause
5. Unparallel complements: either+noun phrase and or+independent clause

Chapter 5
Exercise 16, page 89.
1. At the edge of the Mississippi River in St. Louis stands the Gateway Arch, the world's tallest monument. The stainless steel structure, designed by Eero Saarinen, commemorates the Westward Movement.
3. [No change in the first sentence.] It's not unusual for the temperature to reach 110° in Bakersfield, often the hottest spot in the valley. [Note that *summer* in the first sentence makes *June through September* redundant.]
5. Directed by the U.S. Marshal Service, the federal witness-protection service began in 1968. This program has relocated and created new identities for over four thousand people in extreme danger because they have testified against criminals.

Exercise 17, page 93.
1. Many women ... political status. This effort ....
3. Some married women ... property, but this right ....
5. In 1920 the Constitution ... vote. That amendment ...

Chapter 6
Exercise 18, page 104.
The word *janitor* found its way into the English language as a synonym for doorkeeper. In Scots usage, this word was also the name of a minor school official.

Exercise 19, page 108.
Answers will vary. Here are some possibilities:
1. It was in 1912 that the *Titanic* hit ....
3. There were hundreds of angry parents protesting the senator's position ....
5. There have been countless travelers who have lost ....

Chapter 7
Exercise 20, page 119.
Remember! You won't be using the word *snafu!*

Exercise 21, page 126.
A. Here are some possibilities for the first five in the list: turn down/reject; bring about/cause; bring on/induce; put up with/tolerate; stand for/represent, tolerate
B. (1) suggest, offer, propose; (3) consider; (5) replaces/represents

Exercise 22, page 127.
1. We do not understand why parents buy so many Christmas presents for their children.
3. In his biography of Lyndon Johnson, Robert Caro provides a detailed account of the Senate election of 1948.
5. The overuse of salt in the typical American diet obscures the natural taste of many foods. Nutritionists maintain that if people reduced their dependence on salt, they would find their food tastier and more enjoyable.

Exercise 23, page 135.
Answers will vary.

Chapter 8
Exercise 24, page 143.
Answers will vary.

Exercise 25, page 150.
Answers will vary.

Exercise 26, page 154.
(*Note:* You may have come up with even tighter versions using other kinds of modifiers.)
1. Even though the famous Gateway Arch is located in St. Louis, it is Kansas City that claims the title "Gateway to the West."
3. Thomas Jefferson acquired the Ozark Mountains for the United States when he negotiated the Louisiana Purchase with Napoleon in 1803.
5. When the neighbors added a pit bull to their pet population, now numbering three unfriendly four-legged creatures, we decided to fence in our backyard.

Exercise 27, page 155.
1. To save money (inf phr/purpose), often (adverb/frequency), at my desk (prep phr/place)
3. late (adverb/time), that night (noun phr/time)
5. last week (noun phr/time), to consider ... bill (inf phr/purpose)
7. If ... city (clause/condition), to another city (prep phr/direction)

Chapter 9
Exercise 28, page 162.
1. The president's recent clean-air proposals have been criticized as inadequate by highly placed government officials.
3. No additional punctuation needed.
5. I had back-to-back exams on Wednesday.

Exercise 29, page 168.
1. Having endured rain all week, we weren't surprised by the miserable weather on Saturday. [or "we weren't surprised when the weather turned miserable on Saturday."]
3. We were not at all surprised when the county commissioner, known for her conservative views ... , announced her candidacy ....
5. After I spent nearly all day in the kitchen, everyone agreed ....

Exercise 30, page 172.
1. The first snowstorm of the season in Denver, which was both early and severe, was not what the weather service had predicted.
3. Overspending our budget three times this week probably means eating hot dogs for the rest of the month.
5. When tuition increases as a result of decreases in funding by state governments, students find it difficult to afford a college education.

Exercise 31, page 175.
1. who work in West Virginia (restrictive relative clause); offered by management (restrictive participial phrase); covering wages and safety (restrictive participial

phrase); contract, which expires on Friday at midnight (nonrestrictive relative clause)
3. husband, who was sitting ... platform (nonrestrictive relative clause); mayor, turning to look directly at the senator (nonrestrictive participial phrase)

Exercise 32, page 176.
1. The computer has revolutionized the storage and retrieval of fingerprints, which have been used for criminal identification since 1891, when a police officer in Argentina introduced the method.
3. Because the Northeast has both the highest levels of acid rain and the highest incidence of colon cancer in the United States, researchers suspect there is a causal link between the two.
5. Influenza, or flu, [which is] a viral infection that causes aches and pains in the joints, begins as an upper respiratory infection and spreads to ....

Chapter 10
Exercise 33, page 184.
Answers will vary. Here are some possibilities:
1. Families chose their three favorite board games: Monopoly, Scrabble, and Trivial Pursuit.
3. Three states have over thirty electoral votes: California, fifty-five; Texas, thirty-two; and New York, thirty-one.

Exercise 34, page 188.
1. to tell the truth, infinitive (subject complement)
3. To ignore ... advice, infinitive (subject)
5. to buy up ... stocks, infinitive (appositive)
7. your proofreading ... me, gerund (direct object)

Exercise 35, page 191.
1. that we had a pet boa constrictor in our house (direct object)
3. That the term *First Lady* wasn't used until 1849 (subject)
5. that we reform our spelling system (appositive)

Exercise 36, page 191.
Answers will vary.

Chapter 11
Exercise 37, page 198.
Answers will vary. Here are some possibilities:
1. My sister, who is one of the most conservative people I know, surprised everyone at the family reunion when she showed up in a 1920s-style dress trimmed with beads and feathers, her normally blonde hair dyed red.
3. At the far end of the diner's chrome and plastic counter sat a trucker, an old man with long grey hair, his leathery face a pattern of creases and scars, his fringed jacket worn nearly through at the elbows.

Chapter 12
Exercise 38, page 218.
1. The <u>statement</u> ... was ....
3. Apparently the <u>use</u> of robots ... <u>has</u> ....
5. Correct

Exercise 39, page 222.
1. grief, grieve, grievous, grievously
3. ability, enable, able, ably
5. quickness, quicken, quick, quickly
7. type, typify, typical, typically
9. critic (criticism/critique), criticize (critique), critical, critically
11. appreciation, appreciate, appreciable, appreciably
13. acceptance (acceptability), accept, acceptable, acceptably
15. stealth, steal, stealthy, stealthily

Exercise 40, page 224.
Answers will vary. Here are some possibilities.
1. impassioned, inappropriate
3. futile
5. enthusiastic

Exercise 41, page 226.
1. <u>in</u> a relatively short period of time (noun phrase)
3. to what the guide told us about the trail leading into the canyon (nominal clause) *and* <u>about</u> the trail leading into the canyon (noun phrase) *and* <u>into</u> the canyon (noun phrase)

Exercise 42, page 233.
Answers will vary. Here are some possibilities.
1. Claire has always been interested in children and, when she graduates, plans to work with them. Both she and I are majoring in early childhood education.
3. When …, I had no idea Beth was sick …. Our grandmother took one look at her, called the doctor, and drove her to the hospital. That decision turned out to be a good one: Beth's cramps turned out to be appendicitis.

Exercise 43, page 236.
Answers will vary. Here are some possibilities.
1. I recall with great pleasure the good times that we had at our annual family reunions when I was young. With our cousins and younger aunts and uncles, we played volleyball and softball until dark. Those games were a lot of fun.
3. It seemed to my cousin Terry and me that the grownups were different people at those family reunions. Such memories of family reunions may be true for people everywhere.

Chapter 13
Exercise 44, page 246.
Answers will vary. Here are some possibilities.
1. The cost of repairs to the nation's public transportation facilities—roads, bridges, and railroads—is an expenditure that cannot be delayed much longer if the system is to survive.
3. Normally living in the coastal waters of Japan, the paper nautilus octopus, a rare marine animal, was found recently in the squid nets off Santa Catalina in California.

Exercise 45, page 249.
Management is still taught in most business schools as a bundle of techniques, such as budgeting and personnel relations. To be sure, management, like any other work, has its own tools and its own techniques. But just as the essence of

medicine is not urinalysis (important though that is) the essence of management is not techniques and procedures. The essence of management is to make knowledge productive. Management, in other words, is a social function. And in its practice management is truly a liberal art. [Note: If you put a comma after *practice* in the last sentence, you have improved on the original! A comma would make the sentence easier to read.]

The old communities—family, village, parish, and so on—have all but disappeared in the knowledge society. Their place has largely been taken by the new unit of social integration, the organization. Where community was fate, organization is voluntary membership. Where community claimed the entire person, organization is a means to a person's ends, a tool. For 200 years a hot debate has been raging, especially in the West: are communities "organic" or are they simply extensions of the people of which they are made? Nobody would claim that the new organization is "organic." It is clearly an artifact, a creation of man, a social technology.

Index